D1546432

Malanggan

MATERIALIZING CULTURE
· ·

Series Editors: Paul Gilroy, Michael Herzfeld and Danny Miller

Barbara Bender, *Stonehenge: Making Space*

Gen Doy, *Materializing Art History*

Laura Rival (ed.), *The Social Life of Trees: Anthropological Perspectives on Tree Symbolism*

Victor Buchli, *An Archaeology of Socialism*

Marius Kwint, Christopher Breward and Jeremy Aynsley (eds), *Material Memories: Design and Evocation*

Penny Van Esterik, *Materializing Thailand*

Michael Bull, *Sounding Out the City: Personal Stereos and the Management of Everyday Life*

Anne Massey, *Hollywood Beyond the Screen*

Judy Attfield, *Wild Things*

Daniel Miller (ed.), *Car Cultures*

Elizabeth Edwards, *Raw Histories: Photographs, Anthropology and Museums*

David E. Sutton, *Remembrance of Repasts: An Anthropology of Food and Memory*

Eleana Yalouri, *The Acropolis: Global Fame, Local Claim*

Elizabeth Hallam and Jenny Hockey, *Death, Memory and Material Culture*

Sharon Macdonald, *Behind the Scenes at the Science Museum*

Elaine Lally, *At Home With Computers*

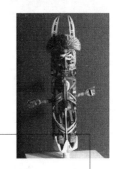

Malanggan

Art, Memory and Sacrifice

Susanne Küchler

Oxford • New York

First published in 2002 by
Berg
Editorial offices:
150 Cowley Road, Oxford, OX4 1JJ, UK
838 Broadway, Third Floor, New York, NY 10003-4812, USA

Berg is the imprint of Oxford International Publishers Ltd.

Library of Congress Cataloging-in-Publication Data

Küchler, Susanne.
    Malanggan : art, memory, and sacrifice / Susanne Küchler.
      p. cm. -- (Materializing culture)
    Includes bibliographical references and index.
    ISBN 1-85973-617-3 -- ISBN 1-85973-622-X (pbk.)
      1. Ethnology--Papua New Guinea--New Ireland Province.   2. Funeral rites and ceremonies
--Papua New Guinea--New Ireland Province.   3. Art--Papua New Guinea--New Ireland
Province.   4. New Ireland Province (Papua New Guinea)--Social life and customs.   I. Title.
    II. Series.
    GN671.N5K83 2002
    305.8'09953--dc21

                                         2002012010

British Library Cataloguing-in-Publication Data

A catalogue record for this book is available from the British Library.

ISBN 1 85973 617 3 (Cloth)
        1 85973 622 X (Paper)

Typeset by JS Typesetting Ltd, Wellingborough, Northants.
Printed in the United Kingdom by Biddles Ltd, King's Lynn.

To Josephine, Isabell and Ian

In Memory of Alfred Gell

Contents

List of Figures and Maps

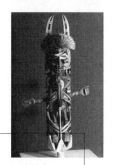

Preface

This study has been a long time in the making. Thus the list of people to thank for help and encouragement along the way is potentially incredibly long: the Volkswagenwerk Research Foundation, which generously funded the first period of 20 months' field-research in New Ireland; the Malinowski Research Fund, which helped in the final year of the Ph.D. at the London School of Economics and Political Science; and the Getty Research Institute for the History of Art and the Humanities, which funded a Postdoctoral Fellowship Year in 1989/90 and a Scholarship Year in Residence in 1995/96, during which most of this work was written.

My colleagues have never failed to inspire and encourage, but special thanks go out to Dieter Heintze, who first introduced me to matters *'malanggan'*, to Maurice Bloch, who encouraged me to pursue a Ph.D. at the LSE, to the late Alfred Gell, who instilled an awe for the English language and a passion for anthropology, and Marilyn Strathern, whose notes on my original thesis I still cherish. Of my colleagues who taught with me at Johns Hopkins University in Baltimore between 1986 and 1990, I would like to thank Gillian Feeley-Harnik, whose work has been a lasting inspiration, Walter Melion, without whom my understanding of memory would not be the same, and Yves-Alain Bois and Michael Fried for their introduction into art history. At University College London I would like to thank Mike Rowlands for his understanding and patience during the many years of juggling teaching and child-care and all my students, in particular Sean Kingston, who helped me to keep going. The warmest thanks, however, go to Janet Hoskins-Valeri, who read an earlier draft of this work.

Special thanks go to all my friends in Lamusmus, Panamafei and Panachais villages, many of whom I can no longer thank. Nothing could have been accomplished without the organizational talent and enduring support of Francis in Panachais village and Saun in Panamafei village.

They and countless others in Lamusmus 2, Panachais and Panamafei whose friendship was like a rock deserve thanks for waiting so long for this to return. I also want to thank my mother for her support, especially in the early days of this work, and Ian, Josephine and Isabell for their understanding.

Introduction

At the centre of this study are objects known under the generic name of *'malanggan'*, which have come to epitomize the dilemma facing art in a disciplinary context that is riddled by the legacy of semiotics and the annihilation of analogy. Long misunderstood, *malanggan* have confounded all attempts at iconographic and contextual analysis. And yet, made as 'skin' and as a 'likeness', of life, they make visible ideas that have come to inform recent rethinking of art and memory in terms of a theory of image and of agency. At once visually complex and yet superbly ordered, *malanggan* tell a story about how art can be thought-like, and, as a vehicle of thought, be the very stuff out of which life is wrought.

To this day, *malanggan* – the funerary effigies used in New Ireland, Papua New Guinea, a ubiquitous collected item in ethnographic museums worldwide – is the generic name of a funerary ritual that culminates in the production, revelation and 'death' of effigies. When installed in a structure that is specifically erected for its display, the effigy is thought to be alive, having been gradually animated during the process of its production. Like the effigies of kings in fourteenth- and fifteenth-century England and France, which matched or even eclipsed the dead body itself, the effigy is attended as though the dummy were the living person himself – being animated and subsequently allowed to die, thus allowing the deceased person's soul to achieve symbolic immortality. The height of the *malanggan* ceremony is the dramatic revelation of the effigy, followed moments later by the symbolic activation of its death. What took often more than three months to prepare is over in an hour, the 'empty' 'remains' of effigies being taken to the forest to be left to decompose or to the mission to be sold to collectors.

We have come to associate *malanggan* primarily with the figure itself. Carved from wood, it is enlivened as 'skin' and is ultimately sacrificed, both effecting in its death the expelling of the dead person and initiating an exchange with the ancestral realm. The death of the object leaves behind a named and remembered image, which is recalled from time to time in states of reverie to re-direct ancestral power to the land of the living. The figure is thus an instance of a polity of images, whose access defines rank, authority and rights to land.

Visually and conceptually, the figure recalls a body wrapped in imagery. Incised to the point of breakage, the emerging fretwork is covered with depictions of birds, pigs, fish and seashells that appear almost lifelike; the same can be said for the figure set within the fretwork, which appears to stare at the beholder with eyes that could hardly be more vivid. It must surely have been the dreamlike quality of the animate surface of *malanggan* that inspired Surrealist artists to collect *malanggan* and draw upon them for inspiration for works such as Giacometti's *Cage* or Henry Moore's sculpture entitled *Upright Internal and External Forms* (Brignoni 1995). Motifs appear enchained as figures stand inside the mouth of rock-cods, framed by many different kinds of fish that bite into limbs and chins, birds that bite into snakes and snakes into birds, and the skulls of pigs that appear to metamorphose into birds. Inner shapes appear enclosed by outer frames in ways that contest the apparent reality of what is depicted, like a vision in a dream. The figures give the impression of making connections visible as processes, but also visibly play with resemblance, as one figure appears to comment on another, being both similar and yet different.

Museum collections of *malanggan* exceed tens of thousands of such figures, perhaps the largest number of figures ever to have been collected from a single cultural area in not more than 130 years. The first figures were collected around 1870, when expeditions were dispatched to the island. Known by then as 'New Ireland', the island had become one of the most important trading posts for the export of copra in the Pacific. Its large existing coconut plantations and natural harbours had made it into a heaven for traders, who had mapped and annexed its plantations early on in the nineteenth century. German Colonial administration was to be followed by the Australian Protectorate and Independence in 1975; yet *malanggan* remained an undiminished part of everyday life in New Ireland. Earlier writing on *malanggan* has presented it as an ancient tradition doomed to follow other 'pre-modern' paraphernalia into oblivion. This study, however, will present *malanggan* as grounded in resistance, rebuilding relations over land, labour and loyalty that provided the foundation out of which post-colonial identity could emerge.

Much has been written about *malanggan* over the last one hundred years, as its figures have continued to attract the attention of curators, collectors and researchers. Personally, I found a museum catalogue published by the curator for Oceania in Berlin most helpful (Helfrich 1973). As a comprehensive visual guide to the extensive holdings of *malanggan*-figures in the museum, the catalogue also lists the place and date of collection for each item. This list, in fact, provided the inspiration for a question that proved to be of the greatest interest to the people of New Ireland when I was talking to them about *malanggan*, yet also turned out to be of lasting significance for my own, theoretically oriented, understanding of what I was to find. For if you compare *malanggan* that appear strikingly similar to the extent of looking almost identical, these include figures collected during a period of over thirty years, and at places far removed from each other – even by today's car-centred standards. In view of the fact that such figures would have been collected soon after the ritual, how could they be so much alike, given the distance that separates them in time and space? It is as though their creators stressed a connection in visual terms, and did this in the absence of the physical remains of objects.

To understand why I found this question exciting, it is important to bear in mind that *malanggan* is practised on an island that is situated to the north-east of Papua New Guinea. As in all island Melanesian cultures, here too social relationships are inseparable from exchange, in which objects stand in for, or do duty as, persons. The theoretical model of exchange is grounded in Marcel Mauss's (1954[1924]) classic study *The Gift* and Bronislaw Malinowski's (1922) famous account of what came to be known as the '*Kula*' of the Trobriand islands. Malinowski described the *Kula* as the circular path taken by necklaces and arm-rings, which are passed between partners from island to island. *Malanggan* had possibly defeated attempts at analysis because it just could not fit this vision, for with *malanggan* what appears to matter most is not the circulation of an object, but the recollection of an image.

Landmark publications on *malanggan* have been those by Hortense Powdermaker (1932), Phillip Lewis (1969) and most recently Brigitte Derlon (1990) and Michael Gunn (1987, 1998), all written from a geographical perspective emulating the mythical origin of *malanggan*. Possibly because of the location of these studies at the 'source' of *malanggan* production, they managed on the whole to avoid the topic of exchange and of memory, as images appear as if rooted in clan land.

This present study, by contrast, has been written from a perspective hitherto ignored – from that of the West Coast, far away from the places where *malanggan* images are believed to have originated. The story told here is thus of the movement and arrest of such images and of the potent, although fragile, connections that 'skins' evoke among the inhabitants of the island.

From the West-Coast perspective it made perfect sense to ask for the path taken by the images. It quickly became apparent that people think about *malanggan* not just as a mental recollection, of which we have the 'real' thing in our museums, but as a kind of resource that is both generative and reproductive in nature. *Malanggan* thus capture a form of property that is not material, but intellectual in kind.

Malanggan are in a visual but simultaneously conceptual manner 'links' that connect, undercutting the colonial legacy of a divisive administrative order that imposed monads of person, property and place. The relentless work of *malanggan* dominates every aspect of life on this island, where all personal names are names associated with images of *malanggan*, passed down from generation to generation as a finite set. As treasured possessions, uniquely important to the assertion and transmission of identity, *malanggan* reflect on the work of Annette Weiner (1992). Her *Inalienable Possessions* examined the strategies of keeping hold of things that are judged to be of profound importance to one's identity and well-being while allowing them to circulate as gifts. 'Keeping while giving' was shown by Weiner to be made possible by things *immeuble* or inalienable, which continue to be attached to their owner although they are given away. *Malanggan* are a perfect example of how to achieve this, by separating a generative and reproductive image from the perishable object and thus bringing forth a political economy built on memory. Yet *malanggan* also raise questions about the use to which memory may be put where images, and not objects, reign.

Remembering to Forget

The work of mourning in New Ireland builds up chains of memory that have the deceptive appearance of duration. Such chains often last more than twenty years, until the final climactic act of the 'finishing' of the dead in *malanggan*. As was observed by Remo Guidieri and Francesco Pellizzi, 'compared with the endless Polynesian genealogies, the genealogical segments of Melanesia are family portraits that quickly fade with the passing of time' (1981: 14). In Melanesia, as exemplified by *malanggan*, the commemorative work for the dead feeds on a memory of which amnesia is the necessary and paradoxical complement. The process of remembering that is incised in the work of mourning is thus at the same time a systematic forgetting of the dead, a process of un-stitching of the tightly woven relations of which the deceased person was so much a part. In New Ireland, one must know how to forget in order to know how to remember.

The work for the dead, then, is a work that creates ancestors, and in so doing establishes a memory. Yet this memory is not filled with things, but with images that are seen as resources from which to re-envision the present over and over again. It is a memory that remembers much forgetting, and that recalls and represents only the better to forget (cf. Guidieri and Pellizzi 1981: 15).

Perhaps not surprisingly, this relation of remembering to forgetting will be experienced as profoundly contradictory from a Eurocentric perspective obsessed with ensuring that remembering can be accurate, enduring and supportive of the accumulation of knowledge (Lowenthal 1993; Bloch 1998). Oblivion appears as dreaded disaster, not a potent site from which to remake the present in the future (Radstone 2000; Hallam *et al.* 2000). Thus all leading treatments of memory undertaken in the last hundred years, as summarized succinctly in Edward Casey's study of *Remembering* (1987), 'have approached remembering through the counter-phenomenon of "forgetting"'. It is, as Casey says 'as if a more direct approach would be futile and question-begging: memory is best understood via its own deficient mode' (1987: 7). Defined as recall of 'forgotten' experience, the study of memory has remained entrenched in the cornerstone of twentieth-century psychology – the study of the unconscious, a supra-human memory whose mechanism is used but not controlled by subject-centred remembering, internalized perhaps, but in a forgetting, self-forgetting special meaning (Halbwachs 1925, 1950; Bartlett 1932).

Virtually all memory theories have assumed the perceptually driven nature of the representations that are active in recollection. Perceptions are thus held responsible for making copies of the external world that constitute both a memory store and the schemata of thought processes. The copies are traces of past experience accumulated and stored in the thesaurus or treasure-house of memory. This notion of representation is embedded in the notion of text- and book-based learning, in which writing constitutes the basic experience of duration.

In order to see that this is not the whole story of memory, it is useful to recall that there have long been understood to be two sides to remembering. These are known as *mneme* and *memoria*: distinctions that we find again in the pairings of *Gedächtnis* and *Erinnerung*, Proust's *mémoire involontaire* and *mémoire volontaire*, Warburg's *Mnemosyne and Sosphrosyne*, Halbwachs's *mémorie* and *histoire* and Benjamin's *Eingedenken* and *Andenken* (Kemp 1991: 87). The first, *mneme*, describes the remembrance by chance of something previously experienced; *mneme* is the ordinary Greek word for 'memory', though often concretized, in which case it means 'something that reminds one' (Latin: *monumentum*). The second, or *memoria*, captures the ability to recall what has been forgotten using referential forms of representation, a process referred to by Plato as *anamnesis*.

Frances Yates (1966) won back *memoria* for the humanities as the classical 'art of memory', which came to describe a collective, unconscious memory. The concern with techniques of recollection became popular as a useful pastime, but also as a device to be deployed by museums and as a reason legitimizing the existence of archives. With the rise of electronic storage systems, however, the accessibility of the memory store and thus the individual connection to collective memory was soon no longer a matter of certainty. Attention turned to the neglected notion of *mnemosyne*, the spontaneous recollection of past experience as captured at the beginning of the twentieth century by the German art historian Aby Warburg in his *Mnemosyne Atlas*. Warburg's project consisted in the arrangement of pictorial and figurative representations, inciting strings of associations that flow outward from gestures, bodily positions and allusions to both popular and esoteric knowledge. Today *mneme* as a mode of remembering opens an exciting new perspective, as it suggests the eradication of the opposition between incorporated and inscribed forms of knowledge and paves the way for understanding visual ways of knowing (Rowlands 1993).

Most important in the attention to spontaneous recollection is the recognition that remembering is inseparable from thinking, rather than being merely a technique that can be taken over by whatever is at hand. Like Marcel Proust's famous encounter with his childhood, which was provoked by eating a *madeleine* cake in his aunt's garden, mnemic recollection recalls what is absent. It does this provoked by, and continuing to provoke, the creation of resemblance, which in Proust's case is the textual analogue to his lost childhood.

Israel Rosenfield observes this intimate relation of thought and remembering in his study of *The Strange, the Familiar and the Forgotten*, as he points out that 'not only can there be no such thing as a memory without there being consciousness, but consciousness and memory are in a certain sense inseparable, and understanding one requires understanding the other' (1992: 3). Rosenfield's challenging and illuminating analysis draws on neurophysiological studies of the brain, which have begun to replace the static model of localized brain function with the dynamic flow of connecting stimuli. Consciousness is argued to emerge as a constantly evolving relation among sets of stimuli, rather than, as was formerly assumed, from snapshots of material 'stored' in the brain and retrieved in remembering. Human memory, he argues, 'may be unlike anything we have thus far imagined or successfully built a model for. And consciousness may be the reason why' (1992: 4).

With this in mind, we can return to the perspective of *malanggan*, which allow us to explore the materiality of 'something that reminds one', not because they are referentially conceived, but because they consist of analogues to thought itself. *Malanggan* tell a story of how to think in, through, and with images that bear no perceptual relation to memorial content, but that visualize thinking through resemblance expressed in material form.

Unlike most monuments that were conceived in the Western post-Renaissance tradition, *malanggan* do not come to stand for memories, formed in the mind (Forty and Küchler 1999). They are not conceived as material objects that, by virtue of their durability, either prolong or preserve memories indefinitely beyond their purely mental existence. Instead, like recent counter-monuments of the Holocaust, *malanggan* effect remembering in an active and continuously emerging sense as they disappear from view (Young 1993). It is thus through the 'death' of the object that the finite past is turned into a site of renewal and of accumulation. As we gather in our collections the figures of *malanggan* that are the remains of object sacrifice, so the creators of these figures collect named images that define their access to the past as a vision for the future in forever new and hope-inspiring ways.

Collections as Remains of Object Sacrifice

An investigation of the ritual death and riddance of artefacts serves as a surprising point of departure for the rethinking of the nature not just of memory, but of collecting. For what we have in collections of *malanggan* tells a story that is hardly yet tapped; this is a story about the inciting of absence as a privileged site of intellectual property, of which collections became the material analogue (cf. Küchler 1997).

Sacrificial economies flourished under colonialism in many parts of the world, as they enabled an institutionalized mode of resistance to colonial intervention in such matters as the regulation of land-ownership and relations of loyalty. In Melanesia, sacrificial economies developed alongside millennarian and cargo cult movements, as the sale of sacrificial remains to Western collectors proved early on to be a successful means of opening the road to the ancestors that was thought to be blocked by the white man. Instead of being left to decompose, the ritually sacrificed objects became the vehicle that reopened the road of cargo to bring, first, guns and cloth, and then money in ever greater quantities.

What we have in masses in our collections, therefore, are the empty, hollow remains of objects of sacrifice that are evidence of an exchange into which we came to be implicated quite unknowingly. We are confronted with a paradox: that we had collected, as transcending commodity-based exchange relations and thus as a reminder of lost traditions, what were actually conceived as the alienable remains of a life-enhancing act of riddance.

Artefacts that were ritually produced for deposition have occupied the interpretative and classificatory skills of generations of archaeologists and anthropologists. Collections of this kind form a commemorative site that can be revisited by scholars, like a Chinese scroll-painting that is written on and altered every time it is unrolled. In fact, however, this appearance is deceptive, as we are really dealing with objects that are the remains of sacrificial acts. The historian Krystof Pomian (1986) indeed argues that we can use the notion of object sacrifice to understand the nature of collecting, because it accounts for a distinct, cognitively founded, exchange value that is capable of transgressing the boundary between the visible and the invisible as 'Gift to God'.

It was no accident that the creation of nineteenth-century archaeological and ethnographic museums coincided with a surge of writings on sacrifice that still form the backbone of an understanding of the exchange value attributed to collectibles. In fact, by taking seriously this connection of the collectible to object sacrifice, a closer look at the theories of sacrifice may point up a new approach to artefacts that have ended up in museums through acts of deposition.

Sacrifice received its most heightened attention in the late nineteenth and early twentieth centuries with the work of Edward B. Tylor (1889) on sacrifice as gift, Robertson Smith's work on sacrifice as a totemic communal meal (1892), and James Frazer's theory of expiation (1922). The contemporary analysis of sacrifice is founded, however, almost exclusively on the comparatively short, yet path-breaking, study by Hubert and Mauss (1964[1906]). The 'new' element contributed by Hubert and Mauss's essay is derived from the development of a 'syntactic' study of sacrifice that entailed viewing it as a global ritual process. A second major, yet much less well-known, definition of sacrifice is as an efficacious representation. Anticipating Hocart (1927), Alfred Loisy (1920) views objects used in ritual as icons that mimetically capture what the sacrifice wishes to achieve. Essential to his view is his divergence from the theory of sacrifice as gift, as he argues that it is the iconic or representational nature of the thing to be destroyed, visualizing the processual nature of destruction itself, that is essential to the 'magical' efficacy of the ritual act. The third definition of sacrifice does not speak of the gift, nor of representational action, but of sacrifice in relation to violence. For Girard (1977), violence is inherent in human relationships, and demands a mechanism for the formation and expulsion of diffuse and reciprocal violence by concentrating it upon a single individual, the sacrificial victim.

In fact, it is Loisy's rather overlooked account of sacrifice that has turned out to be most productive in the analysis of *malanggan* attempted in this study, because it has allowed the uncovering of the working of resemblance in the fashioning of connections that reverberated throughout both ritual and everyday life on the island. More surprisingly, it opened up a new perspective on the centrality of visual analogy in eliciting efficacious ritual action. The nexus of remembering and sacrifice thus requires a third element, that of representation, whose formal and material properties have been persistently ignored in existing analyses of *malanggan*.

Art-like Inventions

Of all aspects of social life, anthropologists are perhaps most reticent about art. The globalization of mass media, of travel and of entertainment have created a diverse terrain with blurred borders and de-territorialized identities. Islands of history and of culture, associated with the Renaissance origins of Western disciplinary concerns with art, appear no longer relevant and capable of serving as categories of study and theory-building. Fred Myers's (1995) call to renounce the privilege of 'thinking in essences' and Alfred Gell's (1992) insistence on 'methodological philistinism' resonate with a deeply felt unease across the disciplines concerned with the study of art about the epistemological purchase of the category.

Yet anthropology is no longer able to relegate the realm of the visual and of art to the periphery of the study of social relations. For, where not long ago we were satisfied with sociological studies of art production and circulation, we now yearn to understand the capacity of images to attract and hold our attention. The growing presence of computer-based learning, backed by advances in cognitive science, has shown that thinking in, through and with images is far more economical and efficient in the transmission of information than language could ever be (cf. Bloch 1991). In fact, visual ways of knowing appear all around us, and are no longer confined to an institutional framework of art consumption. In anthropology, it was Alfred Gell's (1998) *Art and Agency* that redefined the perimeters of the field by arguing that objects that are, as he called it, 'cognitively sticky' are part of the nexus of social relations.

Art and Agency eclectically combines theories of personhood and cognition, and shows that something quite new, yet also familiar and central to anthropological theory, emerges in the wake of this quasi-magical act of synthesis – this being a theory of objectification that is not about meaning and communication, but about doing, and not about persons, but about material entities that motivate inferences, responses, or interpretations. The proposition advanced in *Art and Agency* is perplexingly simple and evolves out of a re-reading of Maussian exchange theory in the light of Marilyn Strathern's (1988) theory of the fractality of personhood – social relations obtain not among persons, but among persons and things, on account of the substitutability of persons by things. Replacing the Maussian theory of prestation by 'art objects', Gell sought to fashion, out of a prototypical and exemplary anthropological theory, an anthropological theory of art – an anthropological theory, moreover, that set out to offer a theoretical definition of art (as 'things provoking attachment') in contradistinction to the existing institutional, aesthetic, or semiotic definitions. The theory thus advanced offers a real alternative to those interested in art from any disciplinary perspective, while it radically shifts the study of social relations in anthropology from the observation of behaviour to the study of material culture.

The notion of a world of things whose look or surface-sheen impels attachment suggests an importance assigned to visual resemblance and visual connections, that has for some time been motivating a rethinking of the pictorial in art-historical writing (Freedberg 1989; Mitchell 1996; Stafford 1996, 1999). Set within a flourishing intellectual economy, *malanggan* may serve as fitting ethnographic counterpart to the theory of visual analogy and of agency. As it traces the creation of 'likeness' in images that are at once performed and made visible as resemblance, this study will lead us to understand the efficacy not just of ritual action, but also of action in the ubiquitous realm of the everyday, in the building of houses, the weaving of baskets, the knotting of fish-nets, and the fencing of gardens. It is here that we will find an answer to the question of why it is that the form given to the images of *malanggan* is *re-collectable*, i.e. both memorable and collectible.

Gathering Places

Like those birds that lay their eggs only in other species' nests, memory produces in a place that does not belong to it. It receives its form and its implantation from external circumstances, even if it furnishes the content (the missing detail) (De Certeau 1984: 86).

New Ireland Province forms a distinctive linguistic grouping of nineteen Austronesian languages together with the adjacent Tolai and Duke of York islands. As one of the northernmost islands of the Bismarck Archipelago that lies off the coast of mainland New Guinea, New Ireland is also the second largest, though of a shape that belies its size. On maps, the island looks like an old-fashioned pistol, with a narrow longitudinal shaft pointing in a northwesterly direction and a wider extension curving away to the south. Thus, while the landmass of the island extends over 220 miles, in some places it is not more than 7 miles wide. Severed from the island along its eastern and western coastline are four smaller island groupings – Tabar, Lihir, Tanga and Djaul, with larger islands, St Matthias and New Hanover, situated at its northern end (Map 1).

Of volcanic origin, the island's interior is faulted in its northern part, with peaks rising to 1,000 metres in places. Limestone deposits in the mountainous interior offer massive cave-structures that were once the site of villages that have only quite recently been abandoned (Ryan, n.d.; White and Downie 1978; White and Specht 1973; Clay 1974). As one drives along the narrow coastal shores and glances up into the vast terrain now claimed by the logging companies, it is perplexing to think that it was all teeming with life only some eighty years ago.

Resettlement along the coast left villages fringed by foreign-owned plantations, by the sea, and by a frequently inaccessible interior, which, along the west coast, drops in places in vertical cliffs four hundred metres down to sea level; along the east coast the interior descends more gently into a wider coastal expanse; yet here too are found plantations limiting the expansion of villages and of gardens.

The shorelines along both east and west coasts are closely followed by a road, today the lifeline of the island, along which villages are perched, often precariously. This is not a sleepy place, but one that is as fast as the trucks that are hurtling along the road from dawn to dusk. Life on the island is totally dominated by an opposing directionality that is embedded in its geography and enhanced by this road. Known as the Boluminski Highway, the east-coast branch connects administrative centres in the far north and south, so that all communication appears to proceed along a longitudinal axis. A narrower west-coast extension was finished only in the late 1970s; this leads off into the interior at the narrowest point of the island. Steep and dangerous at best, and inaccessible during the rainy season, this road leads to the *West-Kara*, who see themselves as living at 'the back of the place' (*lamine pe labine*). From their perspective, one always moves to 'the other side' (*kipul*) in addition to moving to 'Kavieng' (*kipa*) or 'Namatanai' (*kipe*), the two

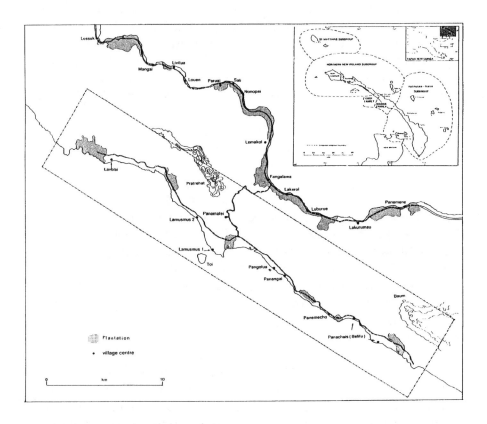

Map 1 Kara and New Ireland.

administrative centres linked by the east-coast highway. The north-west coast is considered as being 'far away' by today's east-coast standard, which expects anything to be accessible by a short car-ride. And yet those who settled along the north-west coast are considered advantaged, for it is in these coastal waters and on these sandy shores that the raw material for the shell-money required for all types of ritual work is found.

Though the East and the West are seemingly cut off from each other by the interior, the mountain that thus separates them also connects them. For in its silence are buried memories that are remembered as if they had happened today. Rituals periodically awaken the memories that lie dormant, hidden beneath the trees. These rituals, however, are far from evoking an ancient tradition, but are the site of an alternative framing of identity, one that is conceived as paving the way for a new beginning. The secret of this new beginning is the connections that are thought to cross-cut the administrative divisions and socio-linguistic distinctions that are the legacy of colonialism.

Connections are, first and foremost, asserted in relation to so-called 'gathering' (*bung*) places, such as tracks, stone walls and fruit-trees, which litter the interior mountains and demarcate the territory of the ancestors (*labu*). Buried beneath the trees and sometimes forgotten, such spaces are the underworld from which the present fashions itself (Küchler 1994). No house is built, no garden planted, no child named without conceiving of it as a 'likeness' (*malanggan*) to the ancestral realm. The story of *malanggan* as told in this book traces the role of resemblance in the forging of connections that link the world of the living and the dead. These connections are a kind of foil or backdrop against which relations in the mundane realm of the everyday are thought about and occasionally challenged.

This emphasis on images that resemble and connect by sheer associative force is peculiar to the North of the island. Images are known under the generic name of *malanggan*, and comprise anything from named designs woven or carved from fibre or wood, to the designs of fences and of houses, to names, songs, dances and the presentation of food (Figure 1.1). While such images constitute the most sought-after exchange item in the North, villages situated in the Centre and the South of the island have begun to acquire *malanggan* images since the 1950s. What Northerners seek in exchange for rights to *malanggan* is the knowledge of magic, and particularly of love magic, which is considered to be of superior efficacy in the southern parts of the island.

The visitor to the island may be blissfully unaware of the frenzy of activity that people in the North associate with *malanggan*. Not a week

Figure 1.1 *Malanggan (Walik)*, Panamecho Village.

will go by without 'work for the finishing of the dead' to be done, leading to the presentation of carvings after often as many as ten years. Yet despite the incessant activity visitors may, quite possibly, not see a single one of the figures that have come to be so abundantly represented in our museums. To the question of what happened to *malanggan*, a person from the North may reply that he too may not have seen a *malanggan* for some time, and sometimes even for years. He may certainly be bemused at the worried look on the face of the visitor – a visitor who may well be concerned that *malanggan* too has finally been overtaken by things modern and Western, like the copper roofing that proudly crowns every house. If he is kind-hearted he may reply that what *malanggan* is about is all around you at all times, and that when it does makes its appearance in the village, its effect is felt for a long time.

In fact, when trying to understand what *malanggan* is all about and how it may impact on what people think and do in the time when it is invisible on the island, it is best to look away from the figure and all the ritual work that it recalls to the tranquil moment when it first emerges as an image to a man sitting daydreaming on the beach. Where does this image come from?

To us, the landscape we encounter, the layout of villages, gardens and houses and the myriad of paths that connect them all, may appear at best metaphoric, at worst the imprint of some hard-to-reconstruct intentions. Yet for the people of the North of New Ireland, these spaces and places are crafted as images that are not just good to think with, but that encapsulate thoughtfulness in the fullest sense of the word. People think in, with and through the images crafted out of the land, and it is here that ideas about the power of resemblance or *malanggan* reside.

The villages, the gardens and the houses that we find in the North are all recent, and bear the scars of careful management of a resource (a land and its children) that came to be experienced as scarce in the years following the imposition of trade and then colonial rule. Diseases killed the young and the old, infertility plagued those who remained, and the land, once plentiful and fertile, was no longer owned by its people. It is deeply felt loss and sorrow that provokes images to come into existence that are capable of recalling what is no longer there.

Landscape and Ritual Culture

While we do have a large number of early expedition reports that date back to the years just preceding the imposition of German colonial rule in 1885, indirect colonial impact can be dated back to at least the 1770s.[1] The interest that the island evoked in the Western world reaches back to the year 1527, when Don Alvaro De Saavedra sailed along the north coast of an unknown island that he called 'Isla de Oro'. The discovery of the island, however, is ascribed to Tasman, who sailed around the island in 1642. Still it remained without name in the official records; this was to change with Dampier, who sailed in 1699 along the coast of a massive island that he called 'New Britain'. Nearly a century later, in 1761, during an exploration led by Carteret, the discovery of a passage that divided this apparently unitary landmass caused the renaming of the island to the north, which henceforth came to be known as 'New Ireland'. Between 1767 and 1848 several schooners sailed along the coast of New Ireland, developing rapidly growing trading networks (*Patrol Report*, May 1956).

Large indigenous coconut plantations along the coast of the island, not to speak of the many natural harbours along its shore, made the island into a haven for the booming trade in copra. The presence of traders on the island left its trace in the firearms and iron tools that were found in abundance on the island in the early to middle 1800s. The ferocity of indigenous warfare during this period is famed in oral accounts and immortalized by Romilly's 1886 report of headhunting near Kapsu (*Deutsches Kolonialblatt* 1885; Romilly 1886). What may have existed as a ritual practice of the 'taking of skin', involving headhunting, appears to have run out of control, as vivid stories recall the scattering and shattering of clans across the North of the island.

No account of *malanggan* exists for the period of indirect contact with the exception of an entry in Abel Tasman's diary dated 6 August 1643 with a sketch of a warrior canoe decorated with massive prow-boards shaped like a transmutation of a bird-pig-human face. While it is not possible to speak with certainty, it appears that *malanggan* as we know it from collections began to take shape only in the late nineteenth century. We know that the warfare finished quite suddenly, having been replaced by feasting, taking by surprise the arriving colonial forces, who were prepared for much greater difficulties (cf. Wagner 1991).

The association of warfare and *malanggan* is attested by one of the most complex *malanggan* carvings, which was collected around 1900 in Paruai village and depicts a warrior canoe. Collected first as the apparent remains of an ancient and doomed tradition, and then as art, *malanggan*-figures skillfully diverted attention away from the burgeoning activity around their ritual consumption, leaving the linkage of *malanggan* to the taking of skin, to exchange and to concepts of life hidden to this day.

Let us assume, for hypothesis' sake, that *malanggan* was not a remnant left over from an old and dying tradition, but a new intervention, a brilliant feat of ingenuity that rapidly proved successful in the combat against loss and sorrow. Where once growth and renewal could be ensured only by the snatching of the skins and the taking of the names of enemies, somehow *malanggan* could achieve the same end through 'technical' means that quickly resonated with new contexts and emerging social relations.

Sociality in the North is impossible to grasp when approaching the question of the nature of social relations from the perspective of kinship. There is no genealogical depth, and no one appears to be permanently resident in any single village. And yet connections are all-important, and are visible, for the brief space of a day, when *malanggan* makes its appearance in the village. These are essentially relations of labour and loyalty, founded upon the work of memory, which silently glues back together what had been severed through marriage and through death.

The new political economy of memory that thus came to be known under the generic name of '*malanggan*' was a response to a growing worsening of conditions in the North that peaked with the imposition of colonial rule in 1885 (Moses 1969). The first official trading-post was established in 1840 by Godefroy and Sons at Mioko, an island in the Duke of York group in southern New Ireland. By 1880, the traders at Mioko in southern New Ireland had formed themselves into a 'German Trading and Plantation Company' as successors to Godefroy. Extensive coastal explorations carried out in 1884 led to the mapping out of sites for plantations in the forms that still dominate the island today. The 1956/ 57 patrol report mentions the existence of 210 recognized plantations on the island, the majority of them on the north-east coast, because of the superiority of the soil in this area.

In the years following the imposition of colonial rule in 1885, traders were followed by missionaries and government officials, who rapidly imposed their presence on the North. Northern New Ireland was exposed to colonial influence earlier and more drastically than central and southern New Ireland. This was because of the concentration of administrative and exploitative strategies on the rapidly developing port in the Kavieng Peninsula in the North, from which the island was made accessible to government inspectors and missionaries. The first project to be initiated by the dynamic officer in charge, Boluminski, was the building along the eastern coast of the island of the highway, that was named after him. By 1904, the road had covered about half the 200km-long coastal range, and remained until the 1960s the longest highway in Papua New

Guinea (Chinnery 1932:11). The road along the west coast was started only comparatively recently, in 1968, and completed in the northern part of the island in 1975.

The construction of the Boluminski highway was the task of the local population, who were first enticed and then, with the imposition of a poll tax in 1906, forced to enrol for work (Rowley 1958). Initially, both men and women worked on the road, because of a serious decline in the population due to ravaging infectious diseases that was noted in the early years of colonial rule (Scragg 1954). By creating a need for cash, the colonial government intended to draw the population of the interior to the coast, where it could be more easily controlled. The recruitment of men and women to work on the road thus led to the formation of first temporary and then permanent coastal settlements by the interior population; readily available sites for these consisted of existing coastal dwellings that had been used as 'fishing abodes' and as defences against the former sea-warriors.

During the first twenty years of the twentieth century the mountain villages were gradually given up, becoming first a resort for the old and the feeble and then temporary abodes for gardening and hunting. Today, there is only one village left in the mountains out of what were clearly once large centres of habitation clustered around four named limestone rock formations famous for their cave-like structures, which are still used today as shelters during hunting expeditions. All four places are situated at the intersections of the present-day dialect areas that segment the North, strengthening the assumption that they may have been used as defence-like structures during the height of the warfare, drawing in people from all the surrounding areas (Map 2).

The most northern centre of past settlement is situated at the foot of a formidable rockface called *Pratrehat* which is visible from afar coming down the road from the North near Paruai village. The second interior village is known as *Baum*, and is followed by *Lourup* and *Lumbin* near Lelet Plateau. Those who did not have existing ties through marriage or habitual land use to the East coast upon resettlement stayed longest in the interior, and only retreated to the West coast when the pressure from the government and the missions became inescapable.

Resettlement had manifold consequences; yet one of these was to be found in the common burial of the dead by a population that, until then, was divided into *a usen* (those of the mountain) and *keleras* (those from the beach). Rawi of Lamusmus 2 on the north-west coast, whose age at his death was estimated at 90 years, recounted this change from the perspective of his experience as a West-coast person:

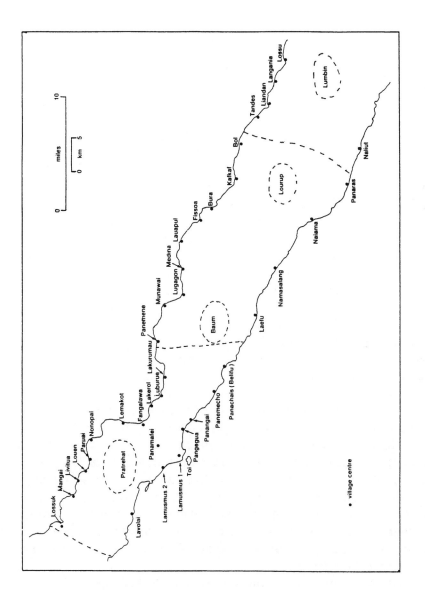

Map 2 Tikana.

When my grandfather Lawin died, his grandmother and mother had already piled up the wood and the men had built a chair made out of bamboo over the funerary pyre. Soon after the skin was cold, the body was burned. No one used to come to a funeral, except those who lived with that person in the same house. Only at the funeral of important men or women would the village attend. Thereafter, we of the coast used to make only *haramgom* and *gisong*. *Malanggan*, that was something only those from the mountain knew about, and we went to see it because we were married to them. Then when they came down to live with us, we began to bury our dead together. Before, only the mountain people used to bury the bones; we used to throw them into the sea. Now, those from the coast have to have a *malanggan* made for them like those from the mountain.

The Australian colonial government, which took over New Ireland in 1914, continued to mould the society they found. A new form of spatial organization was introduced, which was named after its concentrated form *camp*. These camps radically altered the dispersed settlement pattern. The persistence of these camps along the north-east coast, where the movement of settlements is severely restrained by plantation sites, might have contributed to a preference for matrilocal or uxorilocal residence that was noted by Billings (n.d.) for Mangai village and by Lomas (n.d.) for Kulangit. By contrast, along the north-west coast camps were rapidly abandoned with Independence in 1975, with a corresponding norm of patrilocal residence prevailing today.

Together with the change visible in spatial and social organization, central village cemeteries were introduced and cremation as a funerary practice was banned. The implications of these alterations were far more drastic and far-reaching than those of resettlement itself.

Prior to resettlement and co-burial, only the population of the interior buried ashes from a cremation inside a square stone enclosure. The coastal population, on the other hand, deposited the bones of the cremated wrapped in a bundle of *Pandanus* leaves in the sea. Both practices were fused in the ritual work of the new villages that sprang up almost overnight, creating the dual concern with the distancing of the dead and the rooting of ancestral power that will be described for the contemporary *malanggan*.

Perhaps most important, however, was a radical change in the scale of *malanggan* ceremonies, which were attended by more people than ever before. This was certainly partly because of the rising death toll decimating the population in the decades following resettlement, which meant that several deceased persons, all buried in the same cemetery, were commemorated with a single *malanggan*. From well-documented collections we can ascertain, moreover, that several *malanggan*-figures were carved for a single ceremony, rather than just one, which appears certainly to have been the pattern in the two decades leading up to resettlement (Bodrogi 1967, 1971; Heintze 1969, 1987).

Whatever we may assume about how far back in time *malanggan* actually reaches, it is certain that *malanggan* experienced in the early twentieth century an efflorescence in scale, if not in frequency. Moving forward to the present day, we can expect to find life affected by the attention to ritual work.

The Quest for Contiguity

Northern New Ireland, with its population of nearly 70,000 people, is today subdivided linguistically into seven dialect groups. The boundaries between dialect groups coincide spatially with the abandoned settlement sites in the interior. The memory of this common settlement and migration attests to a relatedness and a glimmer of hope in villages where people believe themselves to live as strangers (*namamsei*).

How to reconstitute the sense of being of one clan or of one place is the real dilemma that unites Northerns, evoking a sense of loss that is considered the reason for ill-health and death. 'We are strangers here' (*namam namasei*) is a frequent expression one hears when talking about the village, followed by a eulogy of the route taken in the movement from place to place by those 'who walked together' (*wanen hesuen*), recounting the fragile ties that are linked with security and well-being. Administrative divisions such as the village or district are experienced as arbitrary, a legacy of the colonial administration that had been imposed on local concerns in the years preceding Independence.

Men and women are generally resident in a number of villages at the same time, as they move from place to place during the year to maintain gardens, to harvest fruit-carrying trees or simply to help in the work for the dead, which may preoccupy a relative here or there. One feels safer and more 'at home' living with clan members many miles down the road than in the company of others living in the same village. Yet we will see that retracing the paths of one's clan is not a matter of following stories or intuitions, but of following subtle visual clues embedded in the images that as *malanggan* dominate popular imagination. It is with this search for connections in mind that this book has been written from the perspective of the West-Kara looking outward to the other places and peoples of the North.

While there is no name that could replace the official designation of 'northern' New Ireland, which is actually never used by anyone, there are certain operative names, such as *Tikana* for an administrative conglomerate spanning three dialect areas. Despite being composed phonetically of the names of these three areas, Tigak, Kara and Nalik, Tikana can be translated as 'us severed from roots'. Unless I am specifically pointing to the Kara, I am thus referring to the Tikana as a part of the region that embraces *malanggan* as its core organizing image.

Beaumont's (1976) now classical study of New Ireland languages lends credence to the cohesiveness between the dialect areas that constitute the North. His analysis, while dated, has remained useful in pointing up the interfacing of linguistic and cultural boundaries, which have become more permeable since the rising mobility of an increasingly car-bound population. The affinities he isolated between distinct dialects match administrative divisions. West-Kara census division, for example, is an amalgam of 12 villages and three language groups – called Kara, Nalik and Kuot. Empirical data collected during research support the suggestion that ties of marriage and exchange indeed link the people of this census division. In effect, census-divisions provided a spatial foil for the connections that people trace across villages and dialect areas.

Nowhere is this more evident than among the Kara, whose territory lies between two interior limestone formations known to the Kara as Pratrehat and Baum (see Map 1). The rocky heights of Pratrehat are easily visible from the east-coast road at Mangai village, and serve as a visual reminder that one is crossing the dialect boundary between Tigak in the North and Kara in the South. South of Mangai village, near Lemakot, the interior markedly flattens. It is here that during the late Pleistoscene formation of the island the island upturned and twisted, leaving the northern tip of the island almost severed from its base. Since the early colonial administration and missionization, a footpath led across the mountain at this most narrow point on the island; this footpath in 1968 became a road that today leads as far south as Panaras in Kuot.

A description of Kara villages and house-sites shows at work the crafting of landscape into something that resembles what can no longer be seen, but merely traced in memory and imagined when traversing the now abandoned interior. Where one builds one's house, and with whom one shares part of a garden reflects on places left long ago and on lives that are all but forgotten. As the names of the dead are given to the newborn, imparting to them particular traits and abilities, so new places are conceived as resemblances of formerly familiar places.

As the car leaves Lemakot Mission, at the turn-off at Fangalawa village to the only mountain road it follows a sharply ascending and winding path that traverses a number of scattered settlements of Panamafei village. The sharp ascent is followed almost without interruption by a more rapid descent, ending in a junction known as the eye of the village (*merane bine*). The turn off to the north leads through the villages of Lamusmus 1, Lamusmus 2, and Lavolai, whereas the turn-off to the south leads through the villages of Pangefua, Panangai, Panemecho and Panachais, and further to the villages of west Nalik and Kuot.

To one travelling by car the coast seems almost uninhabited, with only a handful of settlements being situated along the roadside and large plantations seemingly covering any remaining land along both sides of the road. West-Kara village structure is decentralized, each village comprising between 30 to 60 dispersed settlements and between 300 and 600 inhabitants. The named settlements of a village, of which each has between one and five houses, lie scattered along a labyrinth of pathways that traverse the coastal and interior land on either side of the road. Each settlement has its own cemetery and finishes the work for its dead on its own account.

Following the road to the north, one enters an environment different to the one south of the junction. To the north, the landscape widens as the hills retreat and become higher and more rugged. Along the coast, lagoons separate the beach from the reef and provide ideal fishing conditions. Towards Lavolai village the ecology changes from secondary rain forest and rock formations into a predominantly swampy landscape utilized extensively for logging. From the junction to the south the land available for habitation along the coast increasingly diminishes as limestone rock formations sharply descend to the sea at Panachais, forcing the road upwards into the mountains at the southern end of West-Kara.

West-Kara is divided into two administrative districts, which mirror this changing landscape: Ward 4, covering the villages to the north of the junction, from Lamusmus to Lavolai, and Ward 5, covering the villages south of the junction, from Pangefua to Panachais. A brief description of the villages in Ward 4 will highlight certain characteristic features of village organization, such as the pairing of settlements in relation to former settlements buried deep in the forest. A complex pattern of bi-focalization emerges in the consideration of village organization, whereby rights to land are activated through reference to place-names. Any specific claim to land for the purpose of gardening or the harvesting of fruit- or nut-bearing trees must be accompanied

by a detailed recitation of a string of place-names that traces the descent
from the mountain to the coast. Every village is, in addition, divided
into those from the coast (*keleras*) and those from the interior (*utan*)
and in terms of the differential access that such categorization grants
to vegetal and maritime resources.

Lavolai village, in the extreme north of West-Kara, is the smallest of
its villages, with only about 120 inhabitants. Most inhabitants consider
themselves to be descendants of the former settlement Paling in the foothills to the north of Pratrehat. Leaving Lavolai, the road passes through
Kaletawun plantation, which is, with its ten permanent employees,
small by New Ireland standards. Two settlements of Lamusmus 2 are
clustered around the northern and southern borders of the plantation.
These settlements, named Kuntali and Kurumut, are inhabited by
descendants of another former settlement that was situated adjacent
to Paling, called Panalah, likewise situated in the foothills of Pratrehat.
South of these settlements is a 3 km-long stretch of garden area leading
to the other eight settlements of the village Lamusmus 2, all of which
are scattered in compounds of two to three houses, each along footpaths
that traverse the coastal land along both sides of the road.

The southern part of Lamusmus 2 is also known as Pusigeo (Map 3).
Pusigeo was, in fact, the only permanent coastal settlement prior to the
resettlement of the population along the coast. While the northern
settlements of Lamusmus 2 claim extensive ties to the former settlement
of Panalah, the southern settlements are descendants of a settlement
to the south of Pratrehat, called Panehunewut, which is likewise now
uninhabited. Panalah and Panehunewut are remembered to have
existed as a virtually endogamous group that regularly intermarried and
shared rights to *malanggan* and land. Lamusmus 2 thus seemingly repro-
duces in its use of space a duality associated with ancestral grounds in
the mountainous interior. Its border, however, is also the point of fusion
with others, creating a picture of an ever more encompassing whole.
Thus it is the case that those who left Panehunewut to settle with affines
in Panamafei upon resettlement see themselves as more closely related
to those living today in Pusigeo of Lamusmus 2 than to anyone else,
and they all treat each other's homesteads, land and work as one. Both
together share the same relation with Nonopai village to the east, of
which one-half also had to come down from Panehunewut.

The pattern of relatedness in contemporary villages is thus in accordance with the ownership of land as it is perceived to have prevailed prior
to the resettlement of the population along the coast in the early part
of this century. Place-names of long-overgrown settlements serve as

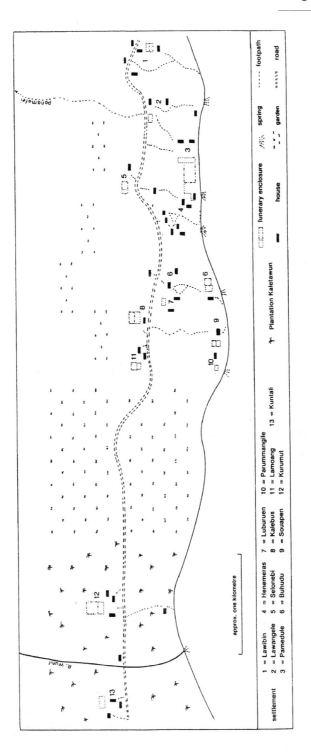

Map 3 Village.

icons of relatedness, drawing together all those who 'have come down together' from a certain 'source' (*rune*). When these inlanders settled along the coast with their coastal affines, complex relationships between different coastal and interior settlements came to be reproduced both in the interior village organization and in its relation to other villages. It is for this reason that a village such as Lamusmus 2 is not only divided into a 'mountain' and a 'coastal' part, separated by a clear spatial divide, but also has a 'partner' village, which likewise grew around an adjacent coastal settlement.

Lamusmus 1 is separated by no visual or spatial boundary from Lamusmus 2, and no one without prior knowledge would be aware of crossing a village boundary. Lamusmus 1 is, with its 64 settlements and over 600 inhabitants, the largest village in West-Kara. Its size may be at least partly facilitated by the width of the coastal expanse here, which allows for extensive settlement and gardening; yet it also reflects the manifold connections that the recollection of settlement history has managed to foster.

In fact, if one inquires into the relationship between Pusigeo and Lamusmus it emerges that historically the relationship alternated between one of war and one of mutual co-operation in defence, which in turn is reflected in the contemporary setting. Every morning one can see groups of women walking along the road in either direction, carrying wrapped parcels of cooked food or areca nut in their baskets as gifts for their sisters in the partner village in whose garden they are allowed to work. Such peaceful gardening co-operations, however, frequently erupt into *dang*, the ban placed on the use of land. Such a ban is imposed on account of an alleged misuse of 'relatedness' in the course of claiming shared rights to land, and can only be lifted during a *malanggan*-ceremony.

Both Lamusmus 1 and Lamusmus 2 have close gardening and feasting ties with the only remaining mountain village, Panamafei, which is inhabited by the descendants of the former mountain settlement of Panehunewut in the foothills of Pratrehat. It is Panamafei village that serves as the nodal point between the northern and southern part of West-Kara, its female inhabitants having intermarried with clans that had moved westwards across the low mountains south of Pratrehat during the period of warfare, as well as with the coastal dwellers of Pusigeo and Lamusmus. Pangefua and Panangai, the villages to the south of the junction, have the strongest ties with Panamafei village and today's east-coast villages. As with Lamusmus 2 and Lamusmus 1, no visible boundary separates these villages, whose most southern settlement borders on a plantation known as Laubul, in which most of Ward

5's population have shares. Panemecho and Panachais to the south of Laubul are inhabited by descendants of the interior settlements around the limestone formation known as Baum. As in the case of Lamusmus 1 and Lamusmus 2, both villages are internally divided into coastal and interior sections, defined in terms of the migration history of their residents. The differentiation is particularly marked in the case of Panachais village, owing to the geographical position of the village, which partially lies along the sandy bay of Panachais, fringed by vertically descending cliffs, and partially in the hilly and rocky coastal land of Belifu to the south. Part of Baum's former inhabitants are also living today in two villages to the south within the Nalik-speaking area.

Today's villages are thus fashioned as a kind of visual resemblance to a lost site through which connections are forged that are in many ways as real now as they were then. Yet it is not just the spatial layout of a village that recalls via similitude, but also things of the everyday, such as the ubiquitous basket woven from coconut fronds, without which no man or woman would leave the house.

The term for 'village' is quite telling, for it is called *bine* in the Kara language, a term that literally translated means 'those who share a basket' (*bi*–basket, *ne*–connecting phoneme). The basket does not symbolize village identity; it crafts that identity in the very weaving of its frame and the nourishment offered by its content. It is not just what the basket looks like that is important, or its texture, whose changing and short-lived surface, turning soft and permeable with age, reminds one of the texturing of both *malanggan*-figures and human bodies, but also what can be done with it, how it is carried, how much it can carry, and so on. Inhabitants of villages from Lamusmus 1 and 2 to Lavolai are known by their distinctive baskets used for gardening, which are carried suspended at the front and the back on sticks held on the shoulder, as well as by smaller personal baskets that feature a handle. The villagers of Ward 5, on the other hand, carry their garden baskets on their heads and their personal baskets under their arms. Specific weaving techniques for rim and handle as well as the shapes given to baskets of different types further distinguish the inhabitants of villages within each ward. As women normally move in marriage just between the two halves of a village, no new techniques tend to be learned after marriage; but the awareness of other techniques and forms is intense.

Baskets are also synonymous with patterns of consumption that conjure up an image of a village as a self-sufficient entity. The daily contents of baskets are offered to anyone encountered on the many paths leading to gardens. As anyone likely to be encountered is considered to be of the same 'source' – figuratively speaking at least, in the sense of referring to common ancestral settlement – in eating the contents of the baskets of others one also eats something that is considered to be 'like' oneself. The associative link of eating with sexual reproduction is underscored in a belief that the ideal marriage is *ulul ine si*, or a 'marriage back to one's roots'.

The village, radiating outward through acts of splitting and pairing, is thus an ideally endogamous unit. The force of 'marrying inside' can be demonstrated with the largest of Pusigeo's settlements, called Henemeras. Henemeras is situated adjacent to the now abandoned communal cemetery along the beach around which all the houses of Lamusmus 2 were clustered. Henemeras is a large settlement with nine houses, three of them on the beach and six on top of the cliff close to the road (Map 4). The settlement is divided into five house-sites, each separated from the others by a stretch of land planted with an array of

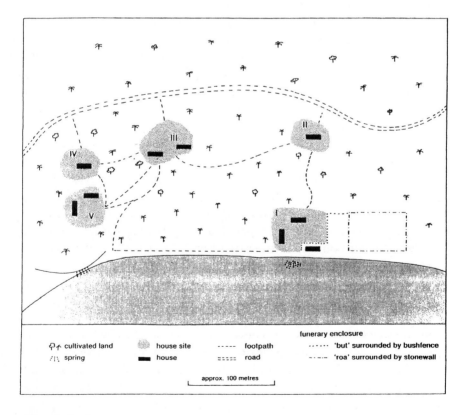

			funerary enclosure
ϙ⸀ cultivated land	▨ house site	----- footpath	······ 'but' surrounded by bushfence
⸝⸝⸝ spring	▬ house	===== road	––··– 'roa' surrounded by stonewall

approx. 100 metres

Map 4 Settlement.

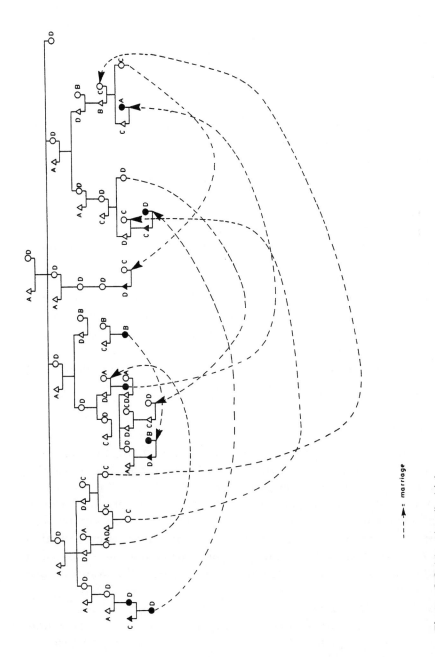

---▸ : marriage

Figure 1.2 Marrying 'inside'.

coconut palms as well as fruit- and nut-trees of various kinds. All occupants of the nine houses consider themselves to be the offspring of four of five sisters and of their mother, Matleroro of Moromaf, who was captured during warfare (Figure 1.2). At the time of the research, the settlement was clustered around its eldest member, a man called Rawi of Moromaf (house-site I), who was about 90 years old at the time.

The part of the settlement that is nearest to the road and is fragmented into the house-sites II, III, IV and V is inhabited by the old man's sister's daughter, his own daughter, her daughters and married son, and the daughter of Rawi's sister's son. House-site I, on the other hand, was inhabited by the old man and his two sons. The geographical split into upper and lower house-sites thus reflects relations between cross-sex siblings, which we will find to lie at the heart of daily concerns in the next chapter.

With Rawi's death, all the houses were abandoned, and, where once life had teemed, secondary forest had soon covered all that remained visible. Where people moved to forged connections to places that had been abandoned in a similar manner long ago. A complex chequerboard pattern appears to be in place, where all your present actions foreshadow both past and future options. The image that the Kara create to capture the complex arrest of movement, alone ensuring the alignment of past and present, of ancestral and living resources, is fashioned to be 'like' a body. We will find this artificially constituted image that is 'like' a body again in the figurative imagery of *malanggan*; yet it is most clearly articulated in the rendering of social space (Küchler 1992).

The Body as Image

The fusion and fission of these multiple, overlapping and ever more introverted domains that separate inside from outside while connecting past and present pivot around the house called *luhu*, or 'source of rootedness'. Like the settlement, the house has only two entrances, one at the 'face' (*none*) and one at the 'behind' (*bak*). Made of sago-thatch roofing (*a vul*) and split-bamboo walls (*arabil*), the house is virtually dark and empty inside, with the exception of a circular fireplace (*hede*) to one side and a central stone- oven (*mun*). This 'place of the womb' (*larune*) resembles the clean-swept outer courtyard (*lamalei*), within whose centre usually towers a single nut-bearing tree. This courtyard is called the 'place that is like ginger' (*ma aleie*), as it is surrounded with an abundance of odorous plants whose sweet (*mamis*) smell (*ngauf*) balances the sour (*mimeric*) smell of the smoke that streams through the roof of the house during the daily lighting of the stone-oven (Figure 1.3).

Figure 1.3 Settlement.

Like the house, the settlement (*bine*) has a 'face' (*none*), which usually is directed to the ocean (*la-ras*) or the road/path (*selen*). Its back (*bak*) is formed by the stonewalled cemetery, which is not a container, but an orifice called 'mouth of stone' (*belehat*) in whose centre is the burial pit or 'rooting place' called *roa*. Next to the 'mouth of stone' is another funerary enclosure, made this time out of bamboo and wood, which is called *sebedo* or 'linking those who are grown from one root' (Figure 1.4). This enclosure surrounds *but*, a term that echoes another *but*, found at the bottom of the stone-oven in the white, finely powdered ashes that are used as a base for ceremonial paint and in the powder that is eaten with areca nut, made of ground coral, both of them believed to effect *mamaluhi*, or active remembering. But, composed phonetically of '*b*' for 'mouth', '*u*' for womb/source and '*t*' for 'split', resonate with a notion of renewal and generative containment that is set into motion in the work for the dead. Occasionally, when the death of an elder is expected, a house is built on *but*, where the elder may live for some months as the 'living dead'.

Unlike the stone-walled cemetery, the *but*'s enclosure is re-built and left to rot in stages that mark the work for each deceased person buried in its adjacent cemetery. As it is never dismantled, but just left to fall

Figure 1.4 *Sebedou* enclosure.

apart, the fence may be in various degrees of decay upon the occurrence
of a new death in the settlement, when it comes to contain the body
of the deceased, which is left there to 'dry' (*mah*) for at least one day.
The process of drying, involving the dripping of the 'water' (*darum*) of
the body into the ground of *but* used to be extended for elders and those
of status until mummification (*vipito*) set in, but has now long been
tightly controlled by the Department of Health and the Mission. Many
years later, upon the death of an elder who is housed for the last months
of life inside a *but*, *malanggan* figures are carved or woven on this ground
to reabsorb in a new 'skin' the watery substance of life arrested in it.

Behind the burial ground and around the sides of the settlement is a
stretch of secondary forest whose size depends on the density of the
population and the space available within the village, called 'the place
of skin' (*laten*). Planted on either side of the settlement, and behind
the burial ground, are usually banana palms (*hut*), breadfruit trees (*be*)
and areca nut trees (*bua*), as well as in certain places coconut groves
(*ni*); all are planted by the present inhabitants of a settlement, and are
dramatically cut down after death as part of the symbolic process of
the removal of 'skin' (*sesere*), which dissolves the identity of a deceased
person.

This secondary forest or 'place of the skin' is thus like a perishable and permeable membrane that envelops each settlement and connects it with all others in the village. With death, this 'skin' is gradually dismantled, to be replaced eventually by a new house-site or 'place of the womb'. Like a cell whose 'inside' becomes 'outside' and again a new 'inside' as it divides and grows, so the growth of a settlement is talked about in terms of the 'changing of skin' marked by a permanent process of inversion.

In these images of social space and its material analogue in baskets we can see at work a plot that enables one to keep to oneself while ensuring growth and continuity. The thinking in, through and with images that resemble one another creates a world that is not divisive, but paved by connections. It is this world that *malanggan* touches and that it brings to life visually and conceptually as a virtuous technique of resistance.

Note

1. Biskop 1975; Brown 1881; Blum 1900; Boluminski 1904; *Deutsches Kolonialblatt* 1885; Chinnery 1932; Friederici 1910; Hahl 1907, 1942; Krämer 1907; Krieger 1899; Meyer and Parkinson 1895; Neuhaus 1911; Parkinson 1907; Ranni 1889, 1912; Romilly 1886; Stephan and Graebner 1907; Strauch 1877; Thilenius 1903.

Matriliny in the Making

> Indeed, contrary to Levi-Strauss's contention that it is the prohibition of incest that makes possible society and the system of reciprocity that underlies sociality, it could be said that it is a recomposed image of androgynous and incestuous unity (or its closest approximation) that stands at the very center of society and is the condition for both hierarchy and exchange. That is, 'keeping to oneself', relatively speaking . . . is the ground against which 'giving away' . . . receives value (Susan McKinnon 1991: 279).

When dusk falls, the sweet vapour of the just opened stone-oven fills the air. The road and the waterfront are deserted at this time, but for an unmarried man of the village who walks by as if by chance, hoping that someone may spot him and call 'Cousin, you come and eat' (*korok, hutman kalak na hangen*). Beaming with pleased surprise, yet averting his eyes, he will come over and sit at some distance to eat from the freshly opened banana-leaf bundle filled with steamed taro (*nuum*) while the women retreat into the house to wait until he is finished and ready to leave.

Daily life in the village is full of solitude coupled with preparedness for attending (*hamarere*) to one's *korok* should they happen to walk by; visiting is unheard-of, and known only as a 'calling' (*nungnung*), which works very much in the manner described above.[1] Baskets are filled with betelnut (*buai*) and lime (*las*), ready for the many, yet brief, chance encounters during the day with same-sex *korok*, while *korok* of the opposite sex are avoided whenever possible.

As a core category of kinship, the relationship between reciprocal *korok* appears to radiate outward from the incest taboo that is observed between brothers and sisters, as it shares with this relationship the imposition of strict rules of avoidance; one has to avoid looking directly at one's *korok*, addressing her by name, sitting or walking next to her,

passing things to her without using a middleman, or being found sleep-
ing or eating in her presence. Avoidance rules are strongest for *korok* of
the opposite sex, yet take the form of a muted joking relationship among
korok of the same sex; one's daily basket of betelnut is mostly for these
latter *korok,* as just one of the many daily and occasional gifts that pass
back and forth between them.[2]

While the classical reading of matrilineal kinship (Schneider 1961)
suggested brother/sister avoidance to prevent conflict, it may also be
interpreted as eliciting relationships, as Roy Wagner (1986:69) argued for
the Barok of southern New Ireland. Avoiding some of the trappings of
the earlier functionalist analysis, this perspective, however, still falls
short of accounting for the nature of hierarchy and exchange in matrilineal societies. This is because it clings to the assumption that it is affinal
relationships that constitute the core kinship category as a consequence
of the incest taboo, with exchange and hierarchy following as derivative
of affinity.

Annette Weiner's (1992) re-analysis of Trobriand kinship points up
a possible alternative perspective on the nature of avoidance: rather than
separating people, it may be seen at least imaginatively, if not actually,
to draw people together. McKinnon (1991) made a similar suggestion
for Tanimbar in Indonesia in arguing for an image of androgynous and
incestuous unity to stand at the centre of society and to provide a logical
conceptual foundation for hierarchy and exchange.

Avoidance rules may thus confound and even be symptomatic of an
endogamous sociality that conceives of units of siblings as the core
kinship category. Among the Tikana, it is sacrifice that conditions an
image of mutual relatedness that unites sibling-units as 'one blood and
one skin'. From the perspective of this re-composed 'body' at the centre
of society, it is sisters, not wives, who define its replacement over time.
In the North of New Ireland, as among the Barok of the South, the
positioning of sisters *vis-à-vis* the endogamous group is framed by the
symbolism of rooting and uprooting that pervades the ritual processes
prevalent in bridewealth and at death.

By elaborating this ritual symbolism in figurative imagery, the Tikana
have found an ingenious way of tracing the movement of their sisters
between places. Otherwise 'closed' groups are artificially expanding, by
means of recreating perishable and permeable 'skins' that are metaphorically uprooted and rooted over and over again, reversing movements
at death that were made during life.

While the Tikana matri-clan thus appears forever on the move, each
move merely contributes to the expansion of the endogamous group

rather than to its demise. In this way, the endogamous group replaces itself as 'one skin and one blood' (*namam retak na deia*) whether marriages are conducted inside it or not (*a ulul ine si*).[3]

The conception of the core kinship unit as consisting of an androgynous and endogamous unit composed of mutually related sibling units has implications for the nature of the sociality thus created. While among the equally matrilineal Trobriand Islands endogamy is synonymous with the localized matri-clan (*dala*) (Weiner 1976), among the Tikana endogamy is an inherently expansive notion that finds its heightened expression in a regionally reconstituted matri-clan. Also, while in the Trobriand Islands regional partnerships fostered through Kula are independent of the movement of sisters in marriage, among the Tikana the ritual work of *malanggan* retraces the scattered matri-clan. By implication, it is one's relationship to one's sister that provides the primary axis of an inherently expansive relationality.

Through patrilateral and patrilocal marriage among the Tikana, a sister becomes a *korok* and the linchpin in a relation of loyalty and labour that is capable of enchaining material and intellectual resources in a continuous and cumulative flow. The endogamous group that results from repeated marriage with father's sister's children (*casuk*) is thus aptly described as 'one growth' (*dahun*).

Gender among the Tikana is a product of becoming at birth part of a set of *korok* relationships that multiply and expand throughout a person's life. When a child is born, the concern is not whether it is male (*uron*) or female (*revin*), but what kind of *korok* it is going to be to whom. As soon as a child can walk it is sent between same-sex *korok* carrying items of food as well as messages, while being kept at a distance from *korok* of the opposite sex. Children also become aware of their gendered position in *korok* relationships through naming; as names are transferred from one generation to another within the village, a child's name will be also the name of at least one *korok* related to at least one of the people who are close to the child, who will then call the child by an additional name.

By the age of four or five, relations with the other female *korok* of a household are becoming so constraining for little boys, who may not address, touch or sit next to them, that they voluntarily move into houses that serve as more or less temporary shelter for the men of various ages. Such houses are not usually built in the settlement, but in the secondary forest or the 'place of the skin' (*laten*), where they may be relocated to more distant locations during times set aside for the preparation of dances (*motiti*). It is also here, in this spatial membrane, that *korok* encounter each other during the day, having left the young and the old behind as the sole guardians of the house.

To Be of One Skin

In the same way as this village space does not consist of a static inside and outside relation, but involves an inversion and blending of the one with the other, the person is composed of perpetually fusing inner and outer elements; that is, of a skin (*tak*) and an inner life-force (*noman*) that permeates the membrane and may escape from it temporarily during sleep or permanently at death. It is this 'skin', composed of a layer of fat and its surface, that is both a container and a passage for the unceasing flow of a regenerative force. Skin is thought of as a substance that is life-giving because it absorbs heat and retains water.

As living, regenerative substance, like earth and plants, a person's skin is thought to be changing from being dry (*meiang*) and seemingly male (*merang*) to being wet (*misirk*) or female (*rehin*) in a process that starts prior to conception and finishes at death. At birth and at death, skin is in its wettest, most permeable, and most female state, while during the rest of life it is gradually hardened through prescribed fasts that extract liquid from the skin until it becomes fully dry or male in the adult man and woman (*merafera meian*); in old age (*labumo*), skin returns again to its wet state through a diet rich in liquid.

Matrilinearity, which is the pervasive concept of sociality throughout New Ireland, is thus neither explainable with the 'logical' entailments of matrilineal descent, nor is it just the outcome of mortuary rituals that isolate and recapture an invisible force whose regenerativity genders social relations through ritual consumption.[4] While it is clearly both of these, it is also and most importantly a processual logic that is inseparable from the operational qualities of skin. Made to be dry and closed during life, the wet skin, which is at once permeable and perishable at either end of life, receives a value through the antithesis thus created. As the invisible inner life-force, in the form of heat and water, permeates skin, it *becomes* the skin that takes on the generative and connective capacity that is the conceptual driving force of the matriliny.

The notion of an androgynous skin, which undergoes periodic states of dryness and wetness, also highlights the at once endogamous and expansive nature of a social group whose permeability is as carefully worked upon as its self-sufficiency. 'We are of one skin' (*namam retak*) is the description of an identity that may incorporate anyone who participates in the many daily and ritual procedures that actively seek to 'make skin' (*retak*). For 'skin' to induce connection in this way it has to be turned into a space full of movement, a passage for the flow of people and things, an entity capable of invoking recognition. Yet, while this kind of skin is connecting as it is softened to the point of dissolution, it presupposes another kind of work, that of the hardening of the skin. The processual dynamic of this closing and opening of skin is activated by drawing attention to certain parts of the body and certain relationships.

Kara language, like all the northern dialects, has no distinct term for body other than that for skin (*tak*). Skin (*tak*) is strengthened (*makasen*) and induced to become more or less wet and permeable or dry and retentive depending on the food one eats (*nggan*). The wet skin of the newborn is 'dried' (*bung*) in being held over the fire by its father's sister just minutes after birth. This process of drying out is continued with the feeding of chewed (*meme*) and dried food, preferably taro tubers roasted over the fire, given immediately after birth and throughout the first two years of life until weaning. The drying of skin is continued through to adulthood and is assisted by food taboos called *alal* that restrict liquids in a variety of forms, including meat and certain kinds of fish, whose red and slimy skin is likened to that of newborn infants.

Health is associated with a strong skin in both men and women, which may be weakened through the presence of visitors (*kumbag*); visitations of all kinds are used to explain illnesses in general, which are thought to result in the gradual permeability and eventual 'loss' (*luk*) of skin. The immanent presence of death is announced to all present by the change of diet from a dry and roasted kind to a liquid one.

Kinship terms amplify this processual nexus of skin and nurture in ways long ago immortalized by one of Edmund Leach's (1967) famous comments: 'Firth', he said, 'understood the fact that kin terms must convey meaning as sound patterns and that contrasts in meaning are likely to correspond to contrasts in sound pattern' (Leach 1967: 127). In Kara, this phonological contrast through which the body emerges as a foil for relatedness is embedded in the transformation of the proto-oceanic form for first person possession –'*ingga* that is also found in the nasalized – *ang* – form – into a clitic – *ak*. Both *ak* and *ang* are common phonological distinctions between social relations and between body parts.

> *tak*, skin (my) *tam, tane, tamam, tami, tadi*
> *rivining*, bone (my)
> *ihak*, cousin (my)
> *i-nang*, mother (my) *i-nam, i-nane, i-namam, i-nami, i-nadi*

Words with the ending *ang* in body terms and in kin terms are linked through associations with food and eating (*nggan/nggen*). *Ak*, on the other hand, links body terms and kinship terms through an emphasis on tactile and visual communication.

Only certain body parts are denoted by the ending *ak*: these nouns are *tak* (skin), *merak* (eye), *mak* (hand) and *wuak* (throat). Other body parts, such as *riwining* (bone), *kining* (leg), *butung* (head), *belang* (mouth), *ngusung* (nose) and *liwang* (ear) have the ending *ang*.

Body parts ending in *ang* are thought to mature and to become strong (*makal*) not on their own account, but through the ingestion of certain food. Only certain kinship categories end in *angg*, and these tend to be those that are required to obey a series of food taboos (*alal*) that aim at the drying of skin: *i-nang*: Mo, MoZ, So, Da, MoBrDaDa, FaZDaDa, *tamang*: Fa, FaBr, So, Da, MoZHu, *maroridning*: MoBr, ZSo, FaBrDaDa(So), MoZDaDa(So) *nang*: Da, So, *e-nang*: FaZ, MoBrWi, BrSo(Da) *aimung*: Wi(Hu)Mo, Wi(Hu)Fa, SoWi, DaHu, FaZHu, *lik*: Da, So(male Ego and outsider). Others ending in *ak* are addressed with the generic term *korok*; *korok* relationships exert constraints upon the child's use of hands, eyes, and voice. They also contribute to the growing wetness of skin through gifts of certain sweet-smelling and 'wet' foods: *paluk*: Si(female Ego), Br(maleEgo), *tiak*: Si, FaBrDa, MoZDa, Br, *ihak*: SiHu, BrWi, MoBrSo, MoBrSoSo, FaZSo, FaZSoSo, *casuk:* Wi, Hu, MoBrDa, FaZDa.

Nerune, the reciprocal term for the grandparental generation and for those two generations removed from Ego, is the only exception to this pattern, being literally the 'source'. *Enang*, father's sister, and *Aimung*, mother- and father-in-law, are intermediate categories, as they are tranformed through marriage into *korok*.

Skin is thought only to be fully hardened in both men and women when those who stand in an *ang* relation to them have ceased to perform the ritual fast of *alal* for the parents', that is their own children's, offspring. This change of diet in the grandparental generation induces an increasing wetness of skin, which usually coincides with the onset of menopause, after which women, as well as their husbands, are able to handle things considered 'wet', such as paints produced from a lime-base or shell-strings, and to eat food that is considered 'wet', such as meat, sweet-smelling fish or creamed taro. The parental generation, at the same time, expecting the first offspring of their own children, have taken their turn in avoiding wet foods.

As the parent's skin thus enters its most consistently dry state ever, the skin of the young adult who is undergoing betrothal (*rarawe hesuen*) is entering the most extreme state of wetness, brought about by a diet rich in meat and creamed taro. Over a period of two to three months, the grandmother of a young man (*rulau*) prepares daily for her son and his spouse one parcel of *kaderu* made of taro and a rich sauce of grated coconut, which is consumed jointly inside the house – this being the only time a man and woman are ever allowed to eat together. The consumption of *kaderu* marks the onset of a period of conception (*burut*) and comes to full completion only with the birth of the child.

Kaderu has to be produced by a post-menopausal woman and is reserved for this occasion and for the carving of *malanggan* figures, when it is consumed by the carver. It is thought to be effective in inducing wetness in those who eat, because of the intense sweetness/wetness (*mis*) of the odorous vapour of grated coconut in its cooked state, but also because of its allusions to connection, made visible in the manner of slicing taro so that it remains joined at the bottom.[5]

As a woman undergoes this process of rapidly increasing wetness in a more pronounced manner, she is called *rehin* or 'rain' for the period in her life in which she can conceive, while men are called *merang*, or 'dry'. With the birth of the child, a strict reduction of wetness in the diet of the mother, interrupted only when she intends to conceive another child, is also followed by the child's father and grandparents, so as to ensure the growing dryness of the infant's body.

It is in the inception stages of wetness, at the onset of a new marriage (*ri hileben*) and conception, as well as after death, that *korok* relationships are coming to the fore. Female *korok* are responsible for contributing to the daily food parcel by bringing meat and sweet-smelling fish. As a sign of their participation in conception, formal gifts for buying shame (*sesemangil*) are passed between future *korok*. These gifts, like the daily ones that flow back and forth between *korok*, are given in public, seen by everyone and accompanied by a speech in a way that is known as 'breaking the "eye" of the tree' (*meremerebak*), which is repeated many times over after death, when *korok* re-form their relationships to each other as sets of siblings after the death of a person. It is these gifts that instigate the notion of shared skin (*namam retak*), with its implied lasting usufructory rights to land, that is cherished among *korok*.

In the hands of *korok*, 'skin' becomes a mobile entity that connects as it is made to dissolve in ritual work. Yet this permeable 'skin' questions the very notion of containment that is at the heart of the endogamous group. The tension between the two sides of 'skin', the skin as container and the skin as passage, is reflected in notions that prevail around 'the place of the skin' (*laten*), which in its animate state figures as the mirror of humanity.

Skin among the Tikana is not just a relational concept, but an entity whose changing surface qualities are shared by land. As with skin, changes in the coloration of the earth indicate its wetness or dryness. The wetness of red earth is anticipated every morning when steam evaporates as the hot morning sun clears the night's dew. Only this earth is considered fertile when planting new taro gardens. The seven-year fallow period for each taro garden is strictly observed and monitored, both by the changing colouring of the earth, from grey, to brown, and back to red, and by the size of the coconut palms planted in the centre of each new garden.

Certain land surfaces literally breathe life; when entering, they virtually hit you in the face with their intense heat and humidity. These places, which are like little oases around deep waterholes or swamps in an otherwise often dry land, are known as the dwellings of *masalei·*.[6] *Masalei* are androgynous spirits of the land that are also known as 'skin changers' (*rulrul*) through their capacity to take on a near-human appearance in skins snatched from victims who have visited these places without precautionary protection or when suffering from an already weakened skin through sorcery (*ngein*). The attack of a *rulrul* results in the temporary possession of the victim, who behaves as if in a dream-like state. The possession is followed by total apathy and, if not cured with magic, by death (Neuhaus 1962: 246). The wetness that emanates from these places, however, turns them also into the preferred ground for planting sago palms and ritual gardens, irrespective of the dangers they harbour.

Another kind of *masalei* is found in dry, barren land located usually at the tops of mountains in the interior. These are the dwellings of giant female pythons, each being named and associated with a clan, to which alone it is harmless. The presence of the snake is recognized by strips of its dried skin, which it sheds regularly, in contrast to the skin-accumulating spirits (*rulrul*).

This conception of clan-spirit land as capable of renewing skin, yet doomed to isolation and bareness, frames the ground against which the wet land with its skin-accumulating spirits receives its value. While being the protective base of a matri-clan, the land of the skin-renewing spirits is unproductive and in itself not an image of continuity. The land of the skin-snatching spirits, by contrast, epitomizes an image of mobility and growth that is claimed by *korok* in the ritual work of bridewealth and death.

The tension between these two images of animated land pervades the performances and images of bridewealth and mortuary feasting. Here it surfaces as the drama of 'obviation', to use Roy Wagner's poignant term for acts of nullification or negation, which in the North are metaphorized in the 'killing' (*luri*) of 'skin' (Wagner 1986: 211–13, 1987). In contrast to what happens among the Barok of southern New Ireland, however, what is fashioned through the negation is not a quasi-supernatural power, but one that is inherent in the notion of 'recollection' (*mamaluhen*). Through negation, the distinction between self-renewal and accumulation is effaced, and a new concept, that of gathering (*bung*), is allowed to emerge.

To Be of One Blood

A woman conceives of herself as a sister (*besak*), and as a *korok*, rather than as a spouse, and will return with menopause to her natal village. While her daughter can return to her mother's land by marrying mother's brother's son, her son's preferred marriage with father's sister's daughter would leave him without title to land, should his father's land in some way not also be his. Among the Tikana, joint land-rights among endogamous sibling-units are the result of blood sacrifice (*kiut*). With *kiut*, one pays, at least in a symbolic sense, with one's sister's blood for 'skin', and is able to fashion the recomposed body of those who are 'one skin and one blood' (*namam retak na deia*).[7]

Today, a female pig that is specifically raised for this purpose inside the settlement and named after the female head of the household is chosen for the blood payment; it is sacrificed (*kiut*) by strangulation, its blood (*deia*) being ritually ingested by the land-owning clans. As a reminder of the blood payment thus made, the name of the sacrificial victim (who is at least symbolically the in-marrying woman or her daughter) is remembered as apical ancestress. Her name figures in any land-dispute as a potent reminder of the fusion of blood and skin that originated the land-holding conglomerate of clans. In recognition of the blood payment and the granting of land-rights, the father's clan makes a *malanggan* figure and gives it to his children as their 'skin', completing the unseverable bond among those who became 'one skin and one blood'.

One such woman who is remembered to have founded a *dahun* with her blood is Matleroro of the matri-clan Moromaf, which through her came to reside in Pusigeo of Lamusmus 2 (see Figure 1.2). As Matleroro died prior to her husband, her unmarried daughter Kei is believed to have been sacrificed (*kiut*) to pay with her blood for the land that Moromaf today owns jointly with two other already co-resident clans.

Another example of *kiut* is remembered by the clan Moroibe, a coastal clan that came to be resident in Panamafei village and conceives itself to be 'of one growth' with the land-owning clan Morotirien, which was annexed in a similar fashion to other clans in its territory. A woman of Moroibe whose offshoots are still resident in Louen in East-Kara is believed to have married a man of Morotirien in Paling as part of an existing *dahun* relationship between the then spatially segregated coastal and mountain clans. During a fight between Paling and Panalah her daughter Pimat was captured and taken to be resident in the settlement Lamaskup, which is situated near the present-day village Panamafei. Pimat married into another offshoot of the clan Morotirien and gave birth to a daughter, known as Hule, who is said to have paid with her blood for the land that Moroibe claims as its own today.

Blood sacrifice as the foundation of an endogamous group explains the fact that New Ireland is one of the few matrilineal societies in which a blood-link is traced through the father's line. Among the Tikana, blood is turned into paternal substance through a sacrificial act that fuses affinal units in expectation of an eternal return. Marriages should ideally be conducted within this skin-and-blood-sharing unit, which usually corresponds spatially to paired villages; yet marriages outside are equally desired, as they provide both for women and for men an increasing radius of *korok* relationships. While each such marriage 'outside' leads to the incorporation of a woman and her offspring into an endogamous group through blood sacrifice, it also creates a chain-like nodal network of *korok* relationships that is of vital importance to the work for the dead.

Bridewealth exchanges are always enacted as capture (*hileben*), either in memory or in anticipation of a blood sacrifice that results from the 'uprooting' (*but ine wai*) of a woman. If marriage is conducted 'inside' a group, *korok* relationships are initiated already in childhood with the buying of shame (*sesemangil*) with the marking of cross-cousins (*casuk*) for marriage. After several months, sometimes years, such *korok* relation-ships are formalized through a bridewealth payment (*ngesen*). *Ngesen* is a term that is composed of *ngen*, literally 'to eat', and *se*, literally 'to count, to unite, to belong to'. The phonetic character of *ngesen* points to the transformation of siblings (*hibisane*) into *korok*, which is acted out as a mock fight leading to the capture of the woman from her natal settlement (*dahun*).

The night prior to this event, a large stone oven (*mun*) is built in the central space of the wife-giving settlement; the couple's (*a ri hileben*) future *korok* arrive with bundles of taro, while their male *korok* carry pigs into the settlement. Each settlement prepares one parcel, called *rut*, to be cooked inside the stone-oven overnight; *rut* are about two-metre-long and one-metre-wide parcels wrapped in *Pandanus* leaves (*haum*), used otherwise for the cooking of fish, yet at this time containing taro tubers that are especially selected for this purpose. Each woman in turn contributes tubers whose colouring, number and size reflect her relationship to her future female *korok* in the opposite group. The smallest taro, given by those who are genealogically furthest removed, yet are still encompassed within the *korok* relationship, such as those who occupy the position of mother-in-law (*enang*), are placed at the bottom, while the largest tubers, contributed by actual and classificatory cross-cousins (*casuk*), are placed on the top. Every woman remembers the size and number of her tubers, because she will have to reclaim tubers of exactly the same kind from the *rut* prepared by the opposite party to become thereby a reciprocal *korok* to the husband's or wife's group.

Each *rut* has to contain one hundred taro (*sangavulu a sangavulu*), which are counted on coconut leaves (*se*, 'to count', 'to unite'); visibly and conceptually, the parcels thus formed anticipate the merging of sibling units. In addition to *rut*, each woman prepares for her future female *korok* one bundle of taro tubers with stem (*lebule*), which is called 'skin' (*tak*); the taro is to be planted in the garden of a woman's new *korok*, so that she is thereby effectively inserting herself into her skin.

Taro plants are the personal property of women, who recognize 24 named types of tubers (*iahes*) in the West-Kara area alone, each type being owned by a matriline and having its own coloration and shape and its own distinctive odorous quality when roasted over the fire. Each woman can tell with exactitude from whom she got each taro-plant and on which occasion, so that she has in her garden literally an assemblage of the total network of affinal relations she controls.

On the day of the marriage payment, the group of the husband invade the settlement of the bride, carrying spears made from the stems of wild ginger (*hi*) and threatening with songs that tell of the time of warfare. The mock attack is met with laughter and mock counter-attacks until the leading *maimai*, who fulfils the ritual role of 'speaker', instils calm. As the excitement subsides, the *rut* prepared by both groups are placed in the centre of the settlement. Both groups assume a spatially segregated seating arrangement on either side of the *rut*, which is in turn further stratified internally according to village membership. The prestation of the bridewealth payment is initiated by the husband's group. Speaker after speaker, each representing a different *korok* and his or her supporters, steps towards the centre and announces whom they follow in making the payment. Every prestation is finished with the exclamation 'to *korok*, for free' (*pene korok, aradem*), with the payment being passed to the other side of the pandanus parcels.

Ngsesen consists of a payment of shell-money and currency, which is given by both groups as *hengiat* (*he* = to cause a link), whereby the bride's payment is said to pull back (*pulltowen*) part of the payment. This merging into a reciprocal relationship is made dramatically visible with the opening of the parcels that provided a physical barrier during the exchanges. Out of nowhere, the leading speaker jumps on to the parcels, dressed like a warrior, with *tenget* leaves stuck in his belt and carrying a spear (*ndol*), and vociferating the place-names with which each group is associated, including those that reach back into the time prior to resettlement. As he reaches the end of the string of names, he pierces the wrapping of the parcels with his spear, and descends to make space for the women, who come forward to claim those taro tubers from the opponent's parcel that mirror exactly those that they had deposited in their own for their *korok*.

Men meanwhile dissect the pigs that have been suffocated earlier in the morning, each given by a group in support of one of their own *korok* and by the couple's siblings; the charred skin of the pigs is cut up length-wise in long stripes of fat in a manner known as 'the cutting of the tree' (*tawai*), otherwise seen only at a burial. The pork fat is carried around in a circular motion by a line of men, with portions being cut and thrown into individual baskets that are placed around the edge of the clearing into which each woman places her taro tubers. This way of distributing food in individual portions that are called 'growth of skin' (*nga buk*) is called 'the meal after the fight' (*mun doien*), and is only repeated on two other occasions, after the burial of a person and after the death of the *malanggan* figure.

Most marriages are conducted 'inside' (*a ulul ine si*) a group whose endogamous nature is expressed in the notion of its being of 'one growth' (*dahun*). If a *dahun* spans a village pair, a woman tends to marry her matrilateral cross-cousins, while her brother will marry his patrilateral cross-cousins, enabling women to return to their mother's natal settle-ment upon marriage. Such marriages 'inside' enchain matri-clans in a process that keeps land held between those who are related through sisters.

When marriages are conducted 'inside', the bridewealth payment tends to be considerably smaller than when the marriage is one defined as 'capture' (*a haio*), dramatized in *ngesen* and involving a group with which no currently existing shared land-rights exist. Each endogamous

dahun is the result of such a past marriage by capture, as only this marriage leads to the permanent residence of a woman and her offspring
in the husband's settlement. Such marriages in effect transpose the
matri-clan in space and create lasting relationships between sisters.

Dahun thus come into existence through a process of 'uprooting',
which is expressed with the metaphor of the tree: a woman who is the
'root of a tree' (*wun ine wai*) is said at marriage to 'break the stem at the
bottom' (*but hanai mane wai la vie*), while a man breaks it off at the top
(*bak hanai mane wai*). Such marriages by capture, which cause uprooting, are frequent occurrences, and often result from participation in the
final finishing of the work for the dead in *malanggan,* when groups attend
to assist each other's *korok* despite the absence of any existing or remembered relation to each other.

Korok relationships do not just enable a conceptualization of the residence pattern of an endogamous group; by retracing the movement of
sisters whose marriage led to the uprooting of the matri-clan, *korok* relationships are extendable into 'branches' (*iaiaran*). Such 'branches', or
'lineages', may connect people resident in different villages, and form
the conceptual background against which usufructory rights in land
are defended.

Moroibe who are resident in Panamafei think of themselves as a branch
reaching back to Louen in East-Kara, and may invoke such relatedness
at times of ritual work, when every single *korok* counts. Offshoots, however, may be seen as branching outward not just from a present endogamous group, but from one of the former settlements in the mountain,
and may thus include all those descended from sisters who may have
moved during resettlement to opposite parts of the island.

When offshoots are perceived as connected in this spatially and
temporally extended fashion, endogamous groups are interlocked as
reciprocal *korok*; such expansive units are called 'a growth that has spilt
apart' (*taune*). A *taune* is a fluid and inherently expansive land-holding
network resonating relationships of loyalty and labour that come to the
fore during ritual work. The spatial nature of this relatedness is emphasized in the corresponding term in Melanesian Pidgin, meaning 'line'.

Metaphors of Sociality

As the *taune* consists of conglomerates of separate *dahun*, sisters are of
primary importance in providing continuing access to the extended
land-holding unit. While both the expanded and localized forms of an
endogamous group consist of intermarrying sibling-units, women as

sisters provide the notional link that enables the retracing of each component to its separate 'source' in an apical ancestress.

For the Kara, the place of origin of its many clans is far away, and is more often than not a matter of interpretation. A common personal name is sufficient ground for assuming that two people are of a common matri-clan, even if the name of the matri-clan differs, as is commonly the case when leaving Tikana for either the Tabar islands or Notsi.

The following origin myth is specific to the clan Moromaf, yet is also known by other clans as a more general story of how people came to be organized according to clan membership. The myth's most striking feature is the theme of containment and release that accompanies the story of a life-giving death:

> At one time, women were washing on the beach of Sallepio island. One of them, a woman called *Manenges*, jumped into the water from the top of a stone. Once in the water, she was swallowed by a large fish with a big mouth (*belehai*). When she became conscious again of her surrounding, she realized that she was caught in the womb (*rune*) of the fish. She took her arm ring (*mulai*), broke it into pieces, and slit open the stomach of the fish. Dying, the fish drifted ashore on the island of the dead known as Tinguen. Noticing the hard surface of the beach, Manenges opened the mouth of the fish and climbed outside.
>
> Manenges gave birth on the island of the dead and named her child 'Moromah'. Her daughter married a man from Omo on the mainland [Kavieng peninsula]. The following villages became places of Moromaf though the movement of one of its women: Tome, Putput, Ngavalus [Nono]. At Nono, Moromaf split. One half moved to Kasseluk and Koplemen, where Moromaf still lives today. The other half moved down south along the east coast, to Mangai [Katendan] and Louen [Panarau]. Again, the unit at Louen split, with one woman marrying a man of Morotirien of Paling [this Moromaf lives today at Lavolai in the settlement Butei] and one woman marrying a man of Morotirien of Panalah [this unit lives today at Lamusmus 2 in the settlement Kurumut] . . .

The fish that swallowed the woman Manenges at Sallepio island is of the family of the rock-cods (*welebam*), and is one of the standard motifs that compose *malanggan*-figures. The particular species of rock-cod represented in *malanggan* and alluded to in the myth of the origin of clans has the characteristic of changing its sex with increasing age, becoming female towards death.

In the myth, the rock-cod's death and the severing of its skin leads to the rebirth of Manenges on the island of the dead. Swallowing and ejecting, emulating death and rebirth, receives its real significance in the drafting of a visual resemblance between clanship and death, as the image drawn by the myth suggests that the clan (*habung*) consists of 'those who are caused to be ancestors' (*habung*), coinciding with the moment at which life-force, personified in Manenges, escapes its container.

While this myth is clan-specific, its form is shared by other coastal clans, with mountain clans believing themselves to have been born in a similar way by being ejected by a female pig. Regardless of the nature of the mythical being whose death gives rise to unceasing relatedness, the force created is inherently mobile and is represented in emblematic names consisting of birds among the Tikana and of sharks in Notsi and Tabar.

In West-Kara, ten named *habung* or clans are living scattered across its eight villages. Certain clans are known under different names, yet are associated with the same name of a bird. Alternatively, the clan name is changed and a new bird is assigned to the clan. This internal fragmentation of clans is explained by incestuous marriages between a classificatory brothers and sisters (*weduk*). The child born from an incestuous relationship is given a different, yet similar, clan name, to increase the radius of its *korok* relationship while retaining its ties to land.

The following tabulation lists the clans resident in the West-coast area and the particular birds with which they are identified. All bird names are also found in all other villages within the Tikana area. Clan names change drastically in Notsi and Tabar, where 'shark'-clans are assigned to moieties, while in the Tikana area the fragmentation and multiplication of clans is believed to have made impossible the use of the moiety as an operative principle.

Moromaf : Mareng (Pidgin: Malip), Parrot
Morokomaf : Rulowlow, Drongo
Moroke : Mareng (Pidgin: Malip), Parrot
Morokomade : Bangbanga (Pidgin: Cocomo), Hornbill
Moromuna : Manuengak (Pidgin: Maningulai), Sea-Eagle
Morumbalus : Balus (Pidgin: Balus), species of Eagle
Morumburume : Balus (Pidgin: Balus), species of Eagle
Moroibe : Regaum (Pidgin: Tarangau), Fish-hawk
Morokala: Juk (Pidgin: Tarangau), Fish-hawk
Morotirien : Tutut (Pidgin: Maningulai), Swamp Pheasant
Morotivingur : Tutut (Pidgin: Maningulai), Swamp Pheasant

Moromaf, Morokomaf and Moroke consider themselves to be related as if they were of one clan. Intermarriage between these three clans is officially discouraged, and co-residence actually does not occur. When asked how they know that they are one 'source' (*wune*), one is referred to the named taro plants that are the common property of their clan-women, who call each other sisters (*diakhin*), and to a fixed set of shared names.

Taro (*iahes*) is a woman's most important property, and this vehicle is transmitted strictly within an endogamous group or its 'branches' (*iaiaran*). Like the taro plant, the banana plant is exchanged between women, whereas specific named varieties are associated with certain clans and are reclaimed at death. Even more than the taro plant, the banana palm is a poignant metaphor of the self-renewal of the matri-clan, as its shoots (*were*) grow back into palms irrespective of how many times a palm has been uprooted. A matri-clan is described as 'the root of a banana palm' (*a wun ine vut*), as it will regrow wherever it is taken.

In theory, each matri-clan has a finite set of names, and each name has to be dissociated from the person to whom it is attached in life before it can be passed on to another. Every generation is, as a result, the mirror image of the previous one. As one accumulates taro plants and banana palms throughout life, however, one also accumulates names. The first name given to a child at birth inserts the child into existing *korok* relationships, and it is this name that is passed on down the generations. The second name given to a child reinserts the child into existing relationships among the scattered fragments of a matri-clan. It is this name that must be made effective by being acquired with money and shell-money in ways that effect its severance from its present carrier. This name is also known as a *malanggan* name, which is attaching sets of images, potential 'skins', to a person, who thus becomes, like an onion, composed of layers that are stripped off one by one, as each layer is turned into a *malanggan*-figure, until death.

The transfer of a *malanggan* name turns a child into a 'member' (*raso*) of *malanggan*. Children who are offspring of women who have married out without effecting the acquisition of land-rights through blood-sacrifice (*kiut*) are known as 'rubbish' (*melon*) and face remaining 'nameless' and unrecognizable by others. The only way out for them is to 'find' a *malanggan*-name through dreaming (*mifen*) and to effect its recognition by paying a carver to carve the name into a figure for a *malanggan* event.

The child who is given the name of a *malanggan* is said to carry the *makasen* or ancestral power that is transferred via *malanggan* on to the living. Both girls and boys of such a category carry a string of shell-money called *meson* around their neck, given to them at the event of *malanggan* or at the ceremony accompanying the first cutting of the hair (*savetbat*). They are marked to become *piren,* men and women with many names and many *korok* relationships, whose full extension will reveal itself only at their own deaths.

In addition to *malanggan*-names there are other names that are associated with certain types of knowledge. Like names of *malanggan*, these too are acquired through a symbolic 'killing' (*tuk*) of the present carrier by the child's *dahun*. Once acquired, these names are passed on within the clan. Thus Rawi, known by his *malanggan*-name, whose first name was Lawin, also had a third name, Mate, which carried with it the specific knowledge of *pigis* that was acquired by his maternal grandfather from southern New Ireland; this *pigis* conferred upon him the ability to dream images, which turned Rawi into an acclaimed song and dance composer. As Mate, Rawi was able to produce many *malanggan*-dances and songs known under the general name *Langmanu*. Rawi gave this name to his son Iang when he was a child. Iang already had five children when his last-born was born, two months prior to Rawi's death and several months after Rawi had moved into the funerary enclosure surrounding *but*. The transfer of the name implied the transfer of the knowledge of the dying man to the newborn infant, also of Moromaf. The little Mate, now grown up, is set to follow his father's and grandfather's footsteps.

Another example of name transmission is that of Logom of Moroibe, resident in the southern part of Lamusmus 1, who knows his name to have been given to him by his maternal grandfather. With the name he acquired the knowledge of 'village work' (*bil a bine*), which includes the knowledge of spells and ritual techniques that are vital to fishing and gardening success. His only daughter, Pipil, stems from his marriage with Kama, Rawi's sister of Moromaf, resident in Pusigeo. His wife died during childbirth, and he remarried a woman from Morotirien with whom he had no further children. Logom took the son of his sister's daughter into his house while he was a child and gave him his name as a sign of the transference of the skills that he conferred upon him.

Since most people co-resident in a village are *korok*, the name transmitted to the child by an elderly person will be unpronounceable to several men and women who share a nurturing relationship to the child, as the same name will be shared by their *korok* through marriage. The more numerous the effective *korok* relationships of an endogamous group are, the more names a person acquires during life. Each unpronounceable name whose absence is marked by its replacement invokes thus a relatedness by virtue of its negation. The significance of absence in the empowerment of a name is vividly expressed in the most common practice of conferring the name of a deceased child upon its sibling. This child is known as a 'spirit child' (*lik bung*), and serves to recall the one who is no longer there.

Names can thus be passed on to effect relatedness; but they can also be empowered through acts of 'killing' to issue forth the cumulative capacities upon which influence and wealth depend. Both the continuity and the efficacy of names depend upon their separation from the physical body and their incorporation into a system of images, for only as a *malanggan* image can a name become the site of accumulation and infinite connectivity.

The Body Politic

The thematic tension between containment and release in the emerging body politic of the Tikana is further highlighted by the existence of two opposing positions of authority – one being inherited, the other acquired, one associated with containment and renewal, the other with release and accumulation.

The first is the position of the 'caught one' (*haio*), who embodies the notion of skin and its regenerative powers. The position is seamlessly transmitted within the endogamous group like the immortal powers of kingship, in that the name and the power associated with the *haio* are transposed upon a pregnant woman who is marked to give birth to the next *haio*.

The second is the position of the 'root' (*maimai*), who appears composed of many and layered 'skins.' This position is acquired in a series of ritual contests that have to be won through a symbolic act of killing. *Maimai* is thus a hierarchical position, based on the cumulative embodiment of the 'gathering' capacity inherent in names of *malanggan*.[8]

Each *dahun* must at all times have both positions filled for it to be considered politically viable. A *dahun* that has no *haio* is not known to have the knowledge of *malanggan* and relies on other neighbouring *dahun* to assist in finishing the work for its dead. Most village-wide *dahun* have at least one *maimai*; yet the right to acquire this position depends upon the existence of a *haio* within a *dahun*. Every clan has in addition at least one *maimai*, who represents their *taune* or their *habung* at even more distant places.

From one perspective, *haio* and *maimai* are diametrically opposed in almost every aspect of their position. Their diverse powers permeate their 'skins' in ways that allow them to be perceived as icons of the story of the life-giving death.

The *haio*, prior to the arrival of missionaries, used to live secluded in the funerary enclosure, and still lives today a life that is comparatively sheltered. She never 'worked' (*haisok*), and was fed a daily diet resembling that of a woman during the period of conception, with lots of meat, fish and other 'wet' produce. The *haio* was forced to stay at one place, while the power of the *maimai* is measured in terms of the frequency and the distance of his movements. Today, the association of the *haio* with the intellectual and creative powers of *malanggan* has allowed its representatives to aspire to positions of learning, with a large number having been educated at university.

Like the woven *malanggan*-figures that are never allowed to die, the *haio*'s powers are thought to 'resurface' (*sevang*) in someone who is taking her place. Like the woven *malanggan*-figures that emulate her powers of self-replacement, however, she cannot increase her powers over others, nor can she control this process of renewal. *Haio*, the caught one, depicts the fraught consequences of not being able to get rid of skin.

Her powers of self-renewal, however, are the very powers that are acquired by the *maimai*. For it is his 'killed' insignia that testify to the negation of involuntary self-renewal and replace it with the active self-fashioning that is likened to the accumulation of skin (cf. Lindstrom 1990).

The term *mai* points to an association of the layering of skin with recollection, as it stresses a form of 'knowing with your eyes' (*masi*). To become a *mai* a man has to have *sesewe*, a piece of tortoiseshell through which strings of shell-money are pulled. This tortoiseshell (*wun*) is incised into intricate patterns representing Orion (*westburut*) and its celestial position at a certain time during the calendrical year. These thin, round filaments are fastened on round pieces of clamshell to become breastplates (*rekap*), which are owned by every male or female *maimai*, their size increasing with the rank achieved in the position. Both *sesewe* and *rekap* are thought to be able to 'pull back' (*wangam*) the strings of shell-money given in exchanges, and demonstrate the *maimai*'s recollective powers.

Sesewe and *rekap* are passed from father to son, but may be worn by the latter only when he is passing through the ritual stages in which he officially acquires their power. Female *mai*, on the other hand, receive their *rekap* and *sesewe* from their mother's brother at a ceremony marking their first haircut (*musbeng*). At this time they are about two years old, and have just been weaned. A *malanggan* has to be made for the occasion, after which the child is named. The girl grows up as *piren*, as a person with a name. When she is a woman past the reproductive age she silently, yet effectively, organizes activities during ritual events. While such a female *mai* may be literally invisible in contrast to the formidable and forever audible presence of her male counterpart, her power and ritual knowledge is undisputed.

Male *mai* are given power in an act called *bur* during a *malanggan* organized by their *taune*. A *mai* has to go through six stages of initiation, each of them acquired with shell-money and currency, until he is known as a permanent *mai*. The money and shell-money is given to the sibling unit from whom the position is acquired. These six stages are paired into two sets, recalling both sets of images of *malanggan* and the spatial and temporal sequence of feasting.

The first two stages are given to the *mai* in the *sebedou* enclosure while he is standing on the ground. He is decorated with lime on his forehead, with leaves of the tenget plant (*si*) on both sides of his waist, and with the *rekap* around his neck; he is also given the stem of the wild ginger plant (*hi*), which is used to ban places from harvest and cultivation (*dang*) and as a spear in ritual warfare. Every single item has to be bought separately with currency and shell-money by his *dahun*, assisted by his *taune*. Afterwards, he is able to direct minor ritual events in his own settlement and in the settlements of his siblings. He may speak only in the central space (*rune malei*), and this while standing still. During other major ritual events that occur within the spatial boundary of his village he can act as an assistant, yet he is not allowed to speak.

The third and fourth stages are given to the *mai* on top of the slit-drum (*garamut*). Again he has to acquire the various ingredients associated with the position. These stages enable the *mai* to direct ritual events concerning his *taune* with his speech. He has to give his speech in the central space while walking slowly up and down.

The fifth and sixth stages are given to a *mai* on top of the platform (*eiben*) used by *malanggan* dancers (*langmanu*) for their performance. He is now a permanent *mai* and can direct ritual events of his *habung* wherever his sisters' *korok* obligations may carry him. In bridewealth payments, he represents simultaneously the village and the people of his clan, and displays the link between the two wherever he goes to attend exchanges outside his own village.

The *maimai* reflects both the link between the village and the region, the *dahun* and the *habung*, and the association of the expansion of this link with power. The link between power and space is visible in his movements during ritual events: speaking and shouting for hours and hours on end with few interruptions for the entire ritual event, he moves up and down, backwards and forwards, across the central space. He does not walk, but runs and gesticulates continuously.

The *haio*, in contrast to the *maimai*, has to live as if poor: unable to free herself by negating her trappings, the *haio* is barred from re-collecting and gathering. Personifying life-force in its contained state, the *haio is* the enlivened *malanggan*. She was only allowed to leave the enclosure within which she was confined prior to missionization when wearing a *malanggan*-mask. One may not address a *haio* by name, sit next to her, or touch her, let alone walk upright past her; a *haio is* the only person ever to sit on a chair made for her, so as to enable people to walk around her without having to crouch on the floor. Only selected women past menopause may supply her with food, which may not be shared by other people, and has to be thrown away when left over. No one may call out (*nungnung*) to the *haio* for areca nut or lime. The *haio* may not enter other houses outside his/her own settlement, and has to await being visited.

To this day, the *haio* is also the only person who does not share a house with other people. She lives in a house called *luhu wewere*, which is itself a *malanggan*. A *malanggan*-house is differentiated from normal houses by the method used in tying the materials together, by the materials used and by the knotted decoration of the house-front, which is made by the same knotting technique (*wuap*) that is used for fishnets. The knotting in the front of the house covers the 'eye' of the house, which is called *were* or 'shoot of a banana-plant', highlighting the *haio*'s capacity for self-renewal.

A living example of a *haio* is Merubeles. According to mission records 78 years old, Merubeles was born a *haio* in succession to her mother's brother Rasot. While her mother could leave it, Merubeles remembers having grown up entirely inside the enclosure into which she was born. The only people who were allowed to enter the enclosure were the elders of her clan. During the *malanggan* event organized to finish the death of Rasot, which occurred when Merubeles was about 8 years old, Merubeles was brought outside (*sohonge*) the enclosure. Her name, Merubeles, is the name of the *malanggan* made for this event.

If the mission had not intervened, she would have carried on an existence inside the enclosure and would have been excluded from marriage. However, the mission did intervene, and Merubeles lived a life in-between. She married a European and spent most of her life in Australia, returning home after her husband's death.

Other *haio* likewise have led an unusual life. Logom was the first doctor trained in Rabaul, New Britain, and worked most of his life both among the Baining of west New Britain and on the mainland of New Guinea. He had been in an enclosure of the *haio* until he was about 6 years old, and was let out through the curiosity of the Catholic priest Father Peekel, who wanted to see him. Another man who was classified as a *haio* was Emos Gomele. Emos was among the first high-school students of New Ireland. Five of his nine children have superior positions in industry and medicine, one of them being a fully trained dentist in Wewak (Spik Province), and another being the assistant director of a construction company in Port Moresby.

Irrespective of the fact that the *haio*'s life is spent outside the enclosure today, not much has changed in the veneration offered to the representatives of this position. As the living testimony of the animation of *malanggan,* they are the intellectual resource of society, though through schooling and jobs much of the opposition that may once have existed between the *haio* and the wealth-accumulating *maimai* has been lost.

The image of the *haio* is conceivable only in its complementarity to the *maimai,* and as such has remained vital irrespective of the changes it has undergone during this century; for the public meaning of 'skin' as a processual entity resides in the *maimai*'s act of accumulation and the *haio*'s powers of self-renewal. By effecting a 'killing', however, the *maimai* is not just confounding by obviating the public meaning of skin. Instead, the *maimai* acts as the sacrificer of an image brought to life as likeness or '*malanggan*' to the recomposed body whose self-sufficiency is attested by the figure of the *haio*. In being the object of sacrifice, this 'skin' is consumed as it is de-animated and turned into an inherently generative and reproductive image whose multiple returns are in the hands of the *maimai*.

Endogamy in the North of New Ireland therefore coincides with the existence of a notion of intellectual, rather than material property. Not objects, but 'gathered' images produced through object-sacrifice fashion a memory-oriented political economy where values are circulated inside a group whose boundaries are forever expanding with every gathering thus affected.

In the light of this material one may ask whether there are two great classes of societies: one that is endogamous and memory-oriented, with values circulating within the group as images, and the other exogamous and object-oriented, with values circulating outside the group in things. This question surely calls for a detailed comparative approach that may be beyond the scope of this work; yet given the complexity of New Ireland ethnography, it cannot be left entirely to one side.

Notes

1. See B. Clay on visiting (1986: 80).

2. See Clay's extensive analysis of the avoidance-defined relationship in Madak: (1977: 42–77; 1986: 26–8).

3. See in contrast Annette Weiner's description of Trobriand kinship as consisting of the nucleus of brother and sister relationship, with an emphasis on the matri-clan as the basic land-holding unit (1976; 1992: 73–7).

4. See David Schneider's now classic account (1961) of matrilineal descent; and Bolyanatz (1994) on the role of mortuary feasting in the construction of the matriliny.

5. *Mamis* means a 'sweet' smell, and *misirk* means 'wet'; the term *mis*, which is the same as the generic term for shell-money, means 'sweet-vapour'.

6. Powdermaker (1933: 35); Groves (1936: 234–5); Lewis (1979: 285); Krämer (1925: 39); Peekel (1910: 1823); Neuhaus (1962: 246).

7. Among the Mandak, blood is interpreted as paternal substance, which initiates social units that are ideally endogamous within the village (B. Clay 1977: 41).

8. Older studies stress the access to wealth: 'The position of the orang in a clan is not inherited . . . the oldest and most influential man of a clan, regardless of the exact relationship to the dead will be regarded as orang. His influence is based on his age, the strength of his personality, and his wealth' (Powdermaker 1933: 41). Dorothy Billings (n.d.), in her study of Mangai village, saw the distinctiveness of the position of the New Ireland *maimai* in the fact that it is 'the only status requirying an installation ceremony' (n.d.: 28). Her definition of the position of the *maimai* stresses the significance of popular support in the acquisition and maintenance of the status (n.d.: 30). The position of the *maimai* is assumed to be based on personal status and individually acquired prestige (n.d.: 23, 30). Peter Lomas (n.d.) gave a picture of the social organization that emphasized the individual actor as manipulator of the political scene: 'emphasis is placed on the leading actor in the ventures, the catalyst who marshalls resources, man power and managerial skill: the entrepreneur' (n.d.: 4).

Sacrifice and Calendrical Rites

> Everything as it moves, now and then, here and there, makes stops. The
> bird as it flies stops in one place to make its nest, and in another to rest
> in its flight. A man when he goes forth stops when he wills. So the god
> has stopped. The sun, which is so bright and beautiful, is one place where
> he has stopped. The moon, the stars, the winds, he has been with. The
> trees, the animals, are all where he has stopped, and the Indian thinks
> of these places and sends his prayers there to reach the place where the
> god has stopped and win help and a blessing (Lévi-Strauss 1964: 171).

The most important, most frequently used Tikana ritual is sacrifice (*gul-utung*). As elsewhere in island Melanesia, ritual actions that include the consecration of an 'offering' induce the realm of spirits to *hamarere* for them.[1] Contrary to what we would expect, however, offerings are not made directly to ancestors, but to named female spirits, *moroa* and *merulie,* who personify the invisible and the powers of renewal attributed to it. *Moroa* is believed to reside on an island beyond the horizon, while *merulie* makes herself felt in earth tremors, which are a frequent occurrence on the island.

Hamarere, the source of well-being and fertility, is the result of a complex exchange between the realm of the visible and the invisible. The vehicle that facilitates a transaction between the visible and the invisible is olfaction (*ngusung*), which is released by leaving the sacrificial object to decompose, so that within it odour comes to be re-encompassed as life-giving force or heat. *Ngusung* among the Tikana means both 'smell' and 'flames', depending on whether it is released or contained.

The primary object of sacrifice is a *malanggan*-figure carved from wood, whose coming to life, death and decomposition play an intrinsic part in the agricultural calendar. *Malanggan* will thus be shown in this chapter to be not just the last phase in the finishing of the work for the dead, but also a calendrical rite that 'makes things move' and brings about the 'turning of the year' (*heles*).

Odour, according to Gell (1977: 27) is defined by formlessness, indefinability and lack of clear articulation, yet is seized upon by the collective imagination across cultures (see Classen, Howes and Synnott 1994). As something that is noted only at the moment it escapes its container, scent is the vehicle of transition *par excellence* and is thus, as Howes argued, 'ideally suited to expressing the notion of contagion or action at a distance' (1987: 384). Ritual symbolism exploits this capacity of odour to trigger a process of recollection, and thus to act as the vehicle of a transmission that metaphorically unites what otherwise exists in separate domains.[2] Its impact on the mnemonic nature of ritual symbolism is grounded in its phenomenal nature, which allows odour to trigger associative thought and remembering long after its last trace has evaporated. Its dependence upon a perishable and permeable figurative container renders odour a vehicle for 'mnemic' recollection, enabling the spontaneous recollection of material that has been rendered absent.

In a comparison of Indonesia and island Melanesia, Howes (1988) observed a tendency for olfaction to be symbolically marked in areas where one finds a concomitant conception of a physical separation between the dead and the living. This is true for the Tikana, where the soul (*verak*) of the dead leaves for an island situated in the north-west called *Tinguen*, only to leave it again for its ultimate destination on an island beyond the horizon called *Karoro*. As ancestral substance (*rongan*), the soul departs for this island after having been recaptured in a *malanggan*-figure whose death and decomposition effects its departure as a 'smell canoe' (*bul ngusung*). At Karoro, it becomes the truly indefinable power of *moroa*, to return with the northwesterly monsoon in the form of uprooted, drifting tree-trunks that carry it as odour back to those who seek to recapture it into containers made as 'skins'.

Offerings to the spirits among the Tikana include not just living things, notably pigs and animated figures, but also vegetal beings that, after having been consecrated, are eaten by the participants in the ritual. Like every sacrifice, the offering requires a subject who performs it or on whose behalf it is performed. Among the Tikana, every village has at least one ritual specialist, called *bil a bine,* who is called upon to perform the most important of the sacrifices.[3]

Rethinking Sacrifice

Sacrifice received its most heightened attention in the late nineteenth and early twentieth centuries with the work of Edward B. Tylor (1889) on sacrifice as gift; Robertson Smith's work on sacrifice as a totemic communal meal (1892); and James Frazer's theory of expiation (1922).[4] The contemporary analysis of sacrifice is founded, however, almost exclusively on the comparatively short, yet path-breaking, study by Hubert and Mauss (1964[1906]). The 'new' element contributed by Hubert and Mauss's essay is derived from the development of a 'syntactic' study of sacrifice that entailed viewing it as a global ritual process. The 'technical' and 'ritualistic' perspective encouraged by Hubert and Mauss enabled a conception of the 'essential' sacrifice abstracted from any particular cultural contexts.

As was pointed out by Valeri, however, the essay contains a tension between two definitions of sacrifice whose relation to each other remains unresolved (Valeri 1985: 64; Mauss 1968–9: Vol. I: 302); they qualify Tylor's characterization of sacrifice as oblation by adding its necessary destruction, but define sacrifice simultaneously as a technique for connecting the sacred and the profane through a victim that functions as a mediator. Implicit in the tension between these two definitions is the recognition of the notion of the sacrificial gift; the corollary of this idea, however, is the belief in anthropomorphic spiritual beings that are conceived as the recipients of the 'gifts', which were unacceptable within the framework of the Durkeimian theory of the sacred as the 'moral reality' consisting of the mutual dependence of individual and society. As a consequence, the notion of the sacrificial gift remained undeveloped.[5]

The second major and still dominant definition of sacrifice is as an efficacious representation, which, like the view of Hubert and Mauss, follows from a holistic perspective on sacrifice. Anticipating Hocart, Alfred Loisy views objects used in ritual as icons that mimetically capture what the sacrifice wishes to achieve (Loisy 1920; Hocart 1927, 1970). Like Hubert and Mauss, he distinguishes sacrifice from other rituals by the destruction of the thing conceived as living. Essential to his view is his divergence from the theory of sacrifice as gift, as he argues that it is the iconic or representational nature of the thing to be destroyed, visualizing the processual nature of destruction itself, that is essential to the 'magical' efficacy of the ritual act. Destruction is viewed as act of arresting the power of an object in a specific place and of translating the object into an image that anticipates the repeatability of this process.[6] It is this position that has been most influential in my thinking about the material, at least partly because of the importance given to decomposition in *malanggan* and the imagistic nature of the vehicle of exchange.

The third definition of sacrifice does not speak of the gift, nor of representational action, but of sacrifice in relation to violence. For Girard, violence is inherent in human relationships and demands a mechanism for blunting and discharging violence.[7] Sacrifice is a mechanism for the formation and expulsion of the diffuse and reciprocal violence that exists between individuals by concentrating it upon a single individual, the sacrificial victim. While a critique of Girard's theory falls beyond the scope of this chapter, it should be said that it encounters the same problem as all psycho-cultural theories, in that it considers culture as a rationalization or cover-up for psychological processes, whose existence however can only be inferred from behaviour in culture (see Bloch 1986).

In seeking the most adequate definition of sacrifice I have been swayed by the importance given in the New Ireland material to the relation between the ritual process and the animation of the sacrificial object, whose destruction forms the core of the rite. In following Loisy (1920) and Valeri (1985) I will maintain the theoretical tradition that views sacrifice as a complex ritual process that cannot be reduced to any of its elements. Unlike Valeri, however, who views the sacrificial ritual as a 'symbolic action that effects transformations of the relationship of sacrificer, god and group', I want to emphasize the figurative and imagistic properties of the sacrificial object and its destruction as central in the activation of a ritual 'awakening' and the fashioning of remembrance as a new beginning, which Nietzsche established long ago as the most important effects of sacrifice (1968: Vol. 4: 60–1).

The symbolic action that effects awakening through erasure consists of the classical three stages as outlined by Hubert and Mauss:

The process is initiated by a perceived lack or imperfection, as in the perceived state of threatening disorder caused by the presence of animate substance 'left over', which if not recaptured and re-channelled into containers may appear in sudden, spontaneous and uncontrollable visions. The sacrificer acts as a medium for channelling animate substance into a container. The second main stage of the ritual process is the ritual 'killing' of the sacrificial object, the symbolic devouring of the offering by the deity. The sacrificer has become inseparable from the offering, and now corresponds to the concept for which the deity stands (Valeri 1985: 71). The third stage of the symbolic action consists of the symbolic and actual de-composition of the sacrificial object. This final dispersal of the sacrificial object, I want to argue, guarantees that the effect of the sacrificial process is not just momentary, but lasting. While the spirit receives the substance that forms the vehicle for relating the visible and the invisible, it is retained as absence, and thus as remembrance. The perceived bilateral relationship between sacrificer and god in the existing theories of sacrifice is not just incomplete, as Valeri argues (1985: 72); it also fails to take into account the materiality of the sacrificial object and its imagistic and analogical nature. By side-stepping the object of sacrifice, existing theories also fail to account for the resurgence of object sacrifice under colonial and post-colonial conditions in the Pacific and for the complex relationship between sacrificial exchange and the emerging monetary economy.

Malanggan is not an isolated phenomenon of sacrificial calendrical rites, but exemplifies a tendency found across Melanesia and Polynesia to emphasize a relation between the ritual process and the animation of a figurative element whose death and subsequent decomposition form the core of the rite (Valeri 1985: 62–5). Kooijman (1984) describes the importance of decomposition among the Mimika in the south-western coastal region of New Guinea: the Mimika produce for their funerary ceremony monumental so-called spirit poles (*mbitoro*) made from the hollowed-out trunk and roots of a mangrove-like tree and composed of superimposed figures. For the Mimika, according to Kooijman, the role of decomposition lies in the freeing and emplacement of life-force: 'the deceased present in the figures on the *mbitoro* were . . . bearers of a vital energy, an impersonal life-force (*kapita*) that accumulated in these images during their stay in the village . . . when the wood of which the images were made disintegrated, the life-force was liberated. After the *mbitoro* had played its part in the ritual, it was brought into the sago marches and left there to moulder and transmit its *kapita* to the sago palms' (1984: 9).

Like the impersonal life-force that temporarily comes to reside in figures such as the Tahitian *to'o* or the Hawaiian *kapu luakini*, *malanggan* figures are animated in the ritual process by absorbing this force as odour; the death and subsequent decomposition of such figures frees, but also immobilizes, this force, and keeps it at a safe distance (Babadzan 1993: 93–9; Valeri 1985: 272–3). This is because decomposition effects a separation of sight from olfaction, within which the invisible force continues to dwell (Valeri 1985: 272–3).

Arrested in the olfactory spaces of temples or gardens, the force freed through sacrifice will not haunt and harm the living;[8] it takes on the character of a memory that enables recognition without itself being repeatable; this had already been defined by Nietzsche as the most important effect of sacrifice (1968: Vol. 4: 60–1). Francesco Pellizi (1995) makes a similar observation with respect to the treatment of certain venerated wooden saints among the present-day Highland Maya in Southern Mexico. Found 'living' in caves where they had spontaneously appeared, 'a magical act, actually a sacrificial one was needed to "kill" the wandering images, so that from that moment on, they would stay in their assigned place of worship, their powers contained within the sacred precinct of the temple' (1995: 9).

The tapping of the distanced domain of the olfactory is possible only through a hold over its imagistic quality that in some way is like the container from which it escaped, and thus allows for the re-incorporation and 'recollection' of odour by sheer analogical force. Among the Tikana, the agent of recollection is the 'gathered' and imaged *malanggan-skin*, which effects the absorption and release of odour in an unceasing exchange with *moroa*.

Retained as mental resource and inherently recallable and reproducible, the imagistic and named remains of the sacrificial object are owned and transmitted as intellectual forms of property in ways described by Simon Harrison as symptomatic of Melanesian ritual economy (1992, 1995). While Harrison extends his argument of the ownership adhering to mental products to all ritual prestige economies, I would like to argue that it is necessary to characterize it as a symptom of a sacrificial economy in which exchange value is not attached primarily to the material thing, but its detachable representational and imagistic properties (cf. Küchler 1988, 1997).

Sacrificial economies flourished under colonialism in many parts of the world, as they enabled an institutionalized mode of resistance to colonial intervention in such matters as the regulation of land ownership and relations of loyalty. In Melanesia, sacrificial economies developed alongside Millennarian and cargo cult movements, as the sale of sacrificial remains to Western collectors proved early on to be a successful means of opening the road to the ancestors, which was thought to be blocked by the white man.[9] Instead of being left to decompose, the ritually sacrificed objects became the vehicle that reopened the road of cargo to bring, in exchange for the collected artefact, first guns and cloth, and then money in ever greater quantities.[10]

What we have in masses in our collections, therefore, are the empty, hollow remains of objects of sacrifice, which are evidence of an exchange into which we came to be implicated quite unknowingly. We are confronted with a paradox: that what we collected as transcending commodity-based exchange relations, and thus as a reminder of lost traditions, was actually conceived as the alienable remains of a life-enhancing act of riddance.[11] At the same time, as the remains of sacrificial objects left as vehicles along the road of cargo, their departure did not mean that the culture was emptied of its treasures, as the notion of salvage collecting suggests. Remaining as a mental resource and asset in the culture is the memory of the image, whose generative and reproductive potential has allowed sacrificial economies to flourish to the present day.

Calendrical Rites and Sacrifice

The imagery of containment and release that pervades every aspect of ritual work among the Tikana points to the confounding of time by space as its operational logic. The ritual symbolism of *malanggan* thus appears to support our understanding of calendrical rites as attempts to abolish time, to annul the past and to return to a primordial era of cosmogonic regeneration.

The peculiarities of this space-oriented model of calendrical rites that seeks to reawaken the past in the present can be usefully compared with a comparable temporal model. In her work on Kodi calendrical rites, Janet Hoskins took issue with Mircea Eliade's position that such temporal rites revolt against the irreversibility of historical time, arguing that the Kodi do not destroy, but imaginatively reflect and re-enact the past, thus revitalizing it (Hoskins 1993: 142). And indeed, Kodi rites invoke a kind of eschatological awakening in the sense of the passive or intransitive German *erwachen*, which allows for the reliving of the past as a vision for the future, thereby cancelling out the present. The Kodi present to us a time-oriented model of remembering fundamental to all political and legitimately historical understanding.

As has been argued by Aleida Assman, this eschatological model of remembering, with its emphasis on the nostalgic and imaginative invoking of the past as tradition, can be compared to what she terms the 'animistic model of remembering', which changes the meaning of awakening to one equivalent to that of the active and transitive German *erwecken* (Assman and Harth 1993: 22–31). This spatially-oriented model, akin to the New Ireland material, enlivens the past by initiating a sudden, momentous collapse of past and present. The mnemic power of animation elucidates transition as metamorphosis, that is as a process of becoming that binds past, present and future into an awareness of the moment (Strathern 1991).

The moment of *Kurzschluss* is achieved by the death of the *malanggan* figure, whose sacrifice effects the fusion of the realm of the ancestors with that of the living in ways yet to be described; it also, however, brings about the 'turning' (*heles*) of the moon (*hulen*) from its position during the dry season in the east to its position during the wet season in the west. The awakening inherent in this moment of turning has its far-reaching implications for the conception of the past, which from the perspective of those who adhere to the calendar of *malanggan* does not have a status separate from the consideration of figures whose fleeting reappearance in villages fashions moments in which all pasts are equally present (see MacDonald 1987).

The calendrical rites that literally 'turn' around *malanggan* dramatize the release and recapture of odour as a single process; this process derives its logical cohesion and predictability from the lunar calendar and its associated winds and tides, which inform every aspect of Tikana work (Figure 3.1). The departure of the 'smell-canoe' with the death of *malanggan* coincides with a number of cosmogonic events, such as the death of sea-creatures on the reef and the mating of the paloloworm in the lagoon. With their focus on the sea, these events mark the transition of the seasons and the 'turning' of the year. The transition is effected by the olfactory exchange initiated by *moroa*; for it is *moroa* who is thought to bring ashore odour at the end of the rainy season in the form of uprooted trees, returning olfactory substances set free by the death of the *malanggan*. *Merulie,* on the other hand, carries on *moroa*'s work on the land in transforming odour into the life-force of the earth (*vie*), which is visible in the early hours of the morning, when heat and moisture create a steaming of the land.

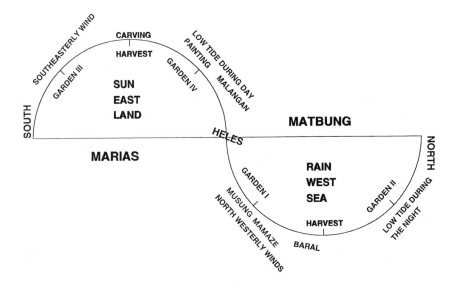

Figure 3.1 The Calendar: The Ritual Cycle.

By reincorporating wetness and heat in gardens and subsequently in the re-composed 'skin' of *malanggan*, a container is created that allows for the 'recollection' of odour, only for it to be released again to effect a return in the following year. Rather than oppositional, the ritual work of re-encompassing *moroa* and *merulie* is thus complementary, and in its complementarity effects the transit of the calendrical year.

To appreciate the significance attributed in calendrical rites to animatorical awakening, it is necessary to recall the geographical positioning of the island. The long and narrow, yet mountainous, island is stretched out in an almost exactly northwesterly to southeasterly orientation. There are two seasons in the twelve-month-long lunar calendar. The first is called *matbung*, which is the rainy season between October and March on the west coast, with its northwesterly and then southeasterly winds, and low tides during the night-time, used for fishing at a time when garden produce is not ready for harvest. The second is called *marias*, which is the dry season between April and September on the west coast, which is the time for harvest and for *malanggan*, and of low tides during the day.[12] The changing positions of the moon and the sun in relation to each other and in relation to the geography of the island are used to determined the monthly calendar of *heles*, the year.[13]

The year starts 'in the centre', when the rising new moon and the setting sun meet in the north-west just above the island of the dead that is called 'Tinguen'. As from the west-coast perspective the moon moves in the course of the year to the south across the sea and the sun to the east across the land, the crossing of the paths of sun and moon marks the transition of the seasons from *marias* to *matbung*. Conversely, as the moon reaches the island in the south and moves across land to the east, *marias* begins and *matbung* comes to a close. The two seasons are associated with wetness (*matbung*) and dryness (*marias*), with a change of food from the sea to food from the land, as indicated in the calendar below.

Matbung 1. Bathu huhus: paloloworm on the west coast (October)
2. Bewue Tas: shark of the sun
3. Biwa langit: month of the shark
4. Manunah: migration of birds to the north
5. Manu roro: aikum, crabs on reef
6. Ialabu sat: numit, month of starving
Marias 7. Ialabu roro: month of the ripeness of fig-trees
8. Dimguh: kukum, star in the east
9. Dim fihihilan: loubala, three stars in the east

10. Tiliwawah: nuts (ngai) half green, half black
11. Tili mismis: nuts black
12. Bathu thutuluk: paloloworm on the east coast

The turning-point of the year, the crossing of the paths of sun and moon and their continuing movement in opposite directions, is marked by the appearance of the paloloworm (*mamaze*) in the lagoon for mating. Just prior to the appearance of the paloloworm a secret ritual is performed on the edge of the reef, known as the 'calling of odour' (*wangam a ngusung*) from beyond the horizon in the west. If the paloloworm is not caught or if it does not appear in the lagoon for some reason, the exchange with *moroa* is not effective and the abundance of crops and thus the possibility of staging *malanggan* ceremonies in the following dry season is endangered.

The agricultural calendar within which the calendrical rites are placed divides the year into four consecutive periods, each period involving the planting and harvesting of in total four gardens, which are worked upon by every resident *dahun*. As the harvesting and planting of consecutive gardens overlap by about one month, each garden has a three-monthly cycle of growth coinciding with the three-monthly pattern of changing winds (*teigh ine bine*) that defines the seasons. As it is the harvest of the gardens that facilitates the onset of each new phase of ritual work, the structure of the agricultural calendar thus engenders the processuality of ritual work; its presence in the structuring of ritual space/time and the figurative imagery of *malanggan* thus finds its motivating force in calendrical considerations.

Gardening, and thus also ritual work, is heavily constrained by other kinds of work that have become the weekly obligatory chores across New Ireland. Mondays are set aside for Church and village work, which includes any repairs and cleaning that may have arisen; a general interdiction is placed on gardening for this day, with the exception of collecting harvests from the garden for the daily evening meal. Tuesday is known as the day for the village-court meetings, which on off-days can be replaced by other kinds of community work such house-construction or copra-cutting. Wednesday is the general market-day, which is adhered to by most women, who at least once a month take their produce to the market in Kavieng or along the road to the south. Once a month, nurses from the local mission hospital carry out their health-checks on this day. Despite the busy schedule of village work, which often tends to invade other days, gardening is a priority and is adhered to at all costs.

The first taro garden of the year is prepared in the weeks following the climactic finishing of *malanggan*; the garden will receive the taro stems (*lebule*) from the ritual garden whose harvest was distributed on the final day of *malanggan*. Planting, however, has to await the appearance and consumption of the paloloworm (*mamaze*). The spatial layout of the garden, with its parallel rows lined by tree-trunks, mirrors the anticipated arrival of the odour (*ngusung*) that drifts ashore during the rainy season in between the vertical and horizontal 'roads' of sharks (*selen bewue*), which are caught during this time along the west coast.

A garden is mapped out in vertically placed and 'drifting' (*baral*) rows of trunks called *wagil* and horizontally placed and drifting *but*, framed by a fence (*vafe*) and containing between eight and sixteen individual plots. In the centre of each garden a fast-growing tree, usually a coconut palm, is planted, mirroring the drifting ashore of an uprooted-tree trunk, which is expected to drift ashore 'head-down' (*kaletung*) together with *wagil* and *but*. The drifting ashore of the tree-trunks should coincide with the second weeding (*ramyt*) of the first taro garden to announce the return of odour and an imminent successful harvest; *kaletung*, the upright drifting tree-trunk, receives offerings (*galetung*) of first-fruits such as banana, taro and coconut, which are left to rot on the stem.

The third month of the first garden is also the month for the preparation of the second garden, involving the clearing of spaces in the secondary forest with slash-and-burn techniques. The turning of the wind from a northeasterly to a southwesterly direction in the third month initiates the harvest of the first and the planting of the second garden. It is this transitory three-month period between *matbung* and *marias* that sees the planning of *malanggan*, either in the home-settlement or in the settlement of one's *korok*, for it is the produce harvested from the second garden that contains the odour returned from *moroa* that will feed the carver of *malanggan*. The harvesting of this second garden again overlaps with the replanting of stems of the taro-plant in the third garden, whose produce will feed the many guests expected for the final days of feasting (*henemos*). The harvested taro is piled up upon platforms that are erected around the settlement, in which the preparations for *malanggan* are about to commence. The taro is cooked daily for the carver by a post-menopausal woman in a manner reserved for those conceiving life; the odour of this cooked taro is thought to be channelled into the wood through the carver's hand and to enliven the wood as it takes on the appearance of a skin. The harvest of the third garden takes place just prior to the culmination of the ritual work in the public revelation and death of the *malanggan*. Its stems are partially stored (those which belong to the residential *dahun*) or are temporarily replanted in small individual plots in the fourth garden, which is prepared without much attention.

Ritual washing (*kei*) in the sea, removing the odour associated with female discharge (*rotap*), has to be carried out by anyone who consumed the taro of the third garden and/or came into contact with the *malanggan*-figure during its display in the cemetery. With this ritual washing the 'smell-canoe' has started its journey back to the island beyond the horizon. As life returns back to normal, preparations are undertaken over the next two months to prepare the first garden of the new year, which is about to begin. The turning of the year is marked by a heightened attention to the sea and a change of diet from garden produce to seafood of all kinds.

While the ritual specialist is most knowledgeable about the positioning of the moon and the stars as indicators of calendrical time, children learn to distinguish the different months by the tides and by the position of the rising moon. The low tides during the day that prevail during the dry season are used extensively for the harvesting of the reef, being earlier each day in accordance with the waxing and waning of the moon, whose cycle also determines evening activities: the full moon during *marias* is used for the practising of *malanggan* dances until late into the night. During *matbung*, in the moonlit nights in which the reef is exposed, everyone who is capable of walking may be found either visiting or fishing.

This pattern of changing tides creates the cyclical frame for the calendrical rites that enliven the yearly lunar cycle. Starting with the onset of the rainy season, offerings directed to the sea serve to move the moon across the sea from the north to the south and back to the land by elaborating on metaphors of drying; rites building up over the period of the dry season, conversely, trace the course of the moon across the land to deploy metaphors of containment that celebrate the coming to life of the figure of *malanggan;* its sudden, momentous death is like the bursting of a bubble, which catapults the moon back into its wet phase on the opposite side of the island.

Thus sacrifices are not just made to *moroa* or *merulie,* but are directed to different domains believed to be their dwellings.[14] *Moroa* is addressed in rites that fall into the transition between dry and rainy seasons when the moon is following its path across the sea in the west; predominantly vegetal offerings, but also 'killed' *malanggan* figures left to dry in the forest, are meant to activate olfaction, whereas *merulie* is the recipient of blood sacrifices through suffocation and of offerings of cooked food during the months of the dry season when the moon moves across the land. As in Hawaii, however, the distinction, based on biblical reminiscence, between sacrificial 'offering' and 'blood' sacrifice is invalid; not only is there no distinction made in language, but the distinction between inanimate and animate on which the opposition is grounded is also absent (Valeri 1985: 62).

The Vocabulary of Sacrifice

Sacrifices that stress containment and those that stress decomposition and release form an inseparable and infinitely repeatable process in being a part of calendrical rites. The most frequently mentioned act of sacrifice is called *kiut*, described already as a blood sacrifice involving the suffocation of a living being. Discussed in an earlier chapter as the only way to assure 'one growth' or *dahun*, acts of *kiut* are today most frequently recalled in the village court as part of the contestation of land rights. *Kiut* is not just an act of obviation, as discussed by Wagner, but involves the offering and consumption of blood among those who are connected as a result as 'one blood'.

Being directed to *merulie*, *kiut*, and with it all sacrifice involving suffocation and the symbolic containment of blood, is also directed to activating the movement of the moon across the land from west to east during the time of *marias*. Pig sacrifices are part of the six main ceremonies marking the stages of bringing to life *malanggan* during carving that were formerly spread out over the entire six months of the dry season, yet are frequently today confined to just three months. As an image of containment, moreover, blood sacrifice is inseparable from images of conception and animation, which reach their most heightened articulation in the coming to life of sculpted *malanggan* figures.

Blood may be a potent image of awakening because it is a bodily substance capable of transformation from a hardened state into a liquefied state. The following myth is retold in detail, as it captures the conceptual centrality of blood in animation. The myth is known as the story of *Hulendap*, and is literally the story of the 'new moon':

> *Hulendap* went into the garden to cut strings. Cutting with a shell into a vine, he cut his finger so deeply that blood poured on to the ground. Taking the shell, he caught some of the blood and placed it under a 'mami' plant. He went home and returned the next day. Looking into the shell he saw that the blood had taken on the form of two eggs. Returning to the garden every day, he observed the content of the shell. Finally he

discovered that the eggs had opened and that two boys, Nangtainese and Nangtalamon, had emerged out of them. The boys stayed in the garden, while Hulendap went home. One day, his wife, Karak, discovered that some of her taro plants were damaged. Enraged, she asked her husband how this could have happened. Hulendap had already built a house inside an enclosure in the garden. Secretly he went into the garden and led the boys into the enclosure. Every day, Karak prepared food for the three men in the enclosure, not knowing of the existence of the two boys. Hulendap brought the boys to the beach every day, where he smeared lime into their hair so that it became white. The boys used to play with spears made out of ginger inside the enclosure. One day, Nangtainese threw his spear and it landed inside the enclosure; Nangtalamon followed him, but his spear landed in front of the cooking house inhabited by Karak. Karak came out and was attracted by the boy. The next day, Hulendap took the boys to the beach to wash their hair with lime as usual, yet while Nangtainese's hair became brilliantly white, Nangtalamon's hair remained dull.

Hulendap knew that Nangtalamon had been with a woman. As they went back to the enclosure, Hulendap asked Nangtalamon to go fishing with him in a canoe. Away from the coast, Hulendap strangled Nangtalamon and took the liver from his body. He hung the body on to a tree growing on the beach and went home to give Nangtainese the liver to eat. Nangtainese, however, wrapped the liver in banana leaves and hid the parcel under the roof of the house. As soon as he could he ran away trying to find his brother. He came to the beach and found the empty canoe. Crying, he ran along the reef calling for Nangtalamon. When he met a group of men he asked them whether they had seen his brother. They answered that he should follow the coast and he would find his brother hanging in a tree. Nangtainese ran and ran until he found the tree. He took down his brother. With the middle rib of a coconut leaf he beat his brother's skin, so that blood poured from his body. He asked him to sit up, yet Nangtalamon fell down again. Again he hit his skin and again he asked him to sit up. When Nangtalamon was able to sit up he hit him again and asked him to stand up. Nangatalamon stood up, yet fell down. Again his skin was mutilated until he could stand up. When he was able to walk, the two brothers went to an island where they knew that men were in possession of bird feathers. They chose the red feathers of the bird Mareng (parrot) and returned to the enclosure of their father. When they saw Hulendap, he wanted to get hold of them. Hulendap shot stones at them to force them to come down, but Nangtalamon and Nangtainese spread out their arms and flew into the air. Today they are still here as the red-feathered bird Mareng.

The recurrent theme of this and other myths like it is the relation of blood to skin. Blood awakens skin to life when contained within it; *Hulendap*'s blood turns into the living appearance of the two brothers. Conversely, the bleeding of skin reawakens Nangtalamon from his deadly sleep and metamorphoses him into a bird. The meaning of '*Hulendap*' is too tantalizing to be overlooked: while *Hulendap* is associated with 'the new moon', the twins are associated with the waning moon, as it is 'dying' on the shore, only to be reawoken and move on like a bird, transgressing the spaces the 'new moon' had enclosed on the land. Like the mythical twins, those who are made ancestors through *malanggan* become birds and fly to the north-west to the island of the dead – just like the moon, which enters its invisible phase with the climax of *malanggan,* to reappear above the island of the dead far away from the land.

Awakening and journeying are intimately related in this myth, which provides an elaboration of the birth and death of *malanggan*. The first awakening, in the form of the transformation of *Hulendap*'s blood into the brothers' appearances, leads to a daily journey between garden and sea that captures the boys' life. The second awakening, through the blood's staining of Nangtalamon's bloodless skin, leads them to re-create their past journeying together. Crucial to the end of the first journey and to the beginning of the second is the moment of appearance and revelation – as Nangtalamon appears in front of Karak, and as the revived Nangtalamon appears with his brother in front of their father. It is, however, the disappearance of the birds from sight that creates the theme of journeying as a metaphor for remembering.·

Their joint departure also captures the bond that blood is thought to effect. The pig sacrifices that are made to the *malanggan* carver over the period of his work thus create a 'likeness' in the same way as Nangtainese and Nangtalamon were created by Hulendap's blood. The image that takes on form over the three months of carving during which the figure comes to life is thus conceived as a mirror image; that is, it becomes an image that is 'like' or '*malang*', not in relation to something outside itself, but, like the mythical twins, to itself. To underscore the self-referentiality of something that is created through the giving of blood, *malanggan*-images are thus always 'split', so that each side faces the other like its mirror; recalling thereby the many adventures of the mythical twins born of blood. Like the twins' enclosed life, that of the *malanggan*-figure inside the enclosure is short-lived. Death and metamorphosis into images of odour and colour are their common fate, yet one that promises the vision of an eternal return.

Olfaction and Transition

Whereas blood sacrifice is most prominent in its regular enactment during the months of *marias* while *malanggan* unfolds, the other domain of sacrifice, called *gulutung*, which falls into the months of *matbung*, is more inconspicuous. Initiated with the death of the *malanggan* figure and the departure of the 'smell-canoe', a series of offerings, which are, like *malanggan*, left to decompose, effect an interchange with *moroa*. In this type of offering, the vehicle between the visible and the invisible realm of Karoro, the seat of *moroa*, is odour (*ngusung*).

Olfaction, as the vehicle capable of transgressing the boundary between the visible and the invisible, is thus central to all sacrifice. However, with the exception of Gell and Howes, who both pointed to the importance of odour in rituals of transition, olfaction has remained an element of ritual symbolism and material culture neglected by anthropologists.[15]

The Kara have a large vocabulary for different odours, which is used among other things to classify taro plants (*iahes*) into named types differentiated into those belonging to the matriline and those belonging to the village. Different *lebule*[16] grow *iahes* or tubers of different coloration, which is visible on scraping away the outer bark. The coloration ranges from white, to yellow, to red, to bluish purple, which are also the colours used in the painting of *malanggan* figures. The classification of tubers, however, is not possible in terms of colour alone, but only when roasting and thereby drying the tuber over the fire; on breaking such a roasted tuber open, the flesh inside is white but the remaining liquid evaporates as odorous steam, by means of which tubers are categorized according to name. Fed as *meme* to the young and the sick, the odorous steam of taro, associated with female reproductive power, is considered beneficial.

The olfactory vocabulary is thus intimately bound up with colour terms, which are also assigned to fish, plants and vegetables, as well as to plant-derived paints. Stephan remarks in his work on southern New Ireland that the paints used in New Ireland were despised by the nearby Duke of York islanders, who considered them inferior because of their strong smell (Stephan and Graebner 1907:37).

The release of odour through heating or decomposition is a common component of all offerings, the most important of which take place in connection with ceremonies performed around *baral*, a site associated with the uncaptured spirits of the murdered, which are known as *pue*. *Baral* is an upturned branch of the kiula tree (*rabai*); it has the shape of a Y and is planted in the centre of a coastal settlement whose habitation

Figure 3.2 *Baral.*

reaches back to pre-colonial times (Figure 3.2). In contrast to the south, where the Y-shaped uprooted trunk of a kiula tree is placed at the entrance to the funerary enclosure, in the north *baral* forms a ritual space of its own, though there are oral accounts of its having also functioned as the entrance to the enclosure of the *haio* and its having been used as the place to deposit the food cooked daily for the *haio*. It may be this connection with the olfactory powers attributed to the *haio's* food and her own association with self-renewal that has propelled the *baral* into the foreground of a sacrificial exchange initiated with *moroa*.

Baral is surrounded by a circle of black obsidian (*benat*), pieces of which are also placed at the bottom of a stone-oven; through repeated cooking, these stones give off a white powder called *but,* which, in combination with coconut juice (*ni*) is used to make *kambang*, a white mixture that when eaten together with areca nut creates a mildly stimulating toxin that is said to 'place or focus the mind' (*la monan*). As a result of ritual actions performed around *baral*, horizontally drifting stems are swept across the sea (*la mon*) during the rainy season as a sign for the arrival of odour as a token of *moroa's* goodwill (*hamarere*). Swimming between these stems are sharks, which are caught during this time of the year all along the west coast by a method known as 'shark-calling' (*ngat bewue*). The songs that are sung in shark-calling are also sung in the direction of *karoro* as part of the ritual performance of 'the calling of smell' (*wangam a ngusung*); these songs address *pue,* the spirits of the slain who failed to be re-encompassed and metamorphosed into ancestors through *malanggan*. Appearing in the guise of sharks, these spirits, who were never allowed to depart and thus could never forget serve as the collectors and carriers of odour in its journey back to land.

Because *but* thus creates both a conceptual and a real passage for the 're-collection' of odour, *benat* are the framing device that makes this placing or focusing of thought possible. Placed in a one-metre-wide circle around the Y-shaped *baral, benat* work like the circular *rekap* worn by the *maimai* as a kind of trapping device that serves to attract and arrest a power in space. Inside the circle are planted red- yellow- and green-coloured tenget (*si*) plants, which serve as powerful attractors of odour because of their colour; colour, as we saw earlier in the example of taro, allows odour to be named (*si-ne*) and thus rooted (*si*). By reason of its synaesthetic capacity, tenget is one of the most important ritual plants among the Tikana; it is worn by the *maimai* in the belt and by *malanggan*-dancers or masqueraders in their costume or their hands, and it is planted around the settlement and the funerary enclosures. Most importantly, however, tenget are used for the calling of odour and of sharks by being washed in water, as well as for the ritual washing (*kei*) that removes the traces of odour from those who came into contact with *malanggan*; the effect of these uses shows tenget's ability to attract odour if it is lacking and repel it when it is present in whatever it touches.

Baral means 'drifting,' its meaning shedding light on its close association with 'the calling of odour' (*wangam a ngusung*), which is the most important calendrical rite performed at the edge of the sea. The ritual is planned and carefully timed for the early morning following the rising of the new moon in *matbung*, as the last full moon of *marias* has vanished, moving 'underground' from the east to the north-west coast. By sunrise of the appointed day, the *bil a bine* has positioned himself on the outermost edge of the reef, which will become fully exposed at dawn with the new moon. As he faces *Karoro* beyond the horizon, he chants songs that call for the drifting ashore of uprooted trees, whose positioning in the water differentiates them as *but*, *wagil* and *kaletung*. While calling for the *moroa* in this way, he washes leaves of the tenget plant taken from the *baral* enclosure, splashing water in the direction of Karoro. The leaves are then planted inside the gardens.

The drifting ashore (*baral*) of uprooted tree-trunks and branches during the rainy season, about two months after this event, is met with *gulutung*, an offering of crops that greets the arrival of *ngusung* or odour, which promises a rich harvest of taro tubers in the gardens. It is again the colour of the item offered and left to rot on the stem that is important, so that each item may be replaced by any other item as long as it is either black, yellow or red. While sometimes such offerings are replaced by store-foods, coconut, banana and taro are still preferred, as they share the capacity to renew themselves in the very process of being left to rot, '*were*' meaning both 'shoot' and 'rotten.'

The calling of odour is most carefully timed, its success depending on two prior appearances that usually coincide with the climax of *malanggan* in the last full moon of *marias* in the east. At full moon in September along the east coast, and in October along the west coast, every living creature in the lagoon and on the reef dies after mating; the event is called *matfue*, 'the reef grows'. Everyone is out after this night on the reef as it is gradually exposed during dawn to collect and then eat the *mat*, or 'dryness'. During the waning moon of *matfue*, gardens are prepared in the forest by burning the undergrowth.

The next important event is expected on the ninth night after the moon of *matfue* has disappeared; this is the appearance of the paloloworm, called *mamaze*, in the lagoon for mating. Shedding their multicoloured, spaghetti-like egg-sacs, *mamaze* are caught by women and carried into the houses, where they are eaten for the next few days until nothing remains. *Mamaze* bring 'heat' and announce the arrival of odour in the gardens; children of all ages are taken to the lagoon to wash in the water of *mamaze*, the youngest of them being thrown in the direction of the rising sun with their faces painted with red ochre (*thai*). Branches of trees that are thought to have a cooling effect are placed against houses inhabited by the old and near the living spaces of those who are for other reasons considered to be in a state of 'hotness', such as menstruating women. They are also forbidden to enter the newly cleared gardens until all *mamaze* have been consumed, lest their odorous qualities should cancel out the 'rooting' of odour in the ground.

With its explicit reference to containment, *mamaze* marks the end of *marias* and opens the new year. Yet *mamaze* is more than a watched-for yearly cosmogonic event. Rather, it is a process of transition marked by three separate events, comprising *malanggan*, *matfue* and *mamaze*, which together trace the escape of odour and its recapture in a new container. This exchange with the invisible is thus dependent upon two interlinked processes of transformation, of creating animate things through the containment and release of odour.

Notes

1. For the Solomon islands see Keesing (1982: 128–42).

2. See Sperber (1975) and Boyer (1994) on the role of remembering in the cognitive efficacy of ritual symbolism.

3. Called *okubine* along east-coast Tikana.

4. It is notable that this theoretical interest in early anthropology coincides with the development of a new type of museum, exemplified in the Pitt-Rivers Museum, which explicitly identified collections as remains or 'burial places of (cultural) memory', safeguarding artefacts against its imminent loss (Pellizzi 1995; Elsner and Cardinal 1994).

5. See Valeri on the theory of sacrifice as an expression of an ideology of 'debt' (1985); on sacrifice and debt see Valeri (1994).

6. Riddance is possibly universally an aspect characteristic of the treatment of offerings: 'the scapegoat must never come back' (Burkert 1983: 45).

7. R. Girard 1977; there are other comparable psycho-cultural definitions of sacrifice, notably that given by Burkert (1983).

8. For comparative studies on the importance of olfaction in Oceania see Gell (1977); Howes (1987, 1988, 1991, 1992); on the fate of odour in early Renaissance culture see Corbin (1986).

9. See Trompf on the wedding of millennarianism and cargoism as typically retaining images of modern technology and scientific achievement (1990: 39).

10. This point was also made by M. Kaplan with respect to Fiji (1990; Kaplan and Kelly 1994).

11. N. Thomas raised a similar argument in relation to Fijian artefacts (1991).

12. The seasons change one month earlier on the east coast.

13. See also Wagner's chapter on 'The Celestial Mechanisms of Gardening' in his work on the Barok of southern New Ireland (1986: 36–48).

14. The east coast calls *merulie, sigeragun* (see Peekel 1910; Krämer 1925).

15. Gell (1977); Howes (1982, 1987, 1988, 1991); Classen (1993). See also Sperber on odour and ritual symbolism (1975).

16. *Lebule* means 'the path of the ancestors'.

four

Building Up The Fire

To this very day, mankind has always dreamt of seizing and fixing that fleeting moment when it was permissible to believe that the law of exchange could be evaded, that one could give without losing, enjoy without sharing. At either end of the earth and at both extremes of time, the Sumerian myth of the golden age and the Andaman myth of the future life correspond, the former placing the primitive happiness at a time when the confusion of languages made words into common property, the latter describing the bliss of the hereafter as a heaven where women will no longer be exchanged, i.e. removing to an equally unattainable past or future the joys, eternally denied to social man, of a world in which one keeps to oneself (Lévi-Strauss 1969: 496–7).

Offerings to *moroa* are an integral part of the 'work for the dead' (*haisok ine mamat);* collapsing the ancestral domain with that of the living, the term *habung* describing both 'those who are made to be ancestors' as well as the extended matriline.[1] Accordingly, the concept of genealogy is absent, with the dead being 'forgotten' (*babangi*) with the completion of the funerary work, their names and skills being transmitted to the living. Death throughout New Ireland, as is eloquently argued by Roy Wagner, is a process of consumption that absorbs and re-channels anything 'left over' from a person's life (Wagner 1991: 329–30, 1986: 146–75; Foster 1990). As elsewhere in New Ireland, the process of consumption is a performative act, involving the creation of predominantly spatial images of containment (Wagner 1987).

Dissolution has become central to the vocabulary of the theory of the fractal person in Melanesian anthropology; processes are captured through which the androgynous substances that compose persons are dismantled so that they can emerge as singular for the brevity of the moment of exchange and reproduction (Strathern 1988). A North Mekeo is 'de-conceived' first at marriage and then finally at death (Mosko 1983); Barok and Siar mortuary feasts 'obviate' previous relationships in finally

killing the dead (Wagner 1986; Bolyanatz 1994); while for the Sabarl
this is a process of disassemblage (Battaglia 1990) and for the Gawa a
'severance' or dissolution (Munn 1986).

Among the Tikana, the work for the dead is fittingly described as 'finishing the dead' (*luri a mamat*); it is a process enacted through multiple,
cumulative images of effacement that culminate in the dramatic death
of a *malanggan* effigy. Here, the process of decomposing persons is first
and foremost an iconic and representational act, in which the thing
to be destroyed visualizes the processual nature of destruction itself.
Thus it is the consumption of material traces of 'skin' in the landscape,
through the eating and leaving to rot of garden produce and the
destruction of the house, that visualizes the changing state of the corpse
and that of the mourners and effects the gradual dissolution of the social
relationships of which the deceased person had been a part. The
physical separation of body and soul is enacted analogically in performances that, step by step, undo the traces left by a person in the social
matrix. Yet this is not the end of the matter. Once the physical traces
of the social body have been effaced, an inverse process of building up
an artificial body as the new container for the soul is set to follow. This
time, the analogical relation between the state of the new body and
the state of the soul is explicitly iconic. The final death and climactic
destruction of the new artificial body completes a process of replacement of persons by things and things by images. By translating the
object into an image that anticipates the repeatability of this process,
power can be arrested in a specific place. It is this last product of substitution, the *malanggan*-image, so easily overlooked in the scheme of
things, that elicits a new beginning as it becomes the focal point and
operative logic of all future attachment.[2]

The work for the dead, in New Ireland, thus does not just restore the
social fabric. Rather, it creates a form of governance that is conceived
analogically, yet in purely visual and conceptual terms. The role of a
polity of images within an emerging body politic will be the subject of
the following chapters. The following detailed account of performances
that translate persons into things and things into images will allow us
to understand better how images can be central to thinking about social
relations in an abstract manner.

Every settlement is responsible for finishing its own dead in a complex
sequence of performances that focus on two, usually adjacent, enclosures.
On one site is a burial enclosure (*a venabut*) whose stone wall (*belehat*)
surrounds the burial-pit (*roa*) where *malanggan* are placed on the night
prior to their spectacular disclosure; adjacent to it is the resting-place

of the dead (*but*), which is also the place where *malanggan* are made – *but* is enclosed by a bamboo fence (*sebedou*) whose material and design is considered to be part of *malanggan*.[3]

While each deceased person is subject to individually timed performances, all those buried in the same cemetery are 'finished' in the same final ceremony, and often with the same sculpted image, the planning of which is initiated by the death of an elder. When all have been made ancestors in this manner, the settlement is abandoned, its stone wall acting as a visible reminder of the many acts of finishing.[4]

Every deceased person is the subject of separately planned ritual work, and every settlement is responsible for the finishing of its own dead. As they are helped by the rest of the village and an extended network bound by loyalty, every household is at any point in time actively planning for its own work as well as for the work of others. Pigs are to be reared, gardens planted, copra cut and sold for cash to be used in exchanges, and shell-money (*burut*) safeguarded and earmarked for the many different stages that complete the work for the dead. Everyone is aware of the different stages of the work that other settlements may be in, and word spreads quickly if decisions are made elsewhere to advance the work of finishing the dead.

The Work for the Dead

The work for the dead is divided into three main stages, each of which in turn is internally subdivided into two parts.[5] These three stages activate secondary burial, as it is described by Robert Hertz in his original study of *The Collective Representation of Death*.[6] The life-force called *ventanun* (or *verak*) that is set free during the first stage of ritual work is transformed into *rongan* in the second and reabsorbed in the third stage into an artificial container that turns it into *rune*, a source for unlimited awakenings.[7] In surprising affinity to the Hertzian scheme, the ritual process effects a transformation of the soul (*ventanun–rongan–rune*), the mourners (*musbad*), and the social group (*dahun–taune–habung*), which results in the fashioning of a life-giving death (Figure 4.1).[8] Performative and self-contained images of uprooting and swallowing pervade each act of 'finishing' and set into motion the 'making of ancestors'.

The three stages and their subdivisions are:

1. *Mamat (kawia to haram gom)*: The first stage is initiated with the burial (*kawia*). Following the two-day ceremony of the burial, the decomposition of the earthly container of the soul associated with

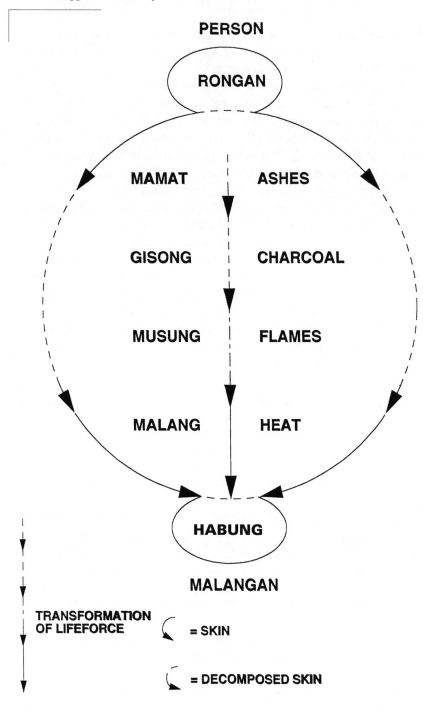

Figure 4.1 The Ritual Cycle.

breath during life and with the shadow after death (*ventanun*) is traced in numerous smaller ceremonies (*hamakterolen*). These ceremonies are organized and attended by the inhabitants of the village of the deceased person. Women harvest and cook and men collectively consume the products of the deceased's garden inside an enclosure built around *but*, where the body is left to rest prior to burial.

2. *haram gom to gisong*: When there is no further produce left in the gardens grown by the deceased, the first phase of this is completed with a ceremony marking the burning of the house of the deceased person (*haram gom*); the ceremony is timed by the harvest of *burume*, the red flower of the *Pandanus* palm, which produces a staining red juice, symbolizing blood, that is eaten together with sago by the local endogamous group. The images acted out in the performance of *haram gom* link it to *gisong*, and thus, while concluding the first, they also open the second phase of ritual work. This second phase is transitional in that it focuses, first, on the transformation of the soul (*ventanun*) into a force associated with heat (*rongan*), and second, on the transformation of the state of the mourners, who, as they expel the deceased from their relationships to each other, emerge as *dahun* made up of sibling-units.[9]

Seen together, both of these phases effect a transition from images of consumption to images of production. While *haram gom* is a two-day event, *gisong* lasts for three days; this increased time devoted to the work corresponds to the growing size of stone-ovens and the growing 'heat' ascribed to the places that metaphorize the changing nature of *rongan* as it is set free. *Gisong* is a three-day event that usually collapses two ritual stages into one: *sesere*, or the 'scraping off the "skin"', during which every last trace of the deceased person's work is effaced; and *sabitbad*, the cutting of the hair of the mourners, which coincides with the erecting of a cement tombstone (*smel*) in the *but*. After this event, nothing further may happen until the burial of an elder inside the same cemetery enclosure initiates the proceedings for the final stage of the work for the dead.

3. *malanggan*: This is a four-day event that completes a period of about three months of carving *malanggan* effigies inside *but*; the preparations for *malanggan* include *wangam a ngusung*, or the calling of odour prior to the planting of ritual gardens. The spirit of the deceased, freed in the preceding stages from its earthly trappings, is recaptured in an artificial container that is carved from wood, woven from vines or moulded from clay. Enlivened and placed on the grave for one night

and the early hours of the next morning, the effigy is killed (*lukfumari*) by symbolically removing its skin, and, like the 'skin' of the deceased person at the onset of the funerary work, consuming it, this time through ritualized exchange. This consumption is completed with the exposure of the effigy's remains in the forest; as the paint pigments and carved planes are gradually erased by the oncoming rainy season, *malanggan,* and with it ancestral power, metamorphoses into a named image of remembrance (*mamaluhen*). Given as *meme* to children or found through dreams, the named image becomes a vehicle that connects the invisible with the visible, the past with the present. Its manifold, yet controlled awakening contrasts with the volatile shades, whose sudden and momentary appearance haunts the living.

The ritual performances following the death of a person proceed in successive stages analogous to the growing heat of a fire, from cold ashes (*mamat*), to glowing charcoal (*gisong*) and finally to the intense heat (*malanggan*) of a fire that has ceased to flame. As the earthly trappings of the spirit are effaced in bodily decomposition and *ventanun* is gradually freed from its container, it is transformed into pure power (*rongan*) – into a dangerous, violent and potentially destructive force associated with female odour (*rotap*) in its released manifestation, and with heat in its contained manifestation in ritual gardens and *malanggan* effigies. Preventive magic (*magi*) and ritual washing (*kei*) are necessary to secure the life of people who come into contact with the odour of death, by sending it to a distant and safe abode.

Rongan that are not recaptured by society and channelled into *malanggan* become *pue*. *Pue* is the power of the slain whose bodies are left to rot or to be eaten. If a village cannot control *pue* it is thought to be threatened by internal feuds, hunger and fragmentation, with people moving away to relatives in other places. The growth and prosperity of a village and the growth or spatial expansion of a clan are thus associated with control over *pue* through sacrifice and the absorption and 'finishing' of *rongan*.

The Building up of the Fire

Death is conceived of as a process whereby skin is removed and fire is extinguished, to be gradually built up again through ritual work. All death occurring prior to old age (*labo*) is considered to be the result of acts of murder (*pue*): either by skin being 'snatched' by spirit beings (*rulrul*), who use these skins to appear in disguise and trick humans, or through sorcery (*ngein*), which strives to weaken the skin, the skin feeling sleepy

(*a tak amat*) and cold (*a tak amadierk*). The only death that is not attributed to murder is the death of a *beiak,* the 'living dead' housed inside
the enclosure (*sebedou*) that also serves as resting-place for the dead prior
to burial[10] (Figure 4.2). *Beiak* are those who have ceased to consume taro
as their main diet and live on liquids that soften the skin and wash it
away in time (see Groves 1933a: 298). The death of these elderly initiates
the planning of the 'finishing' of the work for all the dead buried inside
the cemetery.

Irrespective of where and when a person dies, the body is carried as
soon as possible into the *but.* The place or the house in which the person
died is declared *gom* and may not be entered. While resting on *but*, the
water (*rarum*) of the body is said to drop into the ground. Years later,
where the body had been resting, a cement gravestone called *smel*, the
Pidgin English term for 'odour', will be placed and, years after that, the
'skin' of *malanggan* will be given shape to serve as a new container for
rongan.[11] The length of time a body is left in the *but* is determined by a
principle that links age with the power (*buro*) ascribed to a person. The
power attributed to a person is defined in relation to their activities in
ceremonial exchanges and is measured in the number of names, in the
right to know, to speak and to give. The greater the power at the time
of death, the longer the interval between death and burial.

Figure 4.2 House inside enclosure.

The longest a body is left to dry in the *but* today is five days. Before the restrictions imposed by the Mission and the health department, the oldest and the youngest were left in the *but* to be transformed into *vipito* or mummies by the heat of the sun.[12] The interval between death and burial can be compared to the interval between the second and third stages of the ritual performance. Those who remain longest in the *but* initiate the preparations of *malanggan* and undergo a very abbreviated process of dismantling and reabsorption. Those who are on the lower level of the hierarchy of age and status have to await the burial of a *piren*, a person with many names, in the same enclosure.

Regardless of the interval allowed between death and burial, the spirit (*ventanun*) of the deceased is thought to hover for three days before departing to the island of the dead (Tinguen) in the north-west; it is thought to leave behind a pattern of three crossed-out marks on the beach, which say:

'pabuh o sa lameniau' – you will think of me today
'mahu o sa lameniau' – you will think of me tomorrow
'iansa o sa lameniau' – you will think of me the day after
'o sa bangbangi' – before you will forget me.

Kawia

Kawia, literally to possess land (*ka* = inalienable possession, *wia*=land), is the term used to refer to the burial and to the exchanges that determine who will have control over the ritual work that is about to commence; those who 'win' the body thus take on the ritual work associated with the body's metamorphosis into a *malanggan* effigy.

During the first night in which the body rests in the funerary enclosure a pig is killed by those who aspire to claim rights to recapture the deceased's *rongan* in a *malanggan* of their choice. Rawi's son Iang in the settlement Henemeras of Lamusmus 2 had readied a pig months prior to his father's death. During the night following the old man's death, the pig was killed, and Iang secured his entitlement to the knowledge and land that had been controlled by his father. This pig is called *putu kanai*, meaning the head of *kanai*, a bird that heralds shoals of tuna, which is a theme occurring in the dances of *malanggan*, and here is meant to draw attention to the manifold strategic planning that will occupy everybody for the foreseeable future.

This pig is given to the land-owning sibling unit of the settlement in whose funerary enclosure the person will be buried. The killing of the pig opens the ritualized dispute among co-resident *dahun* over the right to authorize *retak*, the 'making of the skin', which is to reabsorb the life-force. This contest over the body is called *iu a mamat/raunim a mamat* (*vul a mamat* in southern Kara), the 'pulling' or 'swallowing' of the body. It is acted out at the side of the grave immediately after the burial: two groups oppose each other, sitting on either side of a mat, one being composed of the deceased's clan relatives, the other of her *korok*, all being supported by countless others who line up behind each grouping. Money is thrown on the mat, first by the mourning clan relatives, and then by the *korok*; the bids are repeated until a stop is declared by both sides and the *maimai* steps up to count the proceeds.

Those who have offered more and thus have acquired the right to finish the work for this deceased person are challenged with: *O sa wune?* – Will you be up to it? On returning to their homes and while they are sitting around the fire much speculation and thought is given to the work that lies ahead.

During the night following the death, still prior to the burial, the various services associated with the burial are distributed. Each village (*bine*) exchanges these services with its partner-village; the services comprise *meut,* or the wake, *bug,* or the making of a coffin from an old canoe, and *bag auk,* or the digging of the grave (Walden and Neverman 1940: 12).

In the morning of the burial day, a large stone-oven (*mun*) is built and heated by the men, an activity called *udet.* It is situated in the secondary forest encircling the settlement, and will change its position with each successive stage of the proceedings; in the funerary events following *kawia,* as in the bridewealth payment ceremony called *ngesen,* the stone-oven is built in the central space. In *haramgom* and *gisong* the stone-ovens are erected inside the cooking-houses of the resident women, and in *malanggan* in the guest-houses that are occupied by groups separated according to their identity with named *habung* and built where once the house of the deceased person stood. The change in position of the stone-oven from 'outside' to 'inside' metaphorizes the progressive containment of life-force into the source (*rune*) of ancestral power.

When the death of an important elder such as Rawi of Henemeras is announced over the radio, anyone who can claim any kind of relatedness to either him or any of his immediate relatives is expected to arrive. The quantities of food needed to feed these numbers of people are enormous, and preparations have been intense during the preceding days. People arriving during the morning of the burial day order themselves into the existing categories on the basis of their *korok* relationships. Every group has to bring a pig and raw products, such as taro and sweetpotato.

They arrive separately, and remain separate in the places allocated to them, waiting for the work (*haisok*) of *kawia* to begin. The following description of a burial in Panemecho village highlights the orchestration of *malyvi*, of sorrow and remembrance:

> A small footpath led downhill to the settlement of Dupie (Moromaf) on the beach of Panemecho (Rangalis). The group of Moromaf from Panachais and their *korok* of Moroibe and Moromuna of Panachais arrived. Chatter ceased as silently one after the other walked along the narrow path, balancing the pigs and the food over the rocks and steep paths. The pig was carried by four men in the front, followed by Dupie's classificatory sister's son (*marodene*), the *maimai* of Moromaf of Panachais village, and his sisters. The others arranged themselves in order of age and according to their relation to Dupie and the *maimai*. Songs were chanted that can only be heard as a procession approaches a settlement in which a burial or a marriage payment is taking place.
>
> On arriving at the edge of the settlement, the pig and the food were placed on the ground. Without looking around everyone walked swiftly into the *but*, where Dupie's body was being kept. As they stepped over the fence, crying over the body began. Women placed their children on the corpse to prevent the *vethak*, the shade, haunting the children; the dead man now knew the children as well as they once knew him. The crying is taken as an opportunity to lift the cloth from the body to detect signs of sorcery (*ngain*). Thereafter, slowly everyone stepped outside, the men joining the other men in the man's house and the women walking over to the house in which Moromaf of Panemecho had lived since Dupie's death.
>
> The speaker of this group stepped into the centre of the clearing together with men who carried the pig and the food brought by the group. There, he lifted his arm, holding a string of shell-money in his hand. He addressed his classificatory sister, the daughter of Dupie's sister, outlining in his speech the relation between the two sibling units and the reason for their spatial separation. A last outcry *a ram korok* finished his speech. The shell-money was fetched by a child, the pig and the food by young men.

The pigs, the shell-money, the currency and the food presented by each arriving group are given either as *a radem*, for free, as *susuang*, to finish a debt, or as *wurpuran*, to initiate a debt. The nature of the presentation has to be specified in the speech delivered by the speaker representing the donor. None of the pigs, however, are killed (*luk*) on this day or kept by the siblings of the deceased person. After the burial in the afternoon the pigs are given away by the siblings of the deceased to create new debts, which provide the *wun ine*, the source or foundation of the work to follow.

On a sign from the *maimai*, those who have given a pig gather in separate groups to pay for the pigs (*do darak*) they have brought. Both the owner of the pig and also his/her *korok* and siblings throw shell-money and currency on a mat. The payment for the pig is called *caves do*. The *maimai* representing the owner of this pig announces the amount and hands it over together with the pig to the siblings of the deceased person, who in turn give it away to others to initiate debts to be repaid in the work that is yet to unfold. The pigs (*mun do*) given by siblings and offspring, on the other hand, are not exchanged, but are sacrificed by suffocation and distributed to all who are present.

After the buying of the pigs, the coffin is made ready for burial. The bodies of elders are transferred from the resting-place (*but*) to the burial place (*roa*) by dancers of *buma* (the rising bird). The dance with the coffin is classified as part of *malanggan*.[13] The dancers of *buma* decorate their bodies with a mixture of lime (*las*) made from the white ashes of the stone-oven and of the water of a green coconut (*ni*); this mixture is clapped with hollow hands on their faces, shoulders and backs, remaining visible as a leaf pattern (*bai*). Leaves of the tenget plant (*si*) are fastened in the waist belt. In full attire, a group of ten to twenty men and women enter the clearing while singing the songs of *rimbugtio* and dancing in a slow movement backwards and forwards, like the waves of the sea. They approach *but*, enter, and reappear with the coffin. Slowly they advance forward with the coffin to the rhythm (*samsan*) of *redelak*, a rattle made out of shells, to the beat (*seredimet*) of the *garamut*, and to the song of *rimbugtio*. As they approach the stone-walled burial place, people cry and wail, recalling (*malyvi*) the many times they had been together with the deceased at similar occasions. The *maimai* hands over a string of shell-money to the dancers, followed by the *korok* of the dancers, who hand over money. This procedure is called *sui a malanggan*, literally to 'pull the *malanggan* inside'. Thereafter, the coffin is carried inside the *roa* and placed close to the grave (*luk*).

If the coffin is not transferred from the *but* with the dance of *buma*, the carriers are either women (for a deceased woman) or men (for a deceased man). Should both enclosures be at different places in the settlement, in cases where village cemeteries are still in use, the carriers rush with the coffin to the *roa*; the speed being designed to prevent the odour of the body from escaping. As soon as the earth is thrown on top of the coffin, everyone hurries back to the central space in front of the *sebedou* enclosure.

Only after the burial does the work (*haisok*) of *kawia* unfold. The first exchange concerns the ritual services, followed by the exchange of *buma* and by *iu a mamat*, the 'pulling' of *mamat* described above. When the exchanges are almost finished, young men and women uncover the stone-oven and carry the cooked food into the centre of the clearing, where leaves of the breadfruit tree have been spread out. Pigs and taro are lined up in parallel rows alongside the *but*, with their heads facing outward. The placing of the sacrificed pigs (*mun do*), like the positioning of the stone-ovens (*mun*), alters with each advancing stage: facing outward at *kawia*, at *haram-gom* they face inward placed in front of the *but*, are positioned inside the *but* facing outward at *gisong*, and inside the *roa* facing outward at *malanggan*. The transposing of the sacrificial offering effects a shift in emphasis from the visible domain to the invisible, culminating in the offering to *moroa* at the height of *malanggan*.

The food distribution at the burial is specific to it, and is not repeated in any of the other stages. It is called *mun doien*, literally 'the meal after the fight'. *Mun doien* is characterized by the fact that portions of the pork cannot be bought by individuals, but are given to everyone. If there are many groups present from different villages, sticks are lined up in parallel rows, each of them representing a different *dahun*. Along these sticks the food is piled up, creating thereby *ngabuk* or an image of a skin growth, to be fetched by women of the various groups once their names are called by the *maimai* directing the event.[14]

The dissection of the sacrificial pigs, however, is repeated at every stage of the ritual work. *Mun do* are cut up and distributed in a special manner called *tawai*, literally 'the breaking of the stem': starting in the centre, the surface layer of skin and fat is cut from head to tail into long strips, each strip being taken by a young man who forms with others a row and encircles the clearing twice, before each strip is cut into smaller portions, which are thrown, while those carrying them are still walking in a circle, on each food parcel.[15] 'Skin' or *korok* relationships effected through marriage are thus metaphorically ruptured.

The time of the food distribution coincides invariably with sunset. It is a time of hectic preparations for the departure of those who are not going to stay for another one to four weeks in the houses of the settlement. All the pigs that have been received on this day are given away to create new debts (*wurpuran*) to be resolved at the time of *malanggan* (*susuang*) or during the burial in the settlement of the present recipient.

Kawia to Haram Gom

The time elapsing between the successive events following the burial is determined by the ripening of crops and fruit-carrying trees planted by the deceased person; their harvest is taken into the enclosure surrounding the *but*, to be ritually consumed by all the men of the village in small feasts called *marakterolen*, each lasting only a day. The 'place of the skin' (*laten*) created by the deceased person is thus effectively consumed in about the same time-frame as the body is thought to take to decompose in the grave.

The dismantling of 'skin' is marked by the following eight feasts, which provide the basic framework for the ritual work of the freeing of the life-force (*ventanun*):

Vei a sebedou The construction of the fence around the *but* takes place a few days to a few weeks after the burial, while the mourners are still inhabiting the settlement. Each side of *sebedou* is made by a different sibling unit and their *korok*. The bamboo fence of *sebedou* is classified as part of *malanggan*. There are three different types known among the Tikana: the fence (*bas*) of the 'coastal' people, recognized by the use of unbroken bamboo; the fence (*ngit*) of the mountain people, recognized by the use of split bamboo; and the fence (*siliput*) of the *haio*, recognized by the fastening of the bamboo with a knot pattern. The bamboo is carried from the bush into the settlement while singing songs of *malanggan* called *kingiri*.

A biten a labui/dang The land and the lagoon used by the deceased for planting and fishing is declared taboo. In both *labui* and *dang*, stems of the tree called *malemeiasum,* which are believed to have a cooling effect, are stuck in front of and within the space marked out and enclosed for ritual consumption.

Ine wanen hawedok seri The return of the mourners and the beginning of the ritual fast, or *alal*, is marked by a small food distribution attended by the village. Everyone whose *mamaluhen* or mourning is for a *korok* is called up by name and is publicly announced to assume the ritual observances of *alal*. They may not eat taro, cut facial hair, which is left to grow as sign of mourning, or wash their body and clothes more than the absolute minimum.

Tak ape langei a luhu The event marking the return of noise in the settlement takes place as soon as the *burume*, the fruit of a pandanus palm planted by the dead person, is ready for harvest. The red (*bung*) juice of the cooked 'burume' is eaten by the men inside the *but* together with taro and sweetpotato. Its red juice is associated with the cycling of 'blood' and names between successive generations of co-resident units of siblings.[16] Until this event, no one is allowed to sing or shout in and around the houses. Prior to the distribution of food, two fresh green coconuts (*ruwak*), resembling visually the thinning 'skin' of corpse and mourners, are smashed by clapping them against each other inside the house of the deceased or his/her eldest son/daughter. Until the event of *haram gom* all coconuts cut in the settlement have to be opened in the *gom*, the house of the deceased.

Gamsei but Soon after the burial, the children of the deceased mark a small pig, which is sacrificed during this event. The sacrifice marks the spreading of the ashes of the fire left in the house of the dead person.

Punguve This event marks the decomposition of the skin, leaving only the bones in the grave. Those who are children of the deceased person or of his/her brothers/sisters give areca nuts to the siblings of the deceased, and are given by them fruits of the fig tree (*rowen*) planted in the centre of the settlement. This exchange of products of the cultivated land dissolves *korok* relationships tied to the deceased person.

Meda wieien With the completed decomposition of the body, the body has become *wie*, or part of the ground. To mark this moment, all the crops left in the garden of the deceased person are harvested and eaten by the men inside the *but*. Pigs slaughtered for this event are given by the siblings of the deceased and large portions of pork, such as the head or the legs, are given to those who recently had a funeral in their own settlement. The pork will be returned at the ritual events of the recipients' sibling unit. A new sequence is opened, in which affinity based on marriage is transformed into a mutual relatedness between units of siblings.

Hangen a hut Around the time of the burial, the stem of a banana palm was planted next to the house of the deceased person and surrounded by stones. Its capacity for the infinite renewal of its shoots (*were*) makes it into a potent image to conclude the process of the consumption of 'skin' and to effect a transitional phase in the ritual work, which is to be concerned with the state of the freed *ventanun* marked by the finishing of mourning.

About one year after the burial, the banana palm bears fruit. The fruits are taken down and are brought into the house of the deceased, which had been declared *gom* at the time of the death. Here they are left to ripen, whereupon a day is marked on which all the men of the village go out fishing for the day. The fish is cooked together with taro within the house declared as *gom*. Shortly prior to sunset, the men of the village arrive and sit down in the *but*. The bananas are carried into the *but* together with the fish. The food that is left over is left to rot inside the *but*.

After all the men not resident in the settlement of siblings and their offspring have left, those who have ties to the land surrounding the settlement come together to plan the preparations for *haram gom*, the ritual burning of *gom*. The discussions concern the size and the site of the garden to be planted and the number and source of the pigs to be slaughtered at the event. Pigs have to be given both by children and sisters' children and by the siblings of the deceased. They can come from their own produce, can be bought with money and shell-money or can be claimed from established debt relations.

Haram Gom to Gisong

The events of *haram gom* and *gisong* have to be analysed as interconnected instances of a single mediatory process. This links the first phase of the funerary cycle with the second and final phase: a transition is achieved from the ritual consumption of 'skin' and the freeing of *ventanun* to its final reabsorption and containment as *rongan* inside the funerary enclosure where years later *malanggan* will be carved. The images that feature strongly in this transitional phase revolve around the growth of heat, effected through the shifting of stone-ovens into the houses and through offerings of first raw and then cooked food. Affinal relationships associated with the deceased are finally dissolved by focusing on the sibling unit both in exchanges and also in the work carried out by women inside the cooking-houses.

Haram gom

Haram gom is a two-day event, and part of the category of events called *henemos,* characterized by the temporal separation of the cooking and the distribution of food (*mun baing*); the stone-ovens are heated and covered the evening prior to the day of the exchanges. *Haram gom* means 'the burning of *gom*', the house of the deceased person. The burning of *gom* leads to the removal of the house the day after the event.

On the morning of the cooking day, women divide themselves among the available houses according to their relationship with the deceased: separate houses are used by the wife, the sisters and the daughters, each assisted by their clan and *korok*. Each house first prepares *kes*, food parcels given to female *korok* arriving on this day.

Every woman attending a ritual event has to arrive on the cooking day with two baskets of taro or sweetpotato. The baskets are exchanged between the cooking-houses involved in the event, each house transforming the crops of the other into individual food-parcels called *kes*. The cooked *kes* are given to the guests after another exchange that inverts the movement of the raw food. In the afternoon the *rut*, two-metre-long parcels of taro and pork taken from the pigs sacrificed in the morning, wrapped in leaves of the pandanus palm, are prepared. The work is carried out by four selected women, of whom two must be *paluk* (sisters) and two *ihak* (cross-cousins). One *rut* is prepared by each cooking-house, their contents being distributed at the end of the day. The smell of the pork cooked with taro is a reminder that *ventanun* is about to be freed from all its earthly trappings to become *rongan*. The preparation and exchange of *rut,* moreover, undoes relationships associated with the deceased by repeating and inverting the flow of such work at marriage (*ngesen*).

Haram gom culminates in the exchange of food – of rows of baskets filled with raw taro, raw pork and raw sago, as well as of money placed in front of each house, one basket being presented by each woman of a *dahun*, and each row representing a sibling or *korok* of the deceased. While arranging the baskets, both men and women enter into heated discussions about which basket should be given to whom. When everything is ready, all the lines involved in the exchanges simultaneously give away their baskets. Each basket acknowledges and symbolically returns the work that bound together each of the mourners and the deceased during her/his lifetime. The baskets of one house are given to those of the other house, and vice versa. Every time the name of a recipient is called, the acting *maimai* shouts *a ngas a lisin a gom a radem*, 'a *gom* is given to the sun'. With the dismantling of the house of the deceased the next day, *korok* have begun to face each other again as sisters and brothers.

During *gisong*, the presentations are returned by those who have received baskets at *haram gom*. However, cooked portions of pork, taro and sago are returned. This change from raw to cooked food in women's ritual work is associated with the growing heat and intensity of *rongan*, but also with the focus on *but*, which becomes the object of acts of finishing at *gisong*.

Gisong

Soon after *haram gom*, the sibling unit of the deceased has a meeting (*bung*) in which it is decided who should raise a pig and how many pigs might be given at the event to finish or initiate a relationship. The pigs marked within the settlement unit will be used for the days preceding the *gisong*, if the event incorporates the dances of *Langmanu* or of *Medu* that effect the finishing of *but*. The pigs for the final day of the exchanges will come from (1) the siblings and/or offspring of the deceased (*mun do*) and (2) the debts established in the funeral exchanges (*do darak*).

Once the pigs marked by the siblings (*mun do*) have reached medium size, a day is chosen for the clearing of the bush in which the garden will be planted. Taro, in the area of the Tikana, has to grow three months before it is ready for harvest. The growth of the taro is divided into three stages (*hasu, sewuk and rawuk*), the intermediate second stage being the harvest of the leaves of taro tubers. This is the time for clearing a second garden in which the harvested sticks of the taro tubers and the ones acquired in exchanges will be planted after the event of *gisong*. The harvest of the first garden coincides with the collecting of firewood and stones for the stone-oven built in the centre of each cooking-house.

During *gisong*, houses are divided among the sisters of the deceased, each of them being joined by their *korok*. The clan identity of the deceased is now the most important aspect for the organization of the work, which also focuses almost exclusively on female mourners, extending the mourning to all those of the same clan irrespective of their specific relation with the deceased.

Gisong is divided into four parts: (1) *musbad* or *pad magide* – the removal of the head hair of the mourners and the colouring of the hair with charcoal; (2) *lubugbug* – the removal of the fast; (3) *sasarai* – the removal of the ban on the cultivation of the deceased's land or fishing grounds; and (4) *rele but* – the removal of the traces left by the deceased's work.

If the unit inhabiting the settlement has ownership rights to the dances *Langmanu* or *Medu*, the two-day event is preceded by a number of weeks, how many depending on the time needed for the preparation of the decorations of the dancers. During this preparation, the men who will dance have to fast and follow taboos (*alal*) while living secluded in the cultivated land surrounding the village. The following outline of the climax of the ritual event, however, is independent of the performance of a dance.

DAY 1

The women assisting their male and female *korok* arrive in the morning with two baskets of raw food. The same exchanges of baskets and *kes* take place as were described for *haram gom*. When the *kes* are out of the stone-oven (around midday), the ovens are reheated. While the wood is slowly burning down, giving the stones their maximum heat, the banana-leaf parcels of taro (*nuum*) are prepared for distribution in the afternoon.

The activities of the men on this day consist of the thickening of the *sebedou* fence surrounding *but* with a thick coconut-palm screen called *kowebag*. Until the removal of the screen on the final day, only men who are part of the *dahun* organizing the event are allowed inside the enclosure. Those offspring of brothers of the deceased who do not have rights to the particular dance performed on the final day have to give a pig and shell-money in order to become *raso*, members of *malanggan*.

DAY 2

This is the day of *dodolas* (to be given lime), which singles out those of the same clan as the deceased. *Dodolas* is a white substance made out of the ashes accumulating at the base of the stone-oven and the juice of a green coconut, both potent metaphors of heat and renewal; it is slapped with the base of the hand on to forehead, shoulders, back and chest, thus associating the recipients with the finally to be freed *rongan*. Songs of *malanggan* (*kingiri*) can be heard for the first time during this procedure. This day is also the final cooking day, the day on which women and men from distant villages arrive with their baskets of raw food and pigs.

Throughout the day the slit-drum (*garamut*) announces with its rhythm the completion of the final stages of the preparations inside the *but* and the arrival of pigs in the central space. In the cooking-houses three stone-ovens are heated, one after the other, from the early morning until after sunset. The timing of these activities and the co-ordination of the various cooking-houses is in the control of women who act as *maimai*. An unspoken competition exists between the cooking-houses: those who fall behind the others are commented upon, those whose oven bursts into flames and destroys the food are subject to intense gossip. They are suspected of having broken *alal* by handling the food when menstruating or having contact with men during the time of the ritual event.

From the late afternoon throughout the night, the slit-drum (*garamut*) announces (*seredimet*) the number of pigs killed. The sound of the drum can be heard as far as two or three villages away, awaking in everyone excitement and the desire to go to the place on the following day.

DAY 3

During the morning people wait for the last guests to arrive. Around midday, the pigs are paid for (*caves a do*) by their owners and their supporting *korok*. The money paid and the owner of the pig are written down, while the whole donation is given to the siblings of the deceased, who line the up the pigs inside the *but* and, after suffocation, place them (facing inwards) on a platform that symbolically represents the body of the deceased; the distribution of pieces of pork dramatizes the effacement of any trace of the deceased by transforming debts related to the burial into new relations of indebtedness, which will only be resolved at *malanggan*.[18]

Shortly after the pigs have been bought, the mourners gather in the central space; their hair is long, their looks shabby. Quickly they retreat (together with the dancer(s)) into the cultivated land surrounding the settlement. There, they swiftly walk while singing songs of *malanggan* to a tree planted by the deceased. Those who have not participated in the *dodolas* the previous day have to *lelerau* while all are again decorated on the face, shoulders, chest and back with the white lime-mixture. Women are the main centre of attention as they begin to *teterak*, that is to smear their hair with a red powder, called *thai*. *Thai* is made out of ochre found at certain spots near springs in the mountains and burned over the fire while being wrapped in leaves of the areca nut tree (*buai*) and mixed with coconut milk. It is a powder that is also used for the painting of *malanggan* effigies and that is distinguished from the white *las* by its potent odour, which allows one to specify the location where the clay originated. Songs of *malanggan* grow in intensity, interrupted by shouts of *a wethai* and the clinking of the coins that those being painted give to the owners of *thai*, who are normally the sisters of the deceased.

The group of mourners in its fully decorated state is called *biss*, meaning both 'sore' and 'outgrowth' (*rabiss*). The *biss* returns to the footpath leading back to the settlement. If there are dancers of *Langmanu* or *Medu*, women surround the dancers and lead the procession, while men follow behind. Songs of *kingiri* and crying are mingling with the faint rhythm of the slit-drum, when suddenly two men appear from behind; they rush into the forest on either side of the path, cutting down everything that had been planted by the dead person, such as banana and betelnut trees, young coconut palms and coffee or cacao plants.

This is the moment of *sasarai*, the 'scraping of skin', whose drama is accompanied by a sung commentary; these songs invoke the presence of a landcrab called *maiau*, which causes extensive damage to coconut groves by peeling their bark. *Sasarai* removes the ban on the cultivation of land associated with the work of the deceased and dramatically effaces any trace left of his/her life in the village. Emotions soar as men and women remember their walks with the deceased along the path to the gardens, the food they shared and the good times. It is the final moment of letting go of anything that reminds one of the deceased, who will not be mentioned or referred to ever again.

As the *biss* arrives at the boundary of the clearing in whose funerary enclosure the deceased was left to rest prior to burial, it is met by the constant beating of the slit-drum (*garamut*). Here it comes to a halt, waiting for the *maimai* to carry out *sui a biss*, the 'pulling' of the group inside the central space by offering the most senior woman a string of shell-money. If the dance is a *Langmanu*, the sound of the *garamut* lets everyone jump up as the dancers rush towards the coconut screen (*kowebag*) hiding the *but*, bursting through it by pushing the fence inward and beginning to dance. If the dance is a *Medu*, the dancer remains in the central space and attacks the coconut screen with his spear (*thou*). The inward motion of the screen points to the arrest of *rongan* inside the enclosure surrounding *but,* to await there its recapture into a 'skin' of *malanggan*; conversely, the death of *malanggan* and the associated release of ancestral power is effected by an outward motion of the coconut leaf screen surrounding the burial place (*roa*).

After the dance, everyone present has to participate in the *lelerau* in the manner described for *mamat* and *haram gom*. This is called the 'work outside' (*haisok ine malei*), and leads to the renewal of ownership rights to the particular pattern of the decoration and the movements of the dance; inside the enclosure, every *Langmanu* dancer has to buy the decorations of the dance, the platform on which he dances and the lime used for the decoration of his body.

The *lelerau* inside the enclosure also includes payments for the cement gravestone (*smel*) erected on the *but* for this occasion[19] (Figure 4.3). Similar to *malanggan*, *smel* are named designs to which ownership rights pertain; like the *malanggan*, the design of *smel* can be dreamt, but also acquired – unlike *malanggan*, however, the *lelerau* at the base of the *smel* mark not the transfer of rights over ownership, but their incorporation into the *dahun* of the deceased. *Rongan* is effectively arrested as *smel* or

Figure 4.3 Gravestone.

odour inside *but,* waiting to be reactivated and channelled into its new artificial container during *malanggan.*

Those who had followed the *alal* on taro during the period of mourning are given a piece of taro by the *maimai* to transform their status, which is no longer associated with the deceased. When receiving portions of pork at the end of the day from the large pile of carcasses towering on the platform inside *but,* everyone's attention is no longer focused on the past, but on the work still to be done; *but* is finished, and its bamboo fence is left to rot until new work is initiated in the settlement.

Ngusung to Malanggan

Many years may go by and many occasions may have enabled those residing in the settlement to incur further debts by contributing to the work of others until the time comes to think seriously about *malanggan* as the final act of finishing *roa.* Inevitably it is the death of an elder, sometimes already awaited and prepared for, that sets planning into motion in a rather precipitate fashion. The public announcement of the planning of the last stage in the work for the dead is the building of a *luhu gereme,* a house inside *but* within whose walls the wood will be brought to life as a new artificial container for *rongan.*

A meeting is called by the various clans who had taken on the work of the finishing of the dead at their burial inside the shared cemetery space. Decisions are made whether a single *malanggan* is to be made, a decision that depends on the relationships between the deceased that have been buried in the cemetery up to this moment, and also on the money and time available. Female deceased as well as children and adolescents are generally, though by no means always, considered for *warwara* (*oara*), a round *malanggan* woven from vines; those whose death falls during the period of planning *malanggan* are considered for *malanggan* made from clay; while those who died a long time ago and may no longer have a strong representation inside the settlement may be considered to be part of the planning of a *malanggan* carved from wood.

The design chosen for a *malanggan* is subject to further considerations, which depend upon whether designs are currently owned and need to be passed down to the next generation as *meme*, or whether a new design is to be acquired (*sorolis*) or to be innovated through dreaming (*mifen*). The meeting culminates in specifying the number of pigs needed for the work of *tetak* or the making of *malanggan*. The last decision concerns the numbers of pigs to be sacrificed during the production of *malanggan* to the carver (*retak*). The *maimai* who represents the siblings of the person buried most recently in the cemetery arranges pieces of the middle rib of a coconut leaf (*noc*) on the ground. Whoever wants to give pigs, takes out one piece for each pig. At the end of this procedure, the *maimai* knows how many pigs will be available for the weeks prior to the final days of *malanggan,* and decisions can be made about the size of the figure, which corresponds to lengths of time and the number of pigs allocated for carving.

The growth of these pigs determines the timing of *malanggan*. *Malanggan*, however, cannot take place at any time of the year – it is a process that is embedded in the seasonal cycle and the activities of planting and harvesting, as described earlier. *Malanggan* and *ngusung* are therefore instances of the same process, though placed at opposite ends of the calendar year. Everyone waits anxiously for the indicators of the successful 'calling' of *ngusung* as outlined in the preceding chapter. Everything being well, the leading *maimai* is dispatched to approach the *retak* or 'maker of skin', and arrangements are made for his arrival in the settlement where *malanggan* will take place.

Malanggan

The arrival of the carver is marked with a food distribution including at least one pig, given by the sister of the deceased person. The *retak* is given strings of shell-money and currency as the first of numerous payments delivered at each of the twelve stages that mark 'the making of skin' (*tetak*) inside *but*.

Tetak, *the making of skin*

Phonologically, *tetak* embodies the process of splitting (*t*) and of merging (*e*) a skin (*tak*). The onset of carving coincides with the harvest of the second ritual garden, whose produce is heaped on platforms erected around the settlement, most of it to be left there to sprout. The three months usually devoted to carving today overlap with the growth of the third ritual garden, whose harvest coincides with the painting of the *malanggan* and the final week's festivities. This carefully timed procedure is anxiously guarded, depending ultimately upon the goodwill of the carver.

As the force that the carver has to recapture in the wood is freed of its earthly trappings and thus potentially harmful, the carver and any person entering the hut where the carving takes place has to protect himself by smearing over all his joints yellow pigment (*magi*) produced from the blossom of a swamp plant (*iar*) and lime (*las*).[20] To avoid the splitting of the wood through a clash of powers, strict avoidance of contact with women, in accordance with the general rules of fasting, which exclude all sweet-smelling fish or meats or otherwise 'wet' foods or the bodily discharge, is to be observed by anyone entering the carver's hut.[21] Only the carver is given daily a specially prepared parcel of taro (*kaderu*); the sweet-smelling taro prepared by a post-menopausal woman is thought to induce conception and guarantees the coming to life of the wood.

The following twelve stages mark the process of the transformation of wood, the soft wood of *Alstonia scholaris* (*sebah*), into skin in a process closely following that of conception.[22] The subdivisions of stages into groups of three is analogous to the subdivision of the year into alternating cycles of three good and three bad months.

1. *wedele wai* – the cutting of the tree
2. *a meiang* – the drying of the wood
3. *kowebag* – the construction of a screen
4. *tagine marendim* – the marking of the contours
5. *kadenim a bolorane* – the incising of the holes
6. *bolo merane* – the inserting of the eyes
7. *karere* – the cleaning
8. *susuhen sene* – the washing with lime
9. *ki* – the painting

10. *bil a luhu sene malanggan* – the construction of the house
11. *sig lalene* – the transfer into *roa*
12. *kas luhu* – the opening of the house

The stages marking a new interval of successive events are spread out over two days, with cooking and distribution of food being separated in time (*mun baing*). The other stages are marked by a single day of combined cooking and distributing food (*mun mederaf*). The beginning of the second phase (4–6) marks the time of the construction of the cooking-houses for the guests, built on the place of the former *gom*. The houses of the participants in the settlement are extended or rebuilt. Houses built for the event of *malanggan* are about 5m high, 9m long and 6m wide. Cooking houses built for the guests are less monumental and built to be demolished after the event or to be left to rot together with the skin of *malanggan*. The third phase (7–9) is the time of the carrying of large wooden trunks and of large stones for the stone-ovens into the settlement. With the beginning of the fourth phase (10–12), the third garden is harvested. The *korok* of the units co-operating in the performance arrive and take up their places in the cooking-houses built for them in the space of the *gom*. Every cooking-house is occupied by a different *habung* and its affines. This separation is maintained through-out the exchanges. Every day the stone-ovens are heated to cook pigs and taro. During this last week of *malanggan*, the settlement is bursting with activities, laughter and shouting.

The last four days of *malanggan* follow the same pattern as was des-cribed for *gisong*:

DAY 1: Cooking. More women who assist their sisters and *korok* in the main cooking-houses arrive. *Kes* are prepared for these women and *nuum* are cooked for the distribution on the following day.

DAY 2: *Dodolas*. Those who are *raso* or 'members of *malanggan*' enter the *but* to look at the carving. They have to *meremerebak*, to pay for looking at it, thus ensuring that they keep their knowledge of it secret.

DAY 3: At sunset, as soon as the eyes (*mata*) have been set into the *malanggan* and it is declared to be fully alive (*bak*), the effigy is secretly transferred from *but* to *roa*. The heat of the stone-ovens lit continuously throughout the day and the screaming of the many pigs, which arrive all day long and are met by the beating of the *garamut* leave no doubt – standing on *roa* is *malanggan*, hot and dangerous host of the captured *rongan*.[23] The effigy is alive, now that *rongan* has been fully contained in an image likened to the body at birth – soft, porous and odorous skin.

The beating of the *garamut* announces the onset of a night that is truly the high point of the year – a night of songs, dances, inversion, travesty and courtship known as *bot*.[24] As *bot* falls between the awakening of *malanggan* and its imminent death the following day, it marks a transitional passage of profound importance to the concept of the life-giving death; yet the transition it celebrates is also that of the calendrical year, whose 'turning' is to be initiated with the death of *malanggan*. *Bot* takes place inevitably during the full moon, and is divided into three phases, called *sisinung*, *makeo* and *bot*, which dramatize the impending exchange with *moroa*.

The first phase of the evening begins with the distribution of food. This food prepared for *bot* is called *saui*, and consists of scraped taro that can only be eaten during this night, to mark the imminent gathering (*bung*) of *rongan* into an undifferentiated, reproductive source (*rune*). After eating, songs of *sisinung*, known for their wide repertoire and their emotive content, are sung in every cooking-house without interruption for hours, each house singing different songs and competing with the others in endurance. Inside the cooking-houses, *sisinung* is accompanied by a humorous enactment of the negation of the restrictive presence of 'skin' in the lives of the Tikana. Women dress up as men or imitate government officials and approach their female and male *korok*, who are prevented from running away by others, who scream with laughter as those dressed up sit next to, touch and address in a non-respectful, ridiculing manner those whom they never are allowed even to glance at during 'normal' times. Certain women are famous for their performances, which become wilder and more and more provocative as the hours pass.

Upon hearing the sound of the slit-drum that is beaten inside *roa*, people arrive in groups from nearby villages carrying leafless young trees to which tobacco is tied. They sit down in the centre of the clearing and participate in the *sisinung*. During these hours, in which everybody waits for the rising of the moon, violence is prone to erupt; any anger that may have been harboured for some time is thought to erupt with certainty, to be publicly addressed and finished with a payment (*luai*) from both sides the following day.

Once the moon has risen, the guests perform a dance in the clearing called *makeo*. Men dance in a circle around the women, playing on miniature slit-drums made out of pieces of bamboo, while singing songs with explicit sexual content; the movements are slow, the most important being the movements of the hand, in which a leaf of the *tenget* plant is being held, and the movement of the feet, which are like the waves of the sea (*lamon*), moving forwards, backwards, and further forwards.

After about one hour, the large slit-drum (*garamut*) is carried from *roa* into the clearing, and *bot* takes over. Two men start playing the drum, and a few of the older women and men join in the songs of *bot*, while slowly walking hand in hand in the same wave-like movement described above, in a tight circle around the *garamut*. More and more join in as others disappear, their movements tracing ever closer circles around the *garamut* and their songs recalling the arrival of odour along the shores. The night is finished at sun-rise.

DAY 4: With sunrise, the last guests arrive with their pigs. Everybody is resting, waiting for the sun to heat up the place (*hamarere a bine*). Suddenly, on a sign of the acting *maimai*, women who belong to the organizing clan(s) walk into the forest and from there secretly into the thick screen surrounding *roa*, from where they can be heard singing *kingiri* accompanied by the beating of the *garamut*. Many of them cry as they sit, deeply moved, next to the effigy, which has been placed inside a house that has been built for its display. The only man inside the enclosure is the *maimai*, who suddenly pushes the screen surrounding the enclosure outwards, giving the sign for everyone to rush forward over the fallen screen into *roa*.

Nothing but the *garamut* can be heard, as everyone gazes at *malanggan*; some silently sobbing as they are reminded of the many times they have been at similar occasions with someone only recently departed, others whispering to each other opinions about the *malanggan*. It seems as if a long time has passed, though in fact it has been only about a minute, when the *maimai* commands everyone to step forward and *lelerau* at the base of *malanggan*.

Each *habung* present forms a separate line, led by their speaker, and throws money and shell-money at the *malanggan*, from where it is immediately removed and given to a child, who takes it to the owner of the *malanggan*. The *lelerau* is said to 'kill' (*luluri*) *malanggan*, by effecting the transference and thus the stripping of its 'skin'; through the sacrifice of *malanggan*, *rongan* is transformed into *rune*, an absent image to be recalled and revealed over and over again. *Rune* **is** the clan as it is thus 'fed' as *meme* to its many *dahun*.

Once everyone has moved out of *roa* to remove the food from the stone-ovens, the pigs are carried into the burial enclosure and are lined up in front of the *malanggan* house. Painted with lime on his face and shoulders, wearing *tenget* leaves in his belt and carrying a spear in his hand, the *maimai* jumps on top of the pigs and performs the story of the death of the man-eating pig *Lungana*; shouting all the places where *Lungana* stopped, he finishes by exclaiming at the top of his voice while throwing his arms towards the sea *a bul ngusung i lakman:* 'the smell-canoe has left'.

The departure of odour and the 'turning' of the year is completed with the removal of the *malanggan* from the enclosure in the evening of the same day and its exposure in the forest near the edge of a cliff, where the spray of the sea can reclaim its olfactory content.

Minutes after the public killing of *malanggan*, everyone present turns their attention to the distribution of food, which repeats the same pattern known as 'the meal after the fight' (*mun doien*) witnessed also at the funeral. The trucks carrying the many visitors back to their settlements are ready to go when each woman sits next to her basket around the outer edge of the clearing to receive 'the outgrowth of skin' (*ngabuk*), topped by a piece of pork-skin that has been vertically stripped before being cut into portions by men circling the clearing. In consuming this 'skin', they underscore the shared rights in the 'skin' of *malanggan* that they attained in helping to 'kill' it; in taking the parcels with them along the road, the 'roads of skin' (*selen tawaien*) that connect the scattered clan are made present in an unforgettable manner.

Malanggan is completed with the ritual wash (*Kei*). All those who had come into contact with *malanggan* have to participate in the ritual bath in the early morning of the following day. The ritual washing takes place prior to sunrise and the flight of the fishhawk (*tegaum*) on the beach of every village that had been involved in the *malanggan*. *Kei* removes *rotap*, the smell associated with female effluvia that came to be embodied in the *malanggan* effigy during carving. If left on the skin, *rotap* is considered dangerous and potentially fatal, as it would attract sharks (*bewue*) or spirits of the murdered (*pue*). As they enter the water, women kneel in the centre, the men standing in a circle around them. The *dehiu*, a conch-shell on which the mythical victory of the sea over the land is inscribed, is blown, while other men hold large, red leaves of the *tenget* plant (*si*) in their hands. Singing songs of *kei*, men walk around the women, splashing water over them to send off the last traces of odour in the direction of *Karoro*.

The abandonment of the settlement completes the process of ritual consumption and transforms its acts of erasure into 'the burial place of memory'.[25] 'The place of the skin' (*laten*) is step by step erased during the work for the dead, to become with the completion of *malanggan* a new settlement site or 'the place of the womb' (*la runemalei*); conversely, where once stood the houses of the deceased and her/his immediate relatives, grass is allowed to grow, soon to be replaced by gardens and secondary forest. This process of erasing a place 'makes' its name, which thereafter is remembered as point for a potential return.[26]

Among the Tikana, ritual objects thus do not accumulate memory or fame in continuous circulation, as in the famous example of the Kula gift exchange system in the Massim. Instead, the object around which relationships are construed is a temporary phenomenon, inseparable from a ritual process that effects its coming to life, its death and its destruction. The destruction of the figured analogue of relationships allows for new forms of relatedness to be imagined in relation to an inherently generative and reproductive image. Death among the Tikana is thus not just a life-giving process, but also a process of translation of a body and its products into analogously conceived images.

Notes

1. See Clay for the Mandak: 'rather than society reasserting itself at death, Mandak sociality is itself the *product* of mortuary feasts' (1986: 132). See also De Coppet (1980) on the notion of the 'life-giving death' in Malekula; for anthropological and related treatments of death see Huntington and Metcalf (1979); Humphreys and King (1980); Bloch and Parry (1982); Davies (1994); and Hallam *et al.* (2000).

2. See Gell on person-object relation in his *Art and Agency* (1998: 10–25).

3. In central and southern New Ireland, it is only the stone-walled enclosure within which images of containment are activated: see Wagner (1986: 121, 148–70); Clay (1986: 111–32).

4. See Guidieri and Pellizi (1981) on stone altars and ritual forgetting in Malekula.

5. A comparative study of the Lelet plateau in central New Ireland has recently been provided by Brigitte Derlon (1990). Older studies of the funerary cycle are by Girard (1954); Walden and Neverman (1940); Groves (1933b, 1936, 1937); Powdermaker (1932); Peekel (1910); Graebner (1905); Thilenius (1903).

6. Hertz (1907); see also the introduction to Bloch and Parry (1982).

7. The exhumation of the skull common in the Solomon islands and in Borneo for the purpose of the secondary burial is not performed today in New

Ireland, though the use of overmodelled skulls placed on top of carved wooden *malanggan* figures collected in the late nineteenth century suggests that *malanggan* increasingly came to replace the use of the body for the rechanelling of life-force.

8. For the Usen Barok in southern New Ireland Roy Wagner describes *pidik* as the image of containment of a power 'only to be witnessed and revealed' (1986: 122). See also Whitehouse (1992) on memory in Melanesian religious systems.

9. On the transformation of the soul see also Peekel (1910: 821–2).

10. The house is called *luhu wewele* and is considered to be the same as the house inhabited by the *haio*.

11. See Lewis (1973). 'Smel' is the Pidgin term for odour.

12. In 1978, word came out, via a schoolteacher at Panamecho village, that in a cave towering high above the cliff-face of Panachais village were both mummies and deposited *malanggan*-sculptures. The sculptures were taken, amidst controversy, to the National Museum in Port Moresby (Küchler 1983).

13. The dance *buma* is considered to be part of *malanggan*.

14. *Ngabuk* means skin growth or blister, thus emphasizing the extended affinal relationships that are beginning to be dissolved at *kawia*.

15. The entrails are given to those who are 'one blood', the pig's blood being offered to and consumed by the speaker of the group.

16. A woman of Morokomade of Lamusmus 2 reportedly once accidentally cut off a finger of the hand of her infant son while opening a coconut. The finger was buried in the ground and a *burume* planted on top.

17. The use of pandanus for wrapping is found on only one other occasion, this being marriage.

18. One cannot help but notice the similarity between the platform mounted with pigs representing the body of the deceased and the Sabarl axe corpse (Battaglia 1990).

19. These gravestones were described by Phillip Lewis (1973) as replacing *malanggan* effigies, which from the perspective of the 1990s however does not seem to be the case. The confusion may have arisen because of the long intervals that occur (sometimes 10 to 15 years) between the placing of the gravestone at *gisong* and the performance of *malanggan*.

20. Should one follow Peekel's argument of the association between *moroa* and dark nights prior to the new moon, the use of yellow as a protection is heightened in its significance (Peekel 1928: 815–17).

21. When I was allowed to sit in the carver's hut during the carving of a *malanggan* for Teu in Panamafei village, a tense moment occurred while I was alone with the carver and the leading *maimai*: while he was incising and hollowing out the figure, a split appeared along the neck of the figure, at least

potentially because of my presence. Kindly, he took it calmly and agreed to secure the split with a nail and to disguise the spot with charcoal.

22. Krämer (1925: 79–80); Lewis (1969: 47–8); Powdermaker (1933: 135–6) (the Notsi include 6 additional stages marking the initiation of boys into adulthood).

23. See Needham on the role of percussion in effecting transitory states (1965).

24. See Walden (1940).

25. I am using here MacDonald's potent allusion to the notion of the underworld in epic poetry in his 'Burial Places of Memory' (1987).

26. The importance of this metamorphosis of 'place' for an understanding of landscape very different to the Western perceptual definition has been discussed in Küchler (1994).

Images of Malanggan

The mind ascends more easily to attention and devotion in the presence of material images that are arresting because of their verisimilitude (Freedberg 1989: 236).

It is probably the ephemeral quality of the form that disturbs the most, conditioned by a strongly moral sense of artistic economy – all that money for only two performances! (Orgel 1975: 41).

Malanggan is one of the rare ethnographic examples of a funerary ritual that culminates in the production, display and death of figures. The most prominent Western example that comes to mind has been described by Kantorowicz in his *The King's Two Bodies,* in which he describes the importance given to the king's figure in the funerary rites of fourteenth- and fifteenth-century England and France, which matched or even eclipsed the dead body itself.[1] The display of the figure was connected with the new political ideas of that age, indicating that the royal dignity never died, but continued to live in the image of the dead king's jurisdiction until the day his office was transferred. As in the French and English funerary rites at that time, this image was attended as though the dummy were the living king himself. Not of ecclesiastical origin, the practice seems to have been inspired by Herodian's well-known *Roman Histories,* in which he describes the apotheosis of the Emperor Septimius Severus as follows: *'the figure, treated like a sick man, lies on a bed; senators and matrons are lined up on either side; physicians pretend to feel the pulse of the image and give it their medical aid until, after seven days, the figure "dies"'* (Kantorowicz 1957: 427; cf. Bickerman 1929).

Strikingly similar as are *malanggan* and Renaissance funerary statues in their treatment of the figures as the doubles of their dead originals, the comparison between them calls for further commentary; for *malanggan,* like the wooden statue that replaces the king after his death,

111

do more than facilitate a process of reincarnation. As Ginzburg (1991) argued, they may instead be seen to exemplify a side of representation that the contemporary usage of the term has lost sight of. They are not a representation, referential in nature, which adds a public definition to that which it replaces, a person or an event, but represent what is not present by fashioning an image that recalls what is absent into memory (Ginzburg 1991:3–6). While both forms of representation imply the idea of substitution or replacement, the latter is defined by a mimetic element that is missing in the first form of representation. These two sides of representation have thus a fundamentally different relation to remembering. The first, the referential representation, may work as an *aide memoire* by drawing attention to extraneous aspects of what it replaces, most conventionally a people or a nation; whereas the second is fashioned as a *mnemic* site of remembering that makes something that is absent present by enabling an image to be conjured up in memory that 'pictures' what it is really like.[2]

The fragility and ephemerality that the wooden *malanggan* figures share with the Renaissance wooden statues underscore the intrinsic relation between image and ritual institution, in which representation and remembering are inseparably fused. In both cases, a figurative image is crucial to a body politic that is based on the conceptual separation of the mortal body of an individual from her immortal legislative powers; and in both cases, the image engages considerations of intellectual, rather than material, property.[3]

As elsewhere in Melanesia, the notion of intellectual property is, among the Tikana, inseparable from that of the ancestral domain, their translation resting on a system of names. The peculiarity of northern New Ireland ritual culture is that ancestral names are recognized, validated and transferred as skins that are made as 'likenesses' or *malanggan*. The figures are neither portraits of deceased persons, nor are they emblematic in character, as was suggested by Wilkinson in his work on Tabar (1978). Instead, these figures serve as vessels that turn ancestral names into an augmentable and regenerative force that perpetually expands its impact by drawing outsiders into its conceptual frame.

Names among the Tikana become 'skins' as a result of being shaped into figures, but they also become images through the figures' anticipated death and disappearance from sight. The imagistic character of names in New Ireland enables names to be recalled or 'found' spontaneously. This 'finding' of images occurs in a state of reverie or daydreaming that is sometimes induced through toxins.[4]

Malanggan-names and images are regionally distributed, their ritual effectiveness residing in their very capacity to be reproducible and transmittable across boundaries, fusing thereby what has been conceived as separate, distinct, and closed into ever more encompassing entities. All *malanggan*-names, in principle, are thus names carried by persons; and it is the element of recognition that is implied in this relationship that gives to ritual representation its mimetic character. The relation, however, is not referential in the sense that we would expect: that is, figures do not 'look like' the persons who carry their names or are commemorated by them at death. Rather, the relation acknowledges a gap between the representation and the represented in that it is a relation of visual analogy. We will see that each image is thought of as a 'source' that contains a series of potential 'skins' that can be 'projected' or 'produced' out of it. Persons emulate this in their own apparently 'layered' or 'cloaked' constitution, which is granted to them upon receiving the name of a *malanggan* image. Throughout life, a man or woman 'owning' an image and a name of *malanggan* will seek to 'strip' the 'skins' attached to them, passing them on, one by one, to their children. Like an onion, their multi-layered skin is pealed off in this process, which ends in death.

Artefacts of Memory

Almost in order to underscore the verisimilitude between figure and performance, the term *malanggan* refers to any image, whether performed or materialized, that metaphorically alludes to containment and release: it refers to the figures whose animation and death form the core of the ceremony, to architectural structures such as houses and fences that serve as images of containment, and to musical instruments, songs and dances, as well as to names shared by the figures and the living alike. Figures are carved from wood, woven from vines, or moulded from clay in a profusion of named forms that have continued to be recognized and reproduced to the present day.

Malanggan is in more than one way conceived as event. It is a commemorative site whose experience is temporally extended over the months or weeks of making images that serve as points of departure for recollection; these images, however, while inherently temporal because of their fleeting appearance in figures, also implode time by collapsing past, present and future into a point-like moment of revelation (see Strathern 1991, 2001).

Writing about *malanggan* has always proved difficult, as one is confronted, on the one hand, with a staggering quantity of artefacts housed in Western collections, and on the other, with an equally staggering profusion of named, yet absent, images (Heintze 1969, 1987). People readily talk about these images and are able to list names and descriptions of whole series of images to which they have access. It is this polity of images from which rank and status is derived, and that legislates the governance of clan land.

Like a virtual collection, images are ordered, and it is in this order that we can elucidate as a complex tension between constancy and variation in the formal properties of figures. When studying even a single collection of figures one is struck by a visual similarity coupled with distinctiveness that commands one to recall what one has seen before. The form of the artefact thus reveals patterns and dispositions of recognition and recall that are essentially self-referential, pointing back to the forms thus elucidated rather than outward to a context that is either real or imagined. The form visible in a figure in fact works like a hologram, in that it forces one to recall the image (draw it in memory) in two or three dimensions.[5] We will see the importance of image as a case of holography when discussing the forms and technique of *malanggan*; yet here we may recall Roy Wagner's insight that cultural forms may gain their efficacy not because they are 'imposed . . . to order and organise, explain or interpret, a set of disparate elements', but rather because they constitute 'an instantiation of the elements themselves' (Wagner 1991: 166).

Skins Made as Likeness

The term *malanggan* (*malanga, malangga, malangan*) has a number of possible translations. The translation focused upon in this chapter is *likeness* (*malang* = to be like, *an* = noun marker), while that of *heat* was examined in the last chapter as a metaphor for the embodied life-force that animates the artefact (Figure 5.1).

Malanggan is also used as term for 'marking' in the sense of a mnemonic device, rather than of the activity of writing, which is called *karere*. Likeness refers to the process of the 'making of skins' from specific materials, and to the material forms displayed by those figures. In understanding the possible referent of this likeness we must be warned of what Whitney Davis termed the 'projectionist fallacy', which assumes that ideas or concepts are projected out intentionally by artists or come to be seen in images by the beholder (Davis 1986: 199). A carving is

Figure 5.1 *Walik* – Stuttgart 47131.

thus not just alluding to the idea of 'skin', but 'is' skin and thus 'like' a person, able to act as substitute for the mortal body. Yet *malanggan* are not just carved as corporeal likenesses, but are also painted. Coloured planes are tightly wrapped around hollowed-out spaces, and allow the figure to appear to be at once fragile and self-contained. Through paint, understood as substance, the 'skin' thus created is made permeable and is animated like the wet skin of persons anticipating conception. It is, in fact, the painting of the *malanggan* that is thought to enliven the figure. The carving is 'washed' (*susuv*) in white paint made from ashes taken from the bottom of the stone-oven (*but*) and mixed with water from a young coconut (*ni*) until it is covered with a white membrane-like cover. The marks painted over it in black, red and yellow recollect the life-force that was arduously set free through the work for the dead: the more charcoal is used in colouring certain marks black, the longer the time that has elapsed between the last two stages in the work for the dead; the more red ochre is used, the greater the number of pigs sacrificed during the preceding funerary stages; the more yellow pigment from the flowers of a swamp plant that is used, the more powerful the figure is thought to be.

The carved and painted net-like figure becomes a 'trap' for life-force, yet the containment of the *rongan* is only completed with the insertion of 'eyes'.[6] *Malanggan* is unique in its use of 'eyes' that consist of the iris-like suction pods of shells (*Turbo petholaurus*) that are collected by women on the dry reef. The term for the *malanggan* eye is 'banana shoot' (a *were*), its meaning reflecting the generative and reproductive capacity ascribed to the life-force at the stage of its containment.

Like *korok*, *malanggan* figures command attention without speaking or touching and address without naming. Like *korok*, who embrace the connecting force of resemblance radiating outward from the brother–sister relationship, each *malanggan* is a visual assemblage of parts that slot together like the pieces of a puzzle. The parts appear in the form of motifs that are strangely opaque, directing attention away from the subtle combinations that entice recognition. The following is a listing of 27 motifs, and their widely shared associations, that are ubiquitous in collected *malanggan*.

Sang

Clamshell, both open (dead) and closed (alive). The clamshell is in myth associated with death caused by the trapping of the shadow (*verak*) of the skin in the clamshell. In myth clamshells are found at places called *masalei*, at springs of water coming out of the ground. The clamshell was also used as the tool (*dim*) for carving *malanggan* prior to the introduction of steel tools.

D-hiu

Conchshell. The conchshell is associated with a myth about the fight between *palai* (a salamander species) and *wun* (a tortoise), representing the opposition between land and sea; a reminder of this fight and the mythical victory of the tortoise is visible on the surface of the conch-shell.

Raus

Owl. The cry of the owl during the night (*la bung*) is thought to announce a forthcoming death in the settlement. The motif appears always in combination with the rib-cage, the pan-pipe and the paloloworm.

Rulowlow

Drongo, a species of the bird of paradise. The feathers of the *rulowlow* are taken for the head decoration of *Langmanu* dancers (*desah*). The *rulowlow* is thought to be the bird of *malanggan* (*ru* = womb, source).

Those who wear its feathers during the *Langmanu* dance have the right to ban (*labui, dang*) land and sea from cultivation and harvest.

Gomel
Chicken. The word *gomel* is frequently attached to names (Gomelmel, Gomelemun). Chicken feathers are used as the head decoration of the *maimai* during his performance at *malanggan* (*wetkai*).

Cocomo
Hornbill. The carved beak of the hornbill is used as mouthpiece by dancers of *malanggan* dances such as *Langmanu*, *Sorumbual* and *Bual*.

Manuengak
Eagle. On the one hand the eagle is the symbol of the big bird moiety. On the other hand, the cry and the appearance of the eagle above a settlement is thought to be a sign of sorcery.

Iang
Flying fish. *Iang* is the Kara term both for flying fish and also for the yellow paint made out of the bark of a tree for the painting of *malanggan*. *Iang* is also the name of a leaf that is used for the magic of *ngusung*.

Bewue
Shark. *Bewue* is another expression for *pue*, the amalgam of the spirits of the slain.

Wam
Bigmaus or rock-cod. The *bigmaus* is a prominent character in the mythology surrounding death and the birth of a clan. The fish is known to live underneath rocks and to have the characteristic of becoming female with increasing age, being female at death.

Wiu
Dog. According to informants, pigs have replaced dogs as a ceremonial food and an exchange item.

Kapul
Wallaby. The hunting of *kapul* demands ritual fasting. Having eaten its meat, men and women may neither go to the gardens, nor go fishing nor harvest the reef for about four days. The *kapul* used to be traded by mountain people for fish from their coastal affines.

Til

The middle rib of the coconut leaf. *Til* is used for hand movements during dances, for counting, for stitching together the leaves of the *pandanus* palm covering the giant taro and pork parcels during ritual events, and for the decoration of platforms for *Langmanu* dancers.

Kor

Bottle-stop. The *kor* frequently appears in connection with the motif of *da* as a prop for the hole in the shell. *Kor* are made out of leaves of the ginger plant to stop the water pouring out of water containers. The *kor* is the focus of jokes about sexuality.

Tilipats

A mythical figure of the Tabar islands. Tilipats is a small man living in the sea.

Moran

Snakes. Snakes are the embodiment of the power of places classified as clan *masalei*.

Panpipe

The panpipe is used in myth by *rulrul*, beings dwelling at *masalei* places.

Karak

The pointed head-decoration made out of the bark of the breadfruit-tree. This head decoration is said to have been worn by married women in the presence of their *korok*. Today, it is replaced by nappies or scarves.

Rekap

A round piece of clamshell decorated with a pattern made out of the shell of a tortoise. The pattern is said to represent the star *wesburut* (*burut* – pregnant), which appears in the north-west at the time of *marias*.

Bul musung

The spirit canoe. The canoe is said to bring odour to *moroa*.

Bebe

Butterfly. The butterfly symbolizes the movement of the *maimai* while speaking at ritual occasions. It is said, that, like a butterfly, the *maimai* has to run up and down the central space (*rune malei*) while speaking.

Maiau

Landcrab. Scraping off the bark of coconut palms.

Benat

Liver of the slain. The *benat* is a black stone (obsidian) that is preferred for cooking in the stone oven because it absorbs and retains heat. The stone is traded to the north of New Ireland from the central and southern areas of New Ireland, and is occasionally found on the reef. It is used together with other stones (limestones) for the stone-oven (*mun*), and is believed to be essential for the creation of *ru*, or steam, and *but*, or ashes, during the cooking process.

Ngass

Rulrul. The *ngass* is a mythical being associated with *masalei* places.

Taken as what they depict, motifs are listings of images and things associated with life-force. This may explain the fact that we frequently find figures in collections from which parts have been broken off. This breakage is not the result of an accident, but of an act of exchange that reminds one of a similar incident associated with the transferral of land-rights in ancient Roman law, when figures were broken in half to commemorate relations over land. In New Ireland, different groups who join forces to 'kill' a *malanggan* by 'stripping' the skin of the figure may similarly take a part of the figure, either by breaking off a part or by 'keeping' it in the mind (*mamaluhen*). The motif they broke off acts as a material reminder of the sharing of an image, and as we will see, of rights to land. Much strategic plotting is known to occur around these fragments, which entitle their owners to attempt to increase their legitimate share in image and land over time. By looking at such a part, one thus will recall all the other parts that are no longer there.

Motifs are thus interesting not because of what they depict, but because they make visible assemblage and augmentation. You can recall an image for carving only if you know how to combine motifs in ways that enable you to recognize the figure not as unique and singular, but as part of an absent whole. That this is more difficult than it might at first appear is indicated by the fact that there are many stories of so-called 'failed' *malanggan*. Such *malanggan* are generally innovated through dreaming, usually by younger men who have not been given names and thus images of *malanggan* by their fathers, but who are keen to buy themselves into the system. Conversely, *malanggan* who got it 'right' are seen as attractors in their own right, quickly leaving the confines of the village as their images come to be shared by the extended matri-clan.

The interrelation of the parts to an imagined whole enables a figure to be recognizable by a generic name. This name is known as *a wun ine malanggan*, or 'source of *malanggan*' – the term *wune* means 'womb, smoke, and spring'. As a concept, *wune* is associated with certain clans and places of origin, most believed to be situated on one of the three Tabar islands to the north-east of the mainland of New Ireland. From the west-coast and mainland perspective, *wune* are far away, figuratively speaking. Names of *malanggan* owned here are known to have been acquired a long time ago from Tabar, frequently through marriage but also through ties of friendship. The clan Moromah in Lamusmus 2, for example, acquired its *malanggan* name *Lalambais* from a clan resident at Simberi island in Tabar on account of two of their men having become friends when working on plantation sites in Fiji around the turn of the century. Upon the death of the man in Lamusmus 2, Simberi offered to carve one of its *malanggan* at Lamusmus 2. What was acquired by Lamusmus was the right over just a part of the *wune* called *Varim*; yet at least potentially Moromah could approach the Simberi clan again to acquire more parts of the same source.

This story also serves to highlight the concept of generativity and reproducibility that is encapsulated in the notion of *wune*. Whenever a name is revealed in a figure it is slightly varied so as not to loose control over the capacity for future revelations. Each time a *wune* is revealed its new variation is in turn given an individual name, so that with each successive production and transference a 'source' fragments and scatters. This fragmentation and scattering of 'sources' is observable in collected artefacts, which show a progressive reduction in the number of motifs the further west *malanggan* figures were collected.

Despite the fact that new names are imaged through dreaming all the time, there are only six named *wune* for figures carved from wood and a further three for figures woven from vines, while *malanggan* moulded from clay are not thought to have a 'source'. The recognition of a 'source' in wooden figures is in terms of motifs that serve as connecting devices: such connective motifs visualize processes of absorption, containment and release. In woven *malanggan*, the recognition of the 'source' is in terms of the materials used for fabrication, which are taken from the sea, the village, and the primary forest.

There are six main connecting motifs for wooden figures:

1. ***merane hede***: the 'eye of the fire' motif, which is itself a combination of the eye of malanggan, a half-moon shape, a trinket, and a fireplace, which is sometimes surrounded by a snake. This motif is accompanied usually by a fish-head motif, butterflies, flying fish and the snake motif.

2. **kulebmu**: a round fish-bone, shark, flying fish or butterfly motif. A fish-head or bird motif, either alone or in combination.
3. **wagil**: a frame of parallel sticks; often continued into helmetlike extensions and accompanied by horizontal pieces known as 'middle rib of the pig' (*koltimbor*), as well as pig-heads or clam-shell.
4. **da**: coconut-waterbottle with bottle-stop; crowned usually by a figure and surrounded on either side by pig-heads. The motif of the 'middle rib of the pig' is frequently present.
5. **lenguh**: a rib-cage; often accompanied by panpipe and owl.
6. **mamaze**: a polychromic 'feather-like' arrangement, often accompanied by bird and snake motifs.

A sample of sixty photographs were shown to a number of informants of different ages, statuses and genders in a sample group of five villages within Tikana, as well as in Lossu village and Tatau island in Tabar. Even children who had just entered school consistently grouped photographs according to the above-named motifs, while the attribution of names was generally consistent in the adult population. The group of six motifs was seen to consist of three interchangeable sets, each set attracting a certain number and range of the general motifs.

I would like here to introduce a term that appears to me to capture the cognitive efficacy of a 'source' thus recalled by a form. This term is 'pathos', used by Aby Warburg in his mnemosyne-atlas (see Bredekamp 1991; Heckscher 1967). Warburg tried to show, by obsessively arranging and rearranging images from Western culture, the self-referentiality of images that call to mind states of being that are at once present, past and future.[7] He focused on gesture as eliciting emotional response, yet also as deliverable and understandable empathically, that is by means of analogical thinking.

Using the notion of pathos, the question of why the above-outlined motifs should be so eminently memorable may be approached from a new perspective, and indeed becomes quite simple and plainly obvious: *wune* trace the 'becoming' of an ancestor in becoming skin. On closer observation, two central motifs are visually associated with either fish, pig-, or bird-motifs, which are placed in the prominent position of top, bottom or side. Thus, we have really three pairs of *wune* and three sets of analogies:

(a)   eye of fire/fish-bone/fish (rock-cod)
(b)   driftwood/water-container/pig or clamshell
(c)   rib-cage/paloloworm/bird (owl).

The first set of analogies visualizes the relation between fire and life-force that governs the performative structure of the work for the dead; the round fish-bone is less easy to place, but reminds one of the origin myth in which Manenges, swallowed by a rock-cod, sliced the fish's entrails with an arm-ring made of fish-bone, causing it to drift ashore to the island of the dead. Without exception, these two motifs are used in combination with the fish-head, which further strengthens the anal-ogical relation between absorption and skin relevant to the first stage of the funerary cycle and to the process of carving *malanggan*.

The second set of analogies recalls the complete containment of life-force in the *malanggan* figure when it is displayed on the grave as a 'living' kind. The parallel sticks recall the drifting ashore of uprooted trees that carry odour and life-force back to the land. The water-container calls to mind the containment of odour and wetness in the figure at the moment of its display on the grave, associated with the sacrifice of pigs and the ingestion of blood.

The third set of analogies conjure up notions of release associated with the third stage of the making of ancestors through the removal of the skin from the figure and its resulting abandonment and decomp-osition. The owl as the bird of the night (*labu* – the place of ancestors) and the paloloworm, whose egg-sacs are shed and collected by women in the lagoon at the turning of the year, relate the process of decomp-osition to the creation of the ancestral domain as well as to the unceasing exchange of odour with *moroa*.

Pathos as image does not just enable empathic, associative under-standing, that is inherently synthetic (the three sources can also recall the biography of a person in life and in death, as they trace the stages absorption, containment and release). Pathos is also a concept that captures the tendency of *wune* to spread, to be effective in affecting others to take it on. The image appears like a pathogen, as a specific causative agent of an everlasting process of revelation in which images simultaneously serve as material and conceptual vehicles of a process of transmission. One of its effects has been to enable us to talk of a '*malanggan*-culture' in spite of the lack of any other linguistic or nar-rative allusion to cultural wholes, recalling Roy Wagner's allusion to 'the paradox of culture', which is that 'it is made out of culture' (2001: 233).

The Sources of *Malanggan*

Wune thus capture a pathos-formula that facilitates the point-like awakening in which 'all pasts are equally present'. The *wune* described in the following pages are based on a series of interviews in the Notsi, Tabar, Nalik and Kara language areas. It should be born in mind, however, that there is more to a *wune* than the motif combination that allows it to be recognized in a particular figure. Each *wune* has its own songs, its own *malanggan*-house and fence structure, its own way of distributing sacrificial pork and presenting food. When acquiring ownership rights over a *wune* one has to acquire each of its components.

WALIK and LUNUET: KULEBMU and WOWALI (Figure 5.2)

Walik is a source whose theme emphasizes the relation between the eye and the fire, between life-force and its recapturing in a skin of *malanggan* (Walden 1940:21; Powdermaker 1932: 119, 122, 131; Krämer 1925: 75). Together with *Varim* and *Tangala* it is the *wune* with the widest regional distribution. All forms of *Walik* are recognized by the *Mataling* (Tabar/ Notsi) or *Medanehede* (Nalik/Kara/Tigak), the eye of the fire (Krämer 1925: 40, 81; Powdermaker 1933: 132; Walden 1940: 28). The eye is represented by the suction pod of a shell, like all 'eyes' in *malanggan*. Another part of the eye of the fire is called *geleura*, or 'half-moon'. It refers to the position of the half-moon in the month following the appearance of the paloloworm, which indicates the ripening of a wild species of the pandanus plant (*burume*). A further part of the motif is called *gisong* (in Tabar *popolkin*), meaning 'charcoal' and referring to the processual affinity between the agricultural calendar and the ritualization of death – both 'building up the fire' in a gradual containment of odour as heat. The other parts of the motif are known only in Tabar, and are called *wunaor*, or 'quill of feathers' and *sukapwunan*, or 'vine without stem'. Both images highlight the capacity for unlimited growth ascribed to life-force in its anticipated freed state. Feathers grow back once they have fallen out, and vines grow back where they have been cut off.

Walik is recognized also by the manner in which food is distributed, which is known as *mun doien*, 'the meal after a fight'. In *mun doien*, cooked food is heaped in piles according to the number of villages or divisions within villages present at the occasion. It reminds one of the opening of two phases in the work for the dead, one concerning the contestation over the right to effect the transformation of life-force into ancestral name, and the other concerning the transmission of the ancestral name as image.

Two named sources are known to form sub-groupings of *Walik*. The distinction between them is made only on the Tabar islands, while on the mainland their forms are subsumed under *Walik*. These two sources

Figure 5.2 *Walik* – Basle Vb 10583.

are called *Wowali* and *Kulebmu* (Walden 1940:26; Powdermaker 1933: 132). They are distinguished by the imposition of food taboos, which are put into effect for the period in which *malanggan* dominates a village's life. *Kulebmu* specifies that those who own, but also those who most probably will come to own, its 'skin' as a result of the exchanges surrounding its sacrifice may not eat fish. While *Kulebmu* is recognized by fish bones encircling an empty fire-place, in *Wowali* the eye of the fire is merely hidden, as seeing it is thought to lead to swellings under the skin (*buk*). As in *Kulebmu*, *Wowali* leads to an interdiction on consuming anything associated with 'wetness'. Both sources share with *Walik* the fish motif.

Like all the sources, *Walik* has its masked dance, which is performed in the funerary enclosure surrounding *but*, the space where the corpse is kept until burial and where the figure is carved from wood. This dance is called *Langmanu* in Kara, *Langmani* in Nalik, *Bungman* in Notsi and *Kowange* in Notsi.

Lunuet

Thematically related to *Walik* in its reference to the recapturing of life-force, *Lunuet* is an instrument that is played by means of rubbing the surface with the palm of the hand (Messner 1983: 49–56). Played only at night following the death of a person, its sound is likened to the owl called *auish* in Notsi and *raus* in the Tikana languages. Those who hear its sound describe it as the cry of mourning emitted by the dead (*mamaluhen*). In fact, its real sound is at a frequency not heard by the human ear. When it is heard in the village, nobody speaks and nobody ventures out of the house, for it is thought that those who do may come to harm and join the deceased person in the journey to the land of the dead.

MALANGANTSAK and MENDIS (Figure 5.3)

Malangantsak embodies the theme of violence, *tsak* meaning 'to fight'. In its mythical theme and in its material forms *Malangantsak* bears strong similarities to *Varim* (see below); like *Varim*, *Malangantsak* has masks alongside other wooden forms. The masks of *Malangantsak*, however, dance in slow movements inside the cemetery on the space called *roa* to the rhythm of the slitdrum.

Malangantsak is recognized by its songs even before it is revealed and by the pounding of the slitdrum (*garamut*), with a rhythm called 'the head of a pig' at the time of *malanggan*. In its figures, we find the parallel infringing *wagil*, or sticks, characteristically extended beyond the head, as well as other motifs such as the head of a pig or a clam-shell and the middle-rib of the pig.

A prominent image within *Malangantsak* is called *Lasisi*, which is concentrated in the locality of Notsi and is virtually absent in the islands of Tabar. Its material forms resemble both *Tangala* and *Malangantsak* in the shortness and stoutness of their figures and in the pointed extension of *wagil*. It is distinguished from the other two by the frequently, though not exclusively, female features of its material forms and by the extension of the tongue towards the bottom of the chin. *Lasisi* is thought to visualize the sacrifice (*kiut*) of a woman for land.

Mendis

The *wune* with the name *Mendis* evokes the shame between brothers and sisters. The following myth was told by a man called Songis of Tatau island of Sateri:

> At one time a man of Simberi island dreamt the image of Mendis. He gave form to it and called all men to see what he had made inside the funerary enclosure. To show the men what Mendis is about, he told them that he would pass on the image to one of the men present at the event, should he sleep with his true sister; the man was told to go and come back with his sister. He went, but was overcome by shame when seeing his sister; returning to the enclosure without his sister; he was ridiculed by the men and scolded by his brothers. He went and came back empty-handed three times. Finally, he went to his sister and lied to her that she should come with him to pick up a portion of pork inside the enclosure. The woman went with him and both entered the enclosure. The man was overcome by shame and desperation, but succumbed to the wish of his elders; when they were lying on the ground, they were killed by the men

Figure 5.3 Malangganstak – Basle Vb 10550.

present in the enclosure and leaves were thrown over them. This is the shame which is the meaning of Mendis.

During the event for which a material form of *Mendis* is made, men have to take off their waist cloths while inside the funerary enclosure. This behaviour is said to be reminiscent of the transgression of the incest taboo and the shame between brothers and sisters that in myth is the foundation of *Mendis*. As a visual reminder of containment, water is the most prominent motif of *Mendis*. Besides the round coconut shell used as water container (*da*), the most recurring motif in figures associated with *Mendis* is the pig's head and the middle-rib of the pig motif, which recall the incorporation of wetness through sacrifice. Another feature is a triangle on top of the head of figures of *Mendis*, representing the head decoration worn by women in the past. This triangle is called *karak*; *karak* is a female mythical character, central to myths dealing with adultery and marriage between brothers and sisters.

TSUR VARIM and MAMATU; TANGALA and SONGSONG (Figures 5.4 and 5.5)

Tsur Varim or *Tsur* is the Notsi and Tabar term for 'platform' (*eiben* in Nalik, Kara, Tigak); *varim* is a collective noun in the Notsi and Tabar languages. Like *lenguh*, a name associated with the rib-cage prominent in its figurative forms, *Varim* is a personal name given to both men and women.[8] The forms of *Varim* (also known as *Mamatu* in the north) are almost exclusively masks worn by dancers during their movement in the central space of the settlement. The dancers of *Varim* carry spears, tomahawk and *redelak* (called *lalai* in Tabar).

The movement of the dancer of *Varim* is referred to as *kalerala, rala* being a slow downwards movement of the body in the rhythm of the shell rattle (*redelak*), which is shaken forwards by the left hand of the dancer. The movement of the dancer of *Mamatu*, on the contrary, is sideways and upwards rather than forwards and downwards, and is called *titile*. Both *Varim* and *Mamatu* dance in complete silence, noise being made only by the shaking of the shell rattle (*samsam*), which is also for shark-calling. It vividly captures the freed life-force and the anticipation of the return of odour.

Tangala *and* Songsong

Tangala and Songsong are recognized sub-divisions of *Varim* and *Mamatu*; they are figurative in character, sometimes in the shape of a bird, and are recognized by the rib-cage and pololoworm motifs.

Tangala are in the language of Notsi and Tabar mythical beings who are extremely short in stature, yet of great strength. These beings are thought to inhabit the mountain and come down to the coast to fish. In the language area of Nalik and Kara, *Tangala* are known as *Lulura*, and in the area of Tigak and New Hanover (as well as Djaul island) as *Mus*; *Tangala* are thought to have no digestive system, a fact attributed to their violent nature.

Figure 5.4 *Varim.*

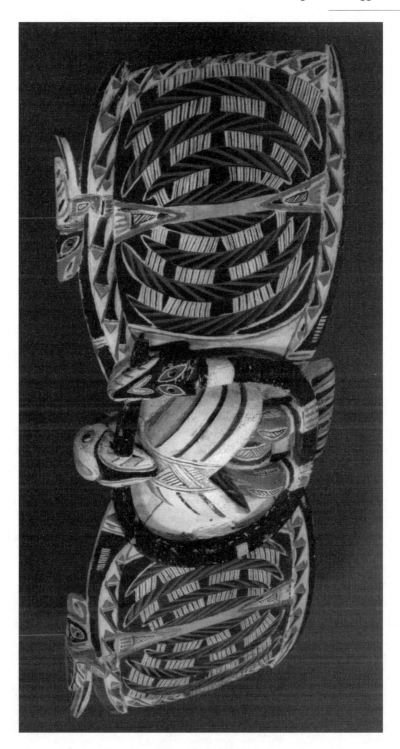

Figure 5.5 *Varim (Lenguh)* – Basle Vb 236.

Songsong

The songs of *Tangala* are used to attract fish, as are those associated with its double, known as *Songsong* (Walden 1940: 39). *Songsong* and *Tangala* are differentiated according to the location of their source and according to the behaviour displayed at the event of *malanggan* (when *Songsong* is being made, ginger is cooked like a pig and eaten prior to the eating of pork). Today, *Tangala* is mainly known on the mainland, while *Songsong* is restricted in its distribution mainly to Tatau and Simberi of the Tabar group of islands. Their forms are recognized by the songs, which name certain fish, parts of the reef and stones that are thought to be places of *masalei*.

Varim *and* Tangala

According to the opinion of several men of the Notsi and Nalik language area, *Varim* and *Tangala* represent the two birds, the big bird and the small bird. It is said that, if a man looks at the forms of either of them, he will think it is one of his *malanggan*; *Varim* and *Tangala* are said to be the most fundamental sources, to which all others could be reduced.

Not only wooden forms are generated out of 'sources', but also those woven into fibre. While generally reserved to capture the life-force of those who died prior to marriage, as well as women, powers are attributed to such woven figures that call for instant destruction through fire. In fact, woven *malanggan* are thought of to be like bones, and are thus associated with male substance. Male, bone-like *malanggan* are thus the containers of largely female and regenerative life-force, which, through burning, is rooted in the ground, while female, permeable and skin-like *malanggan* absorb the largely male life-force that comes to be dissipated across the region. While generally undifferentiated in their form, woven *malanggan* are classified according to the materials used for weaving – these being first banana leaves and stems, second bamboo, and third pandanus.

1. *Marandang* and *Totombo:* Marandang

Marandang is a source that embodies the mythical theme of *pue*, the power of the slain (Walden 1940: 32). The making of figures is part of the magic of making rain. When *Marandang* are made close attention is paid to *baral*, the uprooted tree. The songs of *Marandang* are the songs of calling odour.

Marandang are made out of banana stems and vines, with only the head carved out of wood. The head may not be seen by women, as it is thought to be the temporary abode of *pue*. When occasionally made without a body, the head is too heavy to be worn by a dancer, and is exhibited on a pedestal inside the funerary enclosure.

Totombo
Marandang has a double called *Totombo*, a source that is almost exclusively confined to the islands of Tabar. *Totombo* is made out of banana stems and vines and, like *Marandang*, is not transferred, but kept within the clan.

2. *Takapa* and *Tetegap*
Takapa is a source that is described as *masa* in the Tabar language, *masa* literally translated meaning 'boundary' or 'end', and *Takapa* being a form of denial. *Takapa* is therefore believed to be boundless, a meaning that can be understood in relation to the lack of restrictions placed upon the manufacture of its forms. Anyone is allowed to participate in the making of *Takapa*.

   Takapa is made whenever a person dies prior to having been housed in a funerary enclosure and when the condition of the skin of the corpse supports the suspicion of death by sorcery. The use of bamboo in the construction of Takapa is explained with reference to the practice of *iuh harareo*, literally 'the pulling of bamboo', which reveals the identity of the culprit responsible for the death of the person through sorcery (*ngain*).

Tetegap
Takapa's double is called *Tetegap*. It is a source that is rooted on the mainland in the Nosti area, in contrast to *Takapa*, which is thought to have originated in Tabar. *Tetegap* is differentiated from *Takapa* in the white colour of its forms, compared with the red and yellow colours of the *Takapa*. Like *Takapa*, it is made out of bamboo and vines.

3. *Warwara* and *Kurwunawuna* (Figure 5.6)
The source called *Warwara* (*oara*) has several outstanding features, and is perhaps the most used of the fibre *malanggan*. Like most sources of *malanggan* introduced in this chapter, it is understood to have originated on the island Tabar. Yet unlike all other sources, it is thought to have been invented by women during a moment of reverie (Walden 1940: 24; Lewis 1969: 99–110; Powdermaker 1933: 311, 245–7; Groves 1936: 238–40; Krämer 1925: 67–70). Its predominantly round, disc-like shape sets it apart from figurative figures and likens it to the eye of *malanggan*

Figure 5.6 *Warwara.*

and visualizes one of the most guarded secrets of *malanggan* – that it is a trap whose ability to attract and contain ensures nurture and renewal.

According to mythology, *Warwara* was seen in a daydream by a woman while observing the activity of a spider about to build a nest for its eggs. The following myth was told by a man in the west-coast village Marakat of Tatau island:

> *A woman with her two children used to eat in the enclosure of Witermat. The men went into the enclosure and threw them out. They asked the children: 'Who made your* meme? *Don't you have a father who prepares a garden for you?' Outside the enclosure the mother asked why the men had thrown them out. The children replied they were thrown out because they did not have a father. The mother was ashamed. The children were thrown out of the enclosure again and again. They ran to the mother, crying that they had no father. The mother told them not to worry. She got up and followed the path in between the two enclosures. Walking along this path she was cutting firewood and piling it on*

the sides of the path. She sat down and looked along the path; there she saw a
spider that pulled a thread from one side of the path to the other. The first string
ran above, the second below. The strings crossed and followed the path. The
spider pulled the string so that it became like a house; it went up and around
each corner and cut an eye in its centre. 'This is the house of the spider', she
said and watched how the spider finished its work. Then she got up and filled
her basket with firewood. Calling her children she said: 'I shall give you both
work and you shall carry it out.' She called out: 'tembinnaru', *meaning 'white*
bones'. Then she called 'shurumbor', *meaning 'cooking the hair of the pig'.*
She called these things because she wanted to prevent others from knowing what
they were doing. She disguised their actions with her speech. She called out again:
'kurkareo', *meaning 'breaking bamboo', to disguise the fact that they were*
breaking the vines into two and into four parts. She called 'rerang', *meaning*
'to catch eel in the river' to hide the fact that they were collecting a shell called
kina *and leaves of the Pandanus plant, removing the bark of the vines and*
hollowing out their interior. She called out 'bututun', *meaning to 'wrap the*
eel', to disguise the fact that they were wrapping the vines into the Pandanus
leaves. The men saw the woman and called out: 'Oh Kasolik, Kasoli, a
karawas, karawas, karawas a pane moroa, pane moroa katimget, katimget,
katimget'. *The men knew that someone would come with a* Malanggan; *they*
thought that bewue (pue) *or the spirits of the slain in fight had given the*
Malanggan *and they were afraid. The* Malanggan *entered the enclosure and*
the leaves were loosened to let the vines dry in the sun. The woman called out
'lowiu', *meaning to take the vine for making the* Malanggan, *to disguise the*
fact that the vines were covered with ginger leaves. She called out 'kokoit',
meaning to cut a rope and hiding that they were starting the framework or eye
of the Malanggan. *She called out* 'putkulip', *meaning 'to break' and disguising*
the fact that they were making the bones of the Malanggan *by sharpening their*
ends. Then the Kumbara, *the eye of the spider, was made. Zulip, Saramgum,*
Tor, Titimbelis, Ret, Zugur and Riswis concluded the steps of making warwara.

Warwara is the most guarded secret of any clan; every localized sub-
clan has its own version of *warwara*, and these are often distinguished
only by minute details in the treatment of the central 'eye' section and
by the colouring. Unlike those of the *malanggan* carved from wood,
there is no underlying connection between variations of *warwara*, as
they are assumed to be rooted and immobile. *Warwara's* names are
'silent', in that they are never transferred on to people and should not
be spoken aloud, being known only to those men who participate in
their making, and being forgotten instantly.

Trees and the Growth of *Malanggan*

Figures carved from wood have three different shapes: vertical, horizontal and figurative. The shapes are thought of as an uprooted tree (*but ine wai*): there is the *kaletung*, or stem, the *wagil*, or branch, and the *but*, or leaf-bearing branch. Instantly reminding one of the logs drifting ashore during the rainy season, channelling and announcing the arrival of odour from Karoro, the seat of *moroa*, this connection is affirmed in a famous myth known as Kanam told along the west coast:

> *The place from where* malanggan *comes is* Kanam *(east coast Mandak). Two birds used to live at this place:* Manuengak *(Eagle) and* Bramenekait *(small bird similar to Fishhawk).* Manuengak *showed* Bramenekait *how to catch fish. Above the two birds* Regaum *(Fishhawk) sat and watched.* Regaum *caught them by surprise by flying over the water and catching fish in front of them.* Bramenekait *tried to do likewise, but no fish was left in the water; instead it caught sea cucumbers. Today,* Regaum *catches fish and* Bramenekait *catches crabs. This is the story about the place where* malanggan *comes from. At this place all* malanggan *in existence today had been made by the people living in the two parts of* Kanam, *one part being for those of the big bird* (Manuengak) *and the other part for those of the small bird (Fishhawk).*
>
> *All men from the place* Kanam *made an enclosure called* sasambuam. *A day was determined on which people from other places would come and look at what had been made in this enclosure. Many dances could be seen on this day. Inside the enclosure a dispute between men led to the destruction of the enclosure and of the house built inside it. All the* malanggan *were taken to the sea and thrown into the water.*
>
> *Some* Malanggan *were left – uprooted trees whose trunk had been planted upside down into the ground of the enclosure, called* Kabai; *these* Kabai *were thrown as well into the sea, but, contrary to the others which drifted,* Kabai *sank.* Kabai *is the* Malanggan *of Mandak today, while all other* Malanggan *came ashore at all places in the North of New Ireland. The* Malanggan *made out of vines drifted to Tabar, where they came ashore in the form of sharks that became the* matambu *or ancestors of the Tabar islands.*

The tree visualizes the continuity of the dispersed clan, 'broken off' by women in marriage. Its stem (*kaletung*) is associated with the matrilineal clan, which grows each time a woman moves in marriage and 'cuts the tree at its roots' (*but ine wai*). Its branches (*wagil*) are formed by men who in marriage 'break the top of a tree' (*bak ine wai*) and create roads (*selen*) along which women follow. Its leaf-bearing branches (*but*) are thought to correspond to the affinal units of siblings resident in a settlement and village. As figures are conceptually and actually broken into parts each time they are exchanged, recalling a connection thus formed in relation to both land and *malanggan*-source, so the image is broken into its constituent parts.

The differentiation of forms into stem, branch and leaf implies a hierarchy of complexity and monumentality; forms denoted as stem are vertical and are composed of a number of superimposed figures and motifs. Exhibited in a house built inside the stone enclosure of the funerary complex (*roa*), the vertical forms constitute the 'posts' of the house. Stems, however, are rarely carved today. When asked, people say 'our sisters are not living any longer with us'. This statement has both a practical and a metaphorical meaning. With the scattering of sisters through marriage by capture, people see themselves unable to plant gardens of a size needed to feed the number of people that are thought to be necessary for the production and 'killing' of a stem of *malanggan*. The movement of people away from their place and the expansion of the clan correspond, moreover, to the perceived and actual fragmentation of images. As the clan is scattered, so its 'source' is shattered and scattered into bits and pieces along the roads of marriage.

'Branches' are horizontal forms, which inside the stone enclosure are lined up parallel to the 'eye' of the house, its open front. A branch is said to feature a reduced number of motifs compared with the vertical stem, yet to have at least more than two motifs. In principle, whenever a material form can be dissected into parts that can be given form as independent forms of *malanggan*, it is classified as a branch. A common feature of horizontal forms are figures carved independently and attached to the horizontal forms; the number of figures standing on top of the horizontal form is defined by the number of deceased persons who are turned into ancestors through the making of skin.

A form that is classified as a leaf-bearing branch resembles the shape of a human figure. Figures vary in the number of motifs, which can, like the leaves on branches, be revealed separately.

The metaphor of the tree is not just a static classificatory device that allows figures to be ordered and ranked. Its significance in *malanggan* is rather as a dynamic, holographic principle that visualizes a generative process that allows in principle an infinite number of figures to be carved out of interconnected sources. The horizontal form or branch is thus made as a *projection* (*ruvei* – to pull out) of a detail of the vertical form or stem into an enlarged dimension. A bodily shaped form or leaf is made as a projection of a detail out of a branch. When describing to me this relation between vertical and horizontal forms of a source, men used the analogy of a projector they had seen during events organized by the church. They explained that the same principle operates in the generation of branches: by contrast with the slide projector, however, only a detail of the vertical or horizontal form would be selected and projected – literally 'pulled out' (*ruvei*) – in an enlarged dimension, either horizontal or figurative.

Forms made as 'projections' are made in anticipation of a particular context of exchange called *sorolis*, yet to be described in its fullest detail. *Sorolis* is usually carried out with those outside the *dahun*, normally within the extended clan, and involves the acquisition of complete ownership rights over a source of *malanggan*. It is for this reason that most horizontal forms of figures were collected on the east coast, having been made for *sorolis* by their Tabar relatives, while figurative *malanggan* are most frequently found along the west coast, having been brought there by their east-coast relatives.

Every stem, branch and leaf of *malanggan* is known to have numerous similar forms that are temporary variations upon a common theme. The forms given to the branch or the leaf-carrying branch are differentiated by their name, their motifs, their monumentality, and the pattern painted upon the object. Interconnected endogamous units can share variations upon the same projected form of *malanggan*. As an indication of their common emplacement in the landscape and their joint moves as offshoots of clans from one place to another, they share a single *wune* in either its stem, branch or leaf-bearing branch form; yet each segment has its often minutely different version, as a result of what is called the method of *producing out* (*vei* – to cut) (cf. Strathern 2001).

An example of forms produced out of a form is the leaf called *Sanger-arau* of the source *Sasambuang*. The figurative source is controlled by the clan of Morokomade in Luburue village, which identifies itself with a settlement history in the mountain of Patrehat, like others now resident in other villages such as Panamafei and Lamusmus. The right to generate skins out of the leaf of *Sasambuang* is today in the hands of Gau, a man of Morokomade resident in Luburue village. During his lifetime he has produced out a number of variations acquired by his affines and offshoots of his clan, who likewise have come down from Patrehat at some point in the past. These are the variations of *Sangerarau*:

1. figure sitting in canoe
2. figure standing inside *wilpil* (leaves of coconut)
3. figure standing in an open clamshell

4. figure standing on a closed clamshell
5. figure standing on top of a stone (*benat*)
6. figure standing inside a spear with a bird on the head.

Other forms not listed here have been lost to Gau and his siblings through failing to marry back into the social units who had acquired the forms during exchanges in the past. The knowledge of who has parts of his source is implicit in gardening practice – Gau is hardly ever at home, because he has to tend his many plots, often in different villages, together with those with whom he is connected through the memory of *Sangerarau*.

Those who have acquired from Gau one of his *Sangerarau* cannot consider themselves capable of producing out yet more variations if they wish to carve their *malanggan* – that is, unless Gau should die leaving no sons or daughters who received the name of *Sangerarau* as skin. Instead, they will be able to produce out merely by fragmentation – omitting motifs so as not to pass on to others the right over their *malanggan*. Over time, *malanggan* thus become more and more fragmentary, until they allow only one motif, such as a bird, to be seen. This, however, rarely happens, as the history of ownership is dependent upon living witnesses, who are able to contest rights to *malanggan* on account of having *meremerbak* or 'taken the skins'. When there is no living witness remaining, others take over and reassemble as much as they can link together without infringing the copyright of their neighbours.

What is of concern to New Irelanders is thus not the object or the expression of an idea, which is what is central to Euro-American concepts of copyright, but the idea behind it (cf. Küchler 1987: 629; Harrison 1992: 234; Strathern 2001: 271). What is copyrighted, one might say, is the technology, the knowing 'how' to achieve the desired efficacious result. We saw that the holographic perception of the *malanggan*-image is intimately bound up with a technology that merges quite separate efforts, this being the work of remembering and the work of carving, and it is the synthesis of these two aspects of work, of the mental and the material, that *malanggan* aims to achieve. As thought comes to conduct itself in things, *malanggan* constitute the perfect example of what Alfred Gell has termed 'the technology of enchantment' (1992). In fact, as Marilyn Strathern has pointed out, the notion of copyright is misleading in relation to *malanggan*, for people 'own' them most securely as memories still to be realized: 'The recombination of elements of information, the amalgamation of new and existing forms, the minute variations that may be sufficient to demonstrate crucial intervention, channelling past knowledge to future effect, a limited period of efficacy: this could as well describe *Malanggan* as it describes a patent' (2001: 273).

Patented technology in a state of perpetual transferral is taxing not just to the mind of anthropologists, but to New Irelanders, who are frequently exasperated about the pitfalls that lie ahead when planning a *malanggan*. Village courts meet regularly on matters of *malanggan*, yet solutions are rarely found. The trouble is that there is not enough memory around (not enough children, not enough land, not enough names), but too many recollections (Harrison 1999).

Malanggan Dances

The technology of *malanggan* is not learned by observation, although forms of *malanggan* are known 'with the eye'. Yet this knowing through 'seeing' *malanggan* is tantamount to the gathering of evidence that merely confirms what is already known by other means (cf. Ginzburg 1983). This is because the technology of *malanggan* is inhabited, for it is not only materials such as wood, vines or clay that are sculpted into containers, but also the human body. Indeed, *malanggan* dances are by far the most popular and well-known images. During the nights of *marias*, between April and August, the young and the old are rehearsing dances and preparing their costumes almost daily. Moonlit nights are filled with the chanting of the women, who rehearse in the clearings of settlements, and by the drums of the men, who live secluded in the forest for most of these months, as they have to follow the fast of *alal*. The understanding that is directed to the figures when they are making their ever-so-brief appearance in the cemetery is derived from familiarity with the vocabulary of the dances, which comprises movement, motifs and thematic structure.

Dances are divided into two types: those that are performed by groups of men or women of all ages at public events usually organized under the umbrella of the Church, and those that are performed by masked men as part of the work for the dead. The latter are derivative of the former in both movement and thematic structure, and are thus known and understood intimately by women, even though they cannot themselves participate in their performance. We will also see that the differentiation of masked dances traces the spatio-temporal structure salient in the work for the dead. Like the 'sources' of *malanggan*-images, dances map out the spaces of *but*, *roa*, and *rune malei* within which the drama of the birth of the clan on the island of the dead unfolds.

Even without ever having seen a *malanggan*-figure, one would be able to guess what it might look like by studying dance movements and themes. Dances trace patterned movements into the sand; such patterns recall poetically the endlessly repeated splitting of the matri-clan, and create a map-like figure of its many temporary and kaleidoscopic realignments. The movements are focused on the hands, which are held mostly in front of the body, holding leaves or such-like things that accentuate the slow and stylized movement of the hands. Secondary movement patterns are described by the neck, which are mostly emphasized in women's dances; male dances emphasize leg movements, which are performed in bent positions.

All dances are owned and must be orchestrated by the equivalent of the carver, a man called *bual*. For all those who participate strict *alal* is necessary throughout the period of practising, which may continue over a period of three to four weeks, and for men may involve a period of seclusion in a temporary forest camp. All headgear is made communally by the dance-group, while all wooden masks are made, like the wooden figures, by the carver.

Like the figures, dances are known by 'source' names that serve as points of departure for the generation of seemingly infinite variations upon dances, which are composed of:

(a)   a standard pattern of drumbeats
(b)   parts of costume
(c)   melody patterns and themes expressed in movements of hands and legs
(d)   choreographical elements defining movement in space
(e)   dance parts that follow in sequence (Yayii 1983: 39).

All dances are composed of movement motifs (*titie*). Almost as if to recall physically the linguistic differentiation of body parts into *ak* and *ang* (skin and bones) there are just two movement motifs: the first composed of movements with the hands and the head, usually accompanied by songs, while the second is composed primarily of leg and upper body movements, with a lack of song.[9]

All dances are performed while singing to the rhythm of the slitdrum (*garamut*), by contrast with the dances performed by villagers from southern New Ireland, who dance in silence accompanied by a group of men who sing and play small hand-drums (*kundu*). Southern dances are performed virtually on the spot, with only positional changes of dancers. Dances of *malanggan*, on the other hand, incorporate intricate configurations, with dancers dividing into two or four groups moving in lines and circles, kneeling down, approaching each other and moving away from each other. The space needed for the dancing group expands throughout the dance, while it remains constant in southern dances.

1. The first category contains dances whose decorations and movements are classified in accordance with *malanggan* carved from wood. The right to perform these dances and the right to participate in them is passed on at the time of dancing to those who participate; movement motifs are thus transformed every time a dance is performed.
2. The dances of the second category, on the other hand, do not enter the exchanges of *malanggan*. They are sub-divided into dances of the night and dances of the day. Each grouping is sub-divided into types of dances that are distinguished on the basis of the spatial structure of the dance.

Category 1
1. *Mamatu*, male dance in *rune malei*.
2. *Langmanu*, male dance in *but*.
3. *Nit*, male dance in *roa*.

Category 2
1a. *Makeo*, dances of the *night*, carried out by guests in longitudinal movements encompassing the entire central space (*rune malei*).
1b. *Bot*, *night* dance in circular movements around *garamut*, carried out by guests and hosts.
2a. *Tatanua, Kipong, Rukunau, Pinelewau* – masked dances in *rune malei* carried out during the last *day* of *malanggan*.
2b. *Sorumbual, Bual, Sasale, Silip, Turul, Huluk, Magil, Kandewas, Peng* – group dances with head decorations carried out during the *day*.

In the first category of dances, *Langmanu*, *Nit* and *Mamatu*, only *Langmanu* and *Nit* are said to be *Malanggan* dances proper. *Mamatu*, the only one of the three dances performed in the central space, is supposed to have been introduced from the island of New Hanover in mythical times. In the language groups of Tabar, Nalik and Kara, *Nit* masks are frequently referred to as *Wanis*, and are classified as part of the *Malanggan Varim*; the term *Nit* is more widely used in the Notsi language group.

It is in the Notsi area that the difference between *Mamatu* and *Nit* is insisted on, whereas in the language groups to the north the difference between *Wanis* and *Mamatu* is of greater concern, and debates as to whether a mask is a *Wanis* or a *Mamatu* are frequent. For this reason, I shall refer consistently to the different dancing masks exchanged in the context of *Malanggan* as *Mamatu* and *Nit*, in order to highlight the distinguishing factors in the analysis.

Mamatu: The dance is carried out by one or two masked dancers in the central space at the event of *haram gom*, the symbolic burning of the house of the deceased person. The dancer moves to the rhythm of the *redelak* (shell rattle) held in the left hand of the dancer and shaken sideways and upwards. In the right hand, the dancer carries a spear (*thol*) and a *yellow* (*si kis*) *tenget* leaf, with which he carries out circular movements.

Langmanu: The dance of *Langmanu* is carried out inside the *but* enclosure during the event of *gisong*.[10] The movements of the dancers to the rhythm of the slitdrum (*garamut*) imitate birds and their movements; the movements of the hands are emphasized by the *redelak* held in the left hand and by the red leaf of the *tenget* plant (*si bung*) held in the right hand. The eyes of the dancers are turned upwards, directed to the end of the carved beak of the hornbill (*sehe*), which is carried between the teeth; this gives the impression of the dancers' being in the process of rising up (*malang*) above the ground.

Nit: The dance of *Nit*, performed by one or two masked dancers, is carried out inside *roa* during the final event in the funerary cycle, the event of *malanggan*. The movement of *Nit* dancers is called in the Notsi vernacular *kalerala*, a slow downwards movement of the upper body in accordance with the movement of the *redelak* held in the right hand of the dancer and shaken downwards and forwards, away from the body. In the left hand, the dancer holds a blue-green leaf of the *tenget* plant (*si mereoue*), which is made to vibrate by means of fast circular movements of the wrist. According to informants in the Notsi and Masei area, *Nit* masks were worn by those classified as *haio* when leaving their secluded homesteads inside the enclosures.

Dances of the second category are structured in terms of temporal criteria. They are distinguished from the first category of dances in that the right to participate in them is not restricted by exchange relationships, but by the spatial relationships between people. The temporal structure of night and day distinguishes dances that can be joined by anyone during the performance (night) and dances whose size does not expand, but remains constant (day).

Night: *makeo, bot*
Day: *Tatanua, Kipong, Rukunau, Pinelewau, Sorumbual, Bual, Sasale, Silip, Turul, Huluk, Magil, Kandewas, Peng.*

Night

The dances of the night, *makeo* and *bot*, follow one upon the other during the last night of *malanggan*, when the enlivened figures have been transferred to the gravesite; but *makeo* is optional rather than required. *Makeo* is carried out by guests of a particular village attending the event; the performance is reciprocated by the hosts at a future event of *malanggan* organized by the village who had danced *makeo*. This relationship of debt and reciprocity between villages involved in *malanggan* will be described in the following chapter as *susuang*.

Makeo is danced by men and women in the central space, some men beating small slit-drums made out of bamboo, others holding, like the women, leaves of the *tenget* plant in the right hand. The dance begins in a linear form and proceeds in a circle, whereby the men move in the outer circle around the women, who dance in the centre. The movements of the legs are the same as in the dance called *bot* – one leg slightly raised above the ground, while the other moves in close contact with the ground. The *tenget* leaves vibrate through the fast circular movements of the wrists, while the arms move upwards in the rhythm of the drum. Towards the end of the dance, the men encircle the women closer and closer, with all movements directed inwardly toward the centre.

Bot is a dance that constitutes the climax of the night. The large slit-drum or *garamut* is carried into the central place, taken out from its hidden location behind the thick coconut screen that protects onlookers from the enlivened *malanggan* figure. The hosts, men and women of the village organizing the *malanggan*, begin the dance by moving slowly arm in arm in a circle around the *garamut*. The movements of the legs describe waves, as in the dance of *makeo*. Soon the guests and the hosts intermingle, dancing in rows of four or five people arm in arm around the *garamut*. The songs of *bot*, like the songs of *makeo*, highlight past and present ties of co-operation and competition in the exchanges between villages of different language areas. The Kara know songs of *bot* composed in the language of Tabar and of Nalik and in the language of Tigak.

Bot is distinguished into four named categories: (1) *hai* (to be caught), danced by men and women; (2) *but pene til* (*til*=middle rib of coconut leaf), danced by men – movements are carried out mainly with the hands; (3) *but dehin*, danced by women – movements are carried out mainly with the legs; and (4) *kele lowole*, danced by men and women – the *bot* was performed at the time of hostilities after the return of the men from raids upon neighbouring villages. The people of Mandak and Namatanai in central and southern New Ireland do not know *bot*, but a dance called *merebul*.

Day

The dances of the last day of *malanggan* are divided into those involving masks – *Tatanua, Kipong, Rukunau, Pinelewau* – and those that do not include masks. All dances are commissioned (*nung*) by the village organizing the event of *malanggan* from other villages.

Of the four masked dances, *Tatanua* and *Kipong* are the most widespread and best-known. *Tatanua* is danced more frequently in the Notsi, Big Tabar and Mandak areas, while *Kipong* is danced by the people of the Tikana area. The dances called *Rukunau* and *Pinelewau* are only remembered by the old, but are not currently performed by the young.

Tatanua is recognizable by its wooden mask, whose wide jaw and over-emphasized teeth are characteristic features, as is the pointed head of the mask, whose hair is coloured differently on either side. A red shirt or red barkcloth is worn by the dancer of *Tatanua*. The dance is accompanied by a group of drummers playing on bamboo slit-drums and singers. The movement characterizing the *Tatanua* is the vibration of the red *tenget* leaf in the outstretched arm.

The dance begins with a single dancer; then two dancers approach each other, joined by another four or six. The group of dancers can divide into units of three or four, to finish the dance in the positioning of two units facing each other. After the dance, the participants have to take part in the ritual washing (*kei*).

Kipong is a mask made out of the branch of a sago palm, with its large ears made out of barkcloth and a stiff type of cane. The mask represents the beings of the bush (*la bu*), who populate the myths (*ruskus*) of the people of New Hanover, Tigak, Kara, Nalik, Tabar and Notsi. *Kipong* appear at the time of the food distribution with baskets and demand a share from their female *korok*.

The other day-time dances performed by villages are ranked according to the degree of preparation accompanying the ritual fast of *alal*. The period of learning the movements and songs, fasting and making of decorations generally overlaps with the carving of wood inside the funerary enclosure.

The dances are divided into male and female dances. Only one dance, called *Sorumbual,* can be danced by both men and women. *Sorumbual,* like *Langmanu,* is distinguished by the carved beak of the hornbill held by the dancers between the teeth during the performance. *Sorumbual* demands the most extended and radical observance of the rules of *alal* from all participants.

Buried in the classification of dances and their associated paraphernalia we find a theme that we saw pervading both *malanggan* images and also the agricultural calendar: this theme is one of splitting, and of grouping such split halves into pairs that remain coexistent.

male
1. *bual:* wooden head decoration
2. *sasale*: spear
3. *sisil*: *tenget* in both hands
4. *turul:* dried leaves on chest.

female
1. *magil*: barkcloth head decoration
2. *kandewas:* rattle made from shells
3. *peng*: *tenget* leaf
4. *huluk:* dried leaves on chest.

The songs of these dances are divided into two successive parts:

1. **Pur**, sung on the way from the dressing area in the forest to the central space. There are *pur* for masked dances and for those without masks.
2. **Moditi**, sung throughout the dance (a) by the accompanying drummers in *Tatanua, Kipong* and *Sorumbual* and (b) by the dancers in *Bual, Sasale, Sisil* and *Turul.*

The songs express the theme of the dance and are distinguished into two types: those based on impressions of actual events and composed in understandable words, and those that evolved out of dreams and are composed in a language not understood by the dancers.

Like the songs, the movements of the dance are divided into two, consecutive parts:

1. **Papasang**, the first part of the dance, characterized by the slow rhythm of the drum. Depending on the category of the dance (*sasale* or *bual* for example), *papasang* can be subdivided into two parts. The first of these subdivisions is called *buma* – the dancers move forward raising their legs in time with the rhythm of the drum. According to Lamesisi Yayii, *buma* represents an approaching group of birds in flight (1983: 41). The second part of *papasang* is called *ulet* in the Kara language – the movements of the dancers describe circular, rather than linear patterns, as they split into two or four groups.

2. **Pemoti**, the main part of the dance, characterized by the fast beat of the drum. The category of the dance prescribes the movements of the hands (*mak*), neck (*vuak*) and the direction of the eyes (*merak*). The theme of the dance is developed in the movements of the legs both on the spot and in the space invaded by the dance.

An example of a theme developed in the movements of a dance is the following *bual* called *manu i na kanai*: a man representing a fish (*kulebmu*) appears from underneath the *garamut* and eats the men representing small fish (*talai*); the large fish is then eaten by a bird (*kanai*). The *visual* equivalent of this theme in *malanggan*-figures is known as *Sasambuang*, which consists of a rock-cod ambiguously swallowing or ejecting a figure while being caught by a bird.

Another *bual* is called *manerai*: the dance is about a bird sitting on top of a stem drifting in the sea close to the shore; the bird jumps up and down. A man observes the bird from his house and jumps up and down like the bird. The phrases composing the song accompany the acting of the dancers:

na tuk lului : he is in the house
nuk kailiei i manerai : he calls out
kaili : he calls the bird
nuk tangise : it cries
kakal wep : it turns round and round
geso : what does it do?
tangise kakal put : it cries and turns around.

Bual and *Sorumbual* act out the becoming like a bird, and thus refer thematically to the public meaning of *malanggan*. *Sasale*, on the other hand, has as its theme the splitting of the clan. The splitting of the clan is acted out in the metaphorical theme of a dance called *a tem seseve* – the cutting of a tree with an axe. Another *sasale*, composed in Melanesian Pidgin, refers to the war with Japan, while yet another acts out the meaning of fishing with a string called *men tul kauli* (the three of us go in a canoe) – the meaning being adultery.

The repertoire of dances resembles, therefore, the poetic structure on which *malanggan*-imagery draws. In their combination of song, rhythm and movement, it is these dances that are the real performative and emotive base of *malanggan* that enables its images to be recollected and recognized despite decades separating successive invocations of an image.

The movements of a dance are recognized to be part of a named source by the way in which movement is controlled and arrested. It would be unthinkable to compose a song or dance that would not fit into the order outlined above. While there are a potentially infinite number of different movements possible in a dance, the dance will still be recognized as belonging to a named source.

The following analysis of the dance *Langmanu* will highlight the hierarchical structure that differentiates and ranks named dances generated out of a single source. *Langmanu* (*Langmani* in Nalik, *Bungman* in Notsi and *Kowange* in Tabar) is the general name used to refer to four dances united by the common use of the feather-headdress called *desah*, the yellow chest-bands called *mulai*, the carved beak of the hornbill called *ngusunga* carried between the teeth by the dancers, rattles made out of shells called *redelak*, red leaves of *tenget* called *si bung* and platforms called *eiben* erected for the dancing of those who 'rise like birds'.

Marking the transitional phase in the work for the dead, the freeing of life-force and its rooting in the ground of *but*, *Langmanu* (Figure 5.7) is the most evocative of dances. Accompanied by the rhythm of the slit-drum, which marks the finishing of each part and the numbers of the pigs that are arriving in the clearing, the decorations to be worn by the *Langmanu* dancers are made inside the *but*, which is hidden from the outside by a thick coconut screen. The fabrication of head-gear, chest-bands and platform is drawn out over a period of three days.

The first day is reserved for the public payment (*dodolas*) made by the dancers to the owner of the dance; the dancers, of whom at least one will be an infant, in turn receive *kambang*, white lime clapped in leaf-shaped patterns on their face, shoulders, chest and back, which enables them to become the temporary hosts of the spirit of the deceased. The same day a platform is build on the *but*, its legs consisting of up-turned trees called *baral*, and dancers practise on it, while hidden behind the screen; the melody (*wagele*) and the rhythm (*wetiting*) played by two men on the slitdrum will be heard over and over again over the next three days as 'the bird learns to fly' (*manu i hapas*). On the evening of this day, the head-dresses (*desah*) of the dancers, which are kept from one dance to another, are carried inside the enclosure, decorated with a new red band, and hung on the platform. The head-dress consists of a net (*inau*) made up out of knots (*wuap*) only found in fish-nets (*bone*) and the frontal decoration of the *haio*'s house; the knots, which are made by women and used by men in compliance with ritual taboos, cover the head. The feathers, which are fastened to the net by its knots, are what give the dancers their bird-like appearance.

The second day of preparations is concerned with the fabrication of the yellow chest-band that is made of the bark of the tulip tree (*rotap*), whose olfactory qualities associate it with the site of *baral* and the calendrical rite of the calling of odour. The bark is stripped and beaten (*tuk*) until it becomes a soft, fibrous surface called the 'hair' (*hui*) of the bird. Then roots of wild ginger that have been stored for several days inside the bark of the areca tree to soften them are distributed among the dancers; chewing the roots with areca nut, they spit yellow fluid on to the strips of the beaten bark until it is bright yellow and called

Figure 5.7 *Langmanu.*

mulai. If the colour of the *mulai* is dull, rather than bright, the man concerned is accused of having failed to observe the rules of *alal*, and may be excluded from the dance. *Mulai* are fastened along a string (*rui*) of a length to be able to be fastened cross-wise over the chest and back of the dancer. With the completion of the *mulai*, the final day approaches, and the dancers practise a final time to the rhythm of the slit-drum.

Each *Langmanu* dance is made up out of twelve units, each unit announced by a change of rhythm. The rising of the birds on the platform is possibly the most moving of the performances; the deep sounding of the slitdrum is said to 'turn' the 'liver' (*a ulai angat*), and cause everybody to remember (*mamaluhen*) those who died. Sorrow and celebratory mood mix as *ventanun* are fully freed, about to rise like a bird. Peekel (1928: 459–552) interprets the rising and falling of the dancers, and the turning of the neck from one side to the other, as the rising and sinking and changing position of the moon (*hulen*), which defines the agricultural and ritual calendar alike.

There are four named dances known among the Tikana, each differentiated by a named bird whose movements are imitated by the dancers and by the colour of the decoration of the chest. Two of these four are classified as projections of the other two, and are tied to particular exchange relations. Each dance is differentiated by a decreased number of dancers and by the positioning of the hands of the dancers during the performance. The duality of the dances generated out of *Langmanu* is visible in the spatial position of the dancers, one being danced on the platform, one on the ground:

1. ***Langtegaum:*** *tegaum*, yellow chest decoration and lime (white) body painting, danced on platform (*eiben*), hands on both sides of the body, six or twelve dancers
1a. ***Langkor:*** *kor*, black or yellow chest decoration and lime (white) body painting, danced on platform (*eiben*), hands folded behind the back, four dancers
2. ***Langmareng:*** *mareng*, red chest decoration, red clay (*tar*) body painting, danced on ground, hands on both sides of the body, six or twelve dancers
2a. ***Langmurre:*** *murre*, red or black chest decoration, red clay body decoration, danced on ground, hands folded behind the back, four dancers.

Langmanu has explicit synaesthetic qualities, combining sound with odour and colour, in ways that mark it as ritual work of transitional, but also of instructional, value. These qualities have allowed it to be merged with the 'initiatory' events of the Church, in which boys, but also, more and more, girls, are dressed up as *Langmanu* dancers as they move towards the altar.

Although the polity of images of *malanggan* is inseparable from the ritual institution of which it is a part, the efficacy of its forms cannot be explained by this institution. Far from esoteric, the knowledge of how to make *malanggan*, how to synthesize recall with carving, how to bring about events that are happening with precision and accuracy, how to make things 'work' in the minute detail and in the larger scheme of things is an aspiration to which everyone will subscribe who is a 'member' of *malanggan*. This is an 'enchanted' technology, in the words of Alfred Gell, one that works by makings things not the reflection of thought, but the 'dwelling' of thought, the place where thought can conduct itself freely, over and over again (1992). By thinking in, through and with images of *malanggan*, a holographic worldview, in which every detail projects visions of further more encompassing details, brings to the fore the possibility of an alternative reality, one in which endings are turned into beginnings, distinctions into connections and presents into futures.

Notes

1. Kantorowicz (1957); see also Ginzburg (1991), who examines the relation between word, conception and object in this kind of representation, and Schnepel (1995) who traces the phenomenon of 'twinned beings' across Africa, East India and Renaissance France. An effigy as representation of the king was used for the first time in England in 1327 at the death of Edward II and in France in 1422 for the death of Charles VI. Ralph Giesey (1960), a pupil of Ernst Kantorowicz, documents that since the end of the fifteenth century, a clear separation can be found between the dead king and his image which, as his effigy, was taken in a procession through the streets, while the mortal body went to the grave. He supports the difference first set out by Kantorowicz between the mortal body of the king as individual and the immortal body, associated with the public office of kingship. See also Brückner (1966) on medieval effigies and ritual.

2. Since Aristotle, there have been two sides to remembering: *mneme* and *memoria*; distinctions that we find again in the pairings of *Gedächtnis* and *Erinnerung*, Proust's *mémoire involontaire* and *mémoire volontaire*, Warburg's *Mnemosyne*

and Sosphrosyne, Halbwachs's *mémoire and histoire* and Benjamin's *Eingedenken and Andenken*. The first, the *mneme*, describes the ability to remember by chance something previously experienced, whereas the second, or *memoria*, captures the ability consciously to summon up what was forgotten (see W. Kemp 1991). See also Carruthers (1990) on medieval manuscript reproduction and memory.

3. Wagner analysed the mortuary rituals of the Usen Barok of southern New Ireland in order to demonstrate how the efficacy of their mortuary feasts lies in 'the happening holography': that is in the 'conceptual grasp of the plenitude of things in a single instant' (2001: 233). For Wagner, this 'happening holography' is not a matter of 'direct presentation; it is not perceived in the material so much as it is re-perceived as the sense of indigenous intention to show phenomena in their self-constitution' (1991: 170).

4. See Küchler (1987) and Taylor (1993); for an earlier essay on visual mnemonic systems see Yates (1966).

5. See Strathern (1991).

6. See Gell (1996) on 'traps as art'.

7. See also Connerton on gestures as vehicles of thought (1992).

8. *Lenguh* is known as *bongomas* in Notsi/Tabar.

9. Lamesisi Yayii distinguishes between ceremonial-ritual dances (*Lang Manu, Tetenue, Koluptaine, Kipong*); ceremonial dances (*Sakabual, Bual, Vual, Sasale*); casual dances (*Silip, Uleo, Mequil*) and night dances (*bot, mindal*) and entertainment dances (*Girimsi*) (1983: 47–8).

10. Peekel's (1928) essay on *Langmanu* is the only description aside from my own data.

On Binding and Thinking[*]

> . . . By braiding his sacred cords the king braids social relationships, or, to put it differently, binds men with his cords. The idea that the king is the 'binder' or 'weaver' is reflected in the literal meaning of the title . . . (Valeri 1985: 298).

Pacific artworks are well known for their capacity simultaneously to contain and elicit all prior and future works (Wagner 1987; Strathern 1991). As 'multiples', artworks of this kind counterpoise the Western assumption of the unique object, and thus engage the conceptual frame of modernism in ways that enable us to overcome the latent opposition of Western and non-Western art still rampant in anthropological studies of art (Gell 1998: 6–8). Like Mondrian's grids, such artworks as New Ireland *malanggan* or Trobriand canoe-prows appear to originate from the figural, visualized as a graphic as well as a technical schema, which also serves as the discursive element in art that otherwise resists exegesis (Summers 1989). This chapter sets out to investigate the figural in the art of the Pacific, as it is exemplified by the design structure and 'cross-hatching' of Australian Aboriginal bark-paintings (Morphy 1991), by the looped binding of netbags (MacKenzie 1991) and by my own account of the *malanggan* image (Küchler 1987, 1988; Küchler and Melion 1991).

By revealing the figural in Pacific artworks to be a material trace of alternative techniques of binding, that is of knotting and looping, I hope to open a new perspective on what has become known as the 'epidemiology' of cultural representations (Sperber 1985; Gell 1993). Following earlier uses of the epidemiological model, the question driving this chapter is what enables cultural representations to catch on in certain social and cultural situations and not in others. At present,

* This chapter is based on an article 'Binding in the Pacific' published in *Oceania* Vol. 65 (1999) and reprinted with permission of the publisher.

we have two solutions to such a question: Sperber (1985) argued that susceptibility towards representations must be grounded in the affinity between the cognitive processes governing representations and the cognitive processes sustaining culture. Gell (1993), conversely, saw susceptibility as grounded in the biographical and relational space within which technical virtuosity is selectively appropriated. Binding, in its continuous and yet varied articulation across the Pacific, serves as a perfect example with which both to re-examine these positions and to point to a possible resolution of the conflicting emphasis on the cognitive versus the social in the validation of cultural representations. This is because binding is not part of an esoteric knowledge technology, but is profoundly embedded in the mundane and thus habituated space within which knowledge is externalized; in addition to its embeddedness in the mundane, binding uniquely brings to bear upon material affective and personal as well as mathematical and thus cognitive attitudes and concepts that may help to amplify ways of thinking. Rather than assuming that the figurative expresses ideas that already exist, could it be that its transmission has a dynamic that creates a lasting difference in culture and society?

Rethinking 'templates'

It has become common practice to describe the figural element of art in the Pacific with the term 'template'. 'Templates' are taken to capture the technical and material means that secure the generativity and reproductivity of artworks and to involve geometric and mathematical specifications of some kind, such as the graphic layout and geometric design of 'fore-' and 'back-ground' in Australian Aboriginal barkpainting, or the mathematically precise refiguration of the body in Kula canoe-prows. The problem with the term 'template' is that it is drawn from mechanical modes of reproduction, notably the printing press, and as such embraces notions of linear, homogeneous, separate and local frames of space-time symptomatic of Newtonian physics. The mechanistic world-view, however, is at odds with the 'organic' description of space-time that appears adequate in capturing Melanesian conceptions of events as inseparable, observer-contingent and process-dependent, and as framed by non-linear, heterogeneous, multi-dimensional spacetimes (Munn 1986; Strathern 1990).

Indeed, such an 'organic' view of the universe is not just an adequate description of Pacific concepts of space-time, but has been given validity in the West by the advent of Einstein's relativity theory (Barrow 1992).

Einstein's world broke up Newton's universe of absolute space and time into a multitude of space-time frames each tied to a particular observer, who therefore not only has a different clock, but a different map. Quantum theory, moreover, demanded that we stop seeing things as separate solid objects with definite locations in space and time. Instead, they are delocalized, indefinite, mutually entangled entities that evolve like organisms.

The inadequacy – or should we say 'datedness'? – of the term 'template', and thus of existing descriptions of the figural in art in mechanistic terms, thus hardly needs further elaboration. That term suggests that the formal properties of artworks are fixed by a technical code that is learned as an aspect of esoteric knowledge, and implies in its mechanical description an egocentric and anthropomorphic spatial cognition that is at odds with its conception in culture (cf. Wassmann 1994). Yet what other term, and what set of assumptions, could replace this obviously misleading conception? This question was also raised by the evolving New Genetics, which found itself unable to comprehend the structure of DNA as a dynamic and evolving, 'organic' system as long as it relied on the notion of 'template' as its descriptive vocabulary. In our search for a new model, we may consider following New Genetics, which recently began to look towards the science of topology, a branch of mathematics that developed as computing allowed for the visualization of the behaviour of non-linear, organic space-time. The conceptual key to topology is the geometric constancy of objects under deformation, which topology sees as best exemplified by the behaviour of the knot.

The appeal of the knot as a model for self-organizing, non-linear systems has reverberated over the last twenty years not just in science, but also in the humanities. It is this ubiquitous presence of the knot in contemporary academic thought that, I would argue, shaped the resonances evoked by recent analyses of the figural in Pacific art. I am thinking here of MacKenzie's (1991) acclaimed research on looping technologies in Papua New Guinea and Valeri's (1985) account of binding in Hawaii. These studies point to the fact that the knot is not just uniquely the most important means of fastening across the Pacific, but works as knowledge technology that enables the externalization of concepts, from sorcery to affinity, into a spatial medium (cf. Levinson 1992).

When we rethink what is still present as mechanistic accounts of technique in these analyses in terms of a notion of cultural topology, MacKenzie's (1991: 6) insight into the consistent application of alternative modes of binding – surfacing on the one hand in the loop in non-Austronesian-speaking cultures in the Pacific, and on the other hand

in the knot in Austronesian-speaking cultures – takes on a new significance. Is it possible, one begins to ask, that the non-random distribution
of distinctively bound representations across the Pacific is indicative of
diverse models of spatio-temporal relations? Could the spread of binding in its different logical articulations have facilitated the regional
integration of diverse politico-religious institutions?

Binding in the Pacific

From Polynesia to the non-Austronesian-speaking cultures of mainland
Papua New Guinea, binding appears not just as technique, resonating
in everyday tasks from building to repairing bridges, houses and
containers of all kinds, but also as artwork. Yet despite this almost trivial
and commonsensical presence of binding, the manipulation of string
and the visual and formal properties of products of binding varies from
place to place, with the most pronounced differentiation emerging
between what we call 'looping' and 'knotting' technologies. Looping
involves the pulling of the string through the knot, creating an
expandable mesh that draws attention visually and conceptually to the
threaded string and its continuous run. Knotting, on the other hand,
creates a planar surface that covers the knot. The knot, compared with
the loop, is only visible when unravelled, thus visually and conceptually
drawing attention to a negative, absent space. While we might be readily
inclined to compare examples of looped string with those of knotted
string, carved *malanggan*-figures from the north of New Ireland have
never before been associated with binding. In fact, however, the liminal
position of openwork carving between the loop and the knot enables
us to draw attention to the dynamic relation between the figural and
the social in Pacific art.

Knots and artefacts composed of knots are of paramount importance
to the fashioning of contractual relations across Polynesian island
cultures. Famous examples are the Tongan barkcloths (*gatu vagatoga*),
figuring prominently in ceremonial gift exchanges as the inalienable
property of chiefly lineages; the surface pattern of these mats is the
result of the rubbing of barkcloth over a net spanned across the *kupeti*-
board. Yet it is possibly Babadzan's (1993) exposition on the Tahitian
to'o that illustrates most succinctly the conceptual purchase of artefacts
of knotting.

To'o are bindings of sennit cordage and tapa barkcloth, sometimes
with roughly delineated facial features and limbs woven on to the

outside. At all times, bar the ritual at which the *to'o* was revealed to view, such tightly knotted bindings encompassed a pillar that kept apart and thus connected heaven and earth, and thus invested the *to'o* with god's presence by virtue of contiguity rather than resemblance. The *to'o*, an amalgam of ranked images, were thus embodiments of Oro, the Tahitian god, and control over them was essential to the system of social rank and political power. The correlation between the ranked polity of images and social rank among human beings was given regular and formal expression in a ritual called *pa'iatua,* which, translated, means the 'wrapping of the gods' (Babadzan 1993; Gell 1998: 111).

No one has as yet better revealed the importance ascribed in Poly-nesian culture to binding and to the knotted cord as representation of binding (evidenced in Babadzan's work on Tahiti) than Valeri in his work on the king's sacrifice in Hawaii (1985: 296–300). In Hawaii, a sacred cord (*'aha*) acted as the reference point of genealogy – repre-senting not just the king's relationship with the gods, but also the connecting force of genealogy that 'binds together all other genealogies, since it is their reference point and the locus of their legitimacy and truth' (Valeri 1985: 296). The cord of Hawaiian kingship was not inherited – the undoing of the King's sacred cord dissolving the social bond embodied by the king. The strands obtained from the undoing of the cords were woven into caskets in which the bones of the king are enshrined (Valeri 1985: 298). During the king's reign, the knotting of the cord that celebrated his installation was re-enacted repeatedly as the central organizing rite of the sacrifice of the king. The metaphoric or real 'twisting' of the strands that make up the *'aha* cord enclosed and thereby removed from sight the space where the knot resides, containing and thus arresting the divine powers that come to form the mystical body of kingship.

Across Polynesia, artefacts of binding are thus also a means of wrap-ping, and as such are powerfully associated with contexts and powers of revelation (cf. Gell 1993). Moving to Melanesia, the knot appears to vanish as an artefact of wrapping. This apparent displacement of binding, together with a decrease in emphasis on cloth wealth, appears marked even as one moves from the southernmost islands of the Bismarck Archipelago, such as Vanuatu and the Solomons, to its north-ernmost extensions in New Ireland and New Hanover. And yet a much less obvious rendering of the knot as artefact can be found even in these parts of Melanesia that hitherto have appeared to lie outside the param-eters of Polynesian social systems, with their emphasis on the revelatory powers of the wrap and the ranking of lineages.

Where carving from wood predominates in the ritual arts, as in the north of New Ireland, the idea of the knot as the figural frame for technical knowledge appears far-fetched at first glance. Wood is a rigid substance, so much so that it is difficult to imagine a surface carved from wood as having the quality of stretchable rubber that allows one to image the twisting and tangling of string into a knot. But that wood indeed lends itself to the technical exploration of knotting is revealed by the American artist Brent Collins, whose work visualizes a rather unusual explicit application of knot theory to wood. Many of his pieces display invariant symmetrical relations and uniform thickness, from which one can abstract closed, knotted and linked ribbons curving through space (Francis 1995: 59). The mathematical surface depicted by his artworks indeed constitutes what he calls a 'knot-spanning surface' or a 'framed link', with the knot literally being carved out of the wood and constituting the hollow, negative space of the sculpture.

The entangling of carved planes, common to Collins's knot-sculptures, is strikingly reminiscent of the figural qualities of *malanggan*. 'Made as skins' (*retak*) to contain the life-force of the deceased persons prior to their final expulsion into the land of the dead, *malanggan* figures are not just visual renderings of knots, but partake of the technical vocabulary and skill that is common to a range of knotted artefacts such as nets (both fish-nets and nets used as the basis of the head-dresses worn by *Malanggan*-dancers) and plaited artefacts such as mats and baskets. In fact, the northern New Ireland term for knot, *wu-ap*, is associated phonetically and conceptually with the term for an image-based resource from which *malanggan* figures are derived, which is *wu-ne*, meaning literally 'connected knots' (Figure 6.1).

One may be inclined to suggest that these figures look like story boards visualizing myths of potential importance to the understanding of this culture. In fact, such stories exist and are quite readily provided to those connoisseurs or tourists seeking to purchase them as mementoes of their island experience. In searching for meaning we direct our eyes away from the hollowed spaces clustering between figure and frame. Yet one may wonder about these hollowed spaces; and indeed, it is here, in what is rendered absent through incising, that we find a surprising clue as to what may count as a description of what a *malanggan* is: what we are looking at are complex knot-spanning surfaces reminiscent of the string-figures that form a beloved pastime across the Pacific.

The finding of a knot in the hollowed spaces of the wood distinguishes ritually effective artefacts from those that are considered

Figure 6.1 *Malanggan* and the Knot

'mistakes' – the space framed by the enveloping planes of the carving calls to mind the heap of wood-chips left at the back of the carver's hut, called *rotap*, literally 'salty rubbish', and likened to the dead, uprooted trees that drift ashore once a year from the direction of the ancestral lands. The knot which is visible as negative space thus reflects upon a connection with an ancestral domain that is created through ritualized forgetting, one that is kept at bay at all costs, while recalling its power from time to time to the land of the living (cf. Babadzan 1993).

If a carved knot can in this way be seen to call up what is absent through the creation of negative space, a contrast emerges with the emphasis on life in line, pattern and colour common to the string and looping cultures that predominate on the mainland of Papua New Guinea (MacKenzie 1991; Hauser-Schaublin 1996). Hauser-Schaublin described the experience of ancestral power among the Abelam as captured by the brilliance of the line and the initiant's nettle-beaten body – an embodiment of ancestral power that appears subversive from the perspective of New Ireland, where any claim to personal control over ancestral power is considered deeply ambiguous, and is possible only under the guise of ritualized acts of negation (cf. Clay 1986; Wagner 1987). The knot, which, like all wrappings, exists only to be opened, calls to mind the possibility of containing and thus experiencing ancestral power that is effective only as long as it remains distanced and yet 'recollectable' by covering it in secondary 'skins' whose removal, rotting and re-fabrication inscribes the ancestral domain in cycles of movement and arrest.

Knots are found in many contexts in New Ireland culture, all having in common the fact that they serve as a means of 'binding' in more than just a functional sense. There are knotted stems of the ginger plant that are tied around trees in the forest to demarcate land taken out of cultivation for certain periods of time; usually coinciding with the death of a landholding person, the tying and un-tying of the knot marks the transition of land-ownership that is associated with the right to taboo (*dang*) the land in this manner. There are also nets knotted across the front of certain houses that are the dwellings of the living dead known as '*haio*' or 'the caught ones', who incorporate the knowledge that connects the living to the dead. There are nets worn on the head of *malanggan* dancers, alone able to finish the death of a *haio* by recapturing her life-force, who draw with their movements knotted patterns into the sand that disappear as quickly as they appear. And there are knots tied rhythmically into songs classified as *malanggan*, and fishnets that are knotted and used only with the strictest observance of taboos to avoid the splitting of the netting. Not to be forgotten are basketry and mat-work, whose plaits interweave in ways recalled by the intersecting planes of sculpted and woven *malanggan* – all made not to invite introspection, but to deflect it.

The negative space of the *malanggan*-figure or the invisible underside or inner-layer of mats and baskets recalls an ancestral realm that is positioned beyond the horizon in a land called *Karoro*. Expelled into the land of the dead, the ancestral remains attached to the living by means of the tangled planes of wood and the twisted leaves of the coconut palm, whose seasonal drifting ashore announces the new year of the agricultural calendar. In the same way that magic is needed for the pulling ashore of what is colloquially termed the 'smell' of the dead (*wangam a musung*) in the form of uprooted trees and branches, so the creation of 'skins' carved into wood or bound into coconut leaves that visually and conceptually bind the ancestral to the living cannot be secured by skilled acts alone. The knot that traps the ancestral as it returns to the land of the living has to be found ('seen' – *kalymi*) in dreams. Being able artificially to induce or otherwise voluntarily effect the dreaming of an image that is able to capture the 'smell' (*ngusung*) of the dead distinguishes carvers (the 'joiners of skin' – *retak*) from others who may own knots in the form of named images, but cannot render them effective.[1]

The contractual relation between the living and the dead that is symbolized by the knotted planes of the *malanggan*-figure also extends to land. Thus a contrast emerges with the Polynesian material on knotted artworks: while the sennit binding of the Tahitian *to'o* does not appear to have been made to underwrite symbolically a contract over land made between the living, this is certainly the case with *malanggan*. Like the looped netbags of mainland New Guinea, a *malanggan*-figure is always made for someone who stands in a particular social relation to the current owner of the image.

In being made to be sold (*sorolis*) or lent (*aradem*) to affines or even clan-members who may live in different villages or even different dialect groups as affirmation of a contract over usufructory rights over land, a *malanggan*-figure moves at least notionally every time it is made. Again like a netbag, a figure connects those who made and those who receive the artwork, in that the complex, intertwining planes of a *malanggan*-figure reveal the memory of contractual relations over land. As rights to land are shared and fluid across linguistic and spatial boundaries, so the rights to carve images that evoke such rights are shared; people talk about the 'path' (*selen*) of a named image, which flows like a river from a source (*wune*). Such a 'path' is at least partially discernible and reconstructable, as *malanggan*-figures document the conceptual and actual fragmentation of images in reproduction as they are shared out into smaller and smaller bits along ever-expanding pathways, only occasionally to be reassembled into larger, more complete assemblages.

There are two techniques of creating 'fractal', or breakable figures, each associated with distinct contractual relationships: 'breakable' not just in the metaphorical sense, as points of breakage suggested by the intersections of knotted planes may be targeted when severing a figure after it has served to inform a contract between groups, who each take home one part as reminder of the relation thus effected. Each technique makes use of the knot in different ways: one to render different kinds of knots in the planes carved from wood, of which there are three main named types, and the other to trace the deformation of a knot into its possible forms. Elsewhere (Küchler and Melion 1991) I have pointed to the importance of motifs and motif combinations as tracing the spatio-temporal structure of the ritual process itself and marking it as sacrificial in nature: images of absorption foreshadow images of containment, and beyond that of decomposition and transcendence. It is, however, the technique of carving surface-spanning knots from wood that explains how images are generated and reproduced from an ever-changing and yet fixed repertoire that allows the instantaneous recognition of the named 'source' from which an image is derived. The processuality of ritual itself may be derivative of the process of knotting, which suggests sequences of connecting and opening (cf. Boyer 1994).

This method of creating 'telling' variations in the material forms of *malanggan* is used for the six named image 'sources' of *malanggan*, which are in turn paired into three sets of two. As over 15,000 artefacts have been collected in mainly just six villages over the last hundred years, and the number of actually produced artefacts may be double that, one can easily predict that variations in form will be minute, a suggestion that any collection, however small or scantily sampled, supports. Like the sound of the names that are chanted when a figure is seen for the first and often the only time, or the steps that are traced on the ground when a dance is learned, the knotted shape of a figure contracts, expands and entangles to create for a fleeting moment a container for a knowledge that is tantamount to a testimony -- you know what you have seen.

In behaving like looped artefacts in underscoring reproductive metaphors and relations, yet visually and conceptually alluding to the necessary distancing of the ancestral by means of knotting, the case of *malanggan*-figures falls awkwardly within the neat opposition of the loop and the knot. Yet it is precisely this non-fit that draws attention to the dynamic that keeps looping and knotting as cultural represent-ations within distinct social and historical fields.

The Knot and the Loop

Studies of knots as material renderings of binding in figural, cord-like or patterned form are surprisingly rare in Oceanic ethnography, despite the prominence of an allied technology known as looping, whose conceptual force was recently uncovered by MacKenzie (1991) for the non-Austronesian-speaking cultures of the mainland of Papua New Guinea. MacKenzie's study of netbags showed more than any previous ethnography the intimate link between a technique of binding, in this case that of 'looping', and the externalization and management of knowledge. Her study shows netbags to work as a vehicle of ideas that identify spatio-temporal frames with the continuity of the string, whose continuous run forms the body of the ubiquitous *bilum*. Hauser-Schaublin (1996) recently extended this examination of string-based cultural imagination to concerns with the line and the frond in Sepik River figural art, while arguing for an emerging revelatory 'aesthetic' that is diametrically opposed to the emphasis on the plait and the plane in island Melanesia and Polynesia. Even if we do not want to agree with her identification of the string as 'non-cloth' cultural 'aesthetics', her study is of profound importance for a study of binding in the Pacific, as it suggests a complex and yet systematic contrast between looping and knotting as allied and yet mutually opposed knowledge technologies.

Mathematically speaking, the difference between the loop and the knot lies in their execution only, one being literally the flip-side of the other. As Adams summarizes it succinctly in his introduction to knot-theory, the knot is a *knotted loop of string*, except that we think of the string as having no thickness, its cross-section being a single point.[2] The knot is then a closed curve in space that does not intersect itself anywhere, the most basic form of which is the circle or 'un-knot'. While the knot thus lives in the space visualized by a surface, the loop *is* the surface of intersecting planes.

Returning to my initial considerations of the nature of 'templates', the consideration of the contrast of knotting and looping technologies in the Pacific opens a new, surprising perspective: it appears as if indeed the mechanical description of a template as a technique for reproducing discrete space-time frames within fixed locales is quite apt for an account of looped material culture, yet not for the material renderings of knots, and that we are therefore not dealing with an, albeit vanishing, difference between 'us' and 'them', but with different, though mutually interdependent, ways of framing knowledge. The contrast between the types of binding is brought into sharper relief by considering the differences in the description of each.

Looped netbags as described by MacKenzie (1991) come in a range of numerous different, yet largely 'fixed' and localized 'styles', with bags being defined in terms of different functions associated with the size, texture and finish of each item. Single cultural areas such as the Telefol, as described by MacKenzie (1991: 46–51), distinguish twenty-seven named types of net-bags, and sub-types that are grouped into two categories (large flexible *bilums* and small tightly looped *bilums*) and a further five sub-categories (mouthband *bilum*, father *bilum*, pocket *bilum*, twin *bilum*, red seed *bilum*). The persistence of such categories as well as the techniques that are associated with them broadly frame regional and intra-regional boundaries, as both the bags and the technique of looping associated with them are transmitted along affinal paths. As the construction process and the resulting form of the *bilum* are inseparable from the looping technique selected, a variation in the technique has obvious stylistic consequences. Most important, however, is MacKenzie's observation that technique is learned through observation and imitation, a process that is initiated in early childhood.

In stark contrast to the mechanical description of looping as a *technique* of binding, knotted artefacts are 'seen' and described in terms of figural topologies that emphasize a dynamics of ordering inherent in the patterned *design* of binding. Given the emphasis on a visually mediated 'knowing' or understanding of designs that is acquired through 'dreaming', the execution of knotted forms is not restricted to those who have acclaimed 'rights' to designs. As we saw in the example of *malanggan*, the ownership of a design can be sold, lent or otherwise transmitted, with one carver being hired across the region. As the technical execution of the design is subordinate to the resulting pattern in these knotted artworks, variation of technique is less frequent, and indeed even avoided, as this could enhance the possibility that designs are confused and theft allegations are brought forth.

The variability of design in knotted artefacts is thus governed by factors other than the conditions influencing the transmission of skill-based technique. In fact, as was pointed out earlier with reference to the practice of carving 'fractal' images in New Ireland, the variability of design is a direct consequence of the embeddedness of the design in contractual relations over land that are visually and metaphorically tied into the tangled planes of the *malanggan*-figure.

The 'knotted' planes of *malanggan* figures in New Ireland thus demand to be perceived as a geometric configuration in order for execution to produce acceptable results. In comparison with looped netbags, *malanggan* figures come in limited shapes, sizes, and motifs, with an emphasis on their combination that remains constant throughout the north of the island while allowing for infinite variability at the level of 'surface' design, as in the painted patterns and painted or carved attached motifs. The stability of pattern is the result of the subordination of technique to the spatial framing of the image. Rather than 'finding' the design of the figure in the wood during carving, the geometric contours of the image are drawn on sand or on to the wood that is used for carving, thus allowing improved or innovative techniques of fabrication only minimal scope to influence the resulting product. It is this geometric design of a *malanggan* that is owned and exchanged in the north of New Ireland as knowledge technique, quite unlike the New Guinea netbag described by MacKenzie (1991), which is validated in terms of its technical execution and exchanged as an artefact.

The emphasis on the configuration of design rather than its execution also explains the frequently lamented decline in the degree of visual openwork in *malanggan*. Noted as negative by the Western connoisseur, who measures aesthetic appeal in terms of skilful execution, the decreasing three-dimensionality of carving does not bother anyone in New Ireland, as even a sketched, more or less painted design would do if time and attention are demanded for tasks other than the preparation of feasting.[3] At the same time, figures are seen as belonging to the same 'source' or knot-type, even if one is executed in wood and the other in fibre, and even if place and time of execution are unconnected.

Making such comparisons, which are by definition unverifiable, as the artefact is destroyed or sold after its use in ritual, implies that the experience to which reference is made lies outside the making of ritual artworks in the mundane tasks of binding. Yet should we imagine people walking around with an abstract image of a knot, its different types and possible deformations, in their heads, which then just gets projected on to a given medium? Or should we imagine that pattern is deduced from the structures inherent in the practical operation of knotting? These quite plausible solutions to the problem of pattern production and recognition ignore an aspect of pattern that has become known as self-organization, whose explanation has become crucial to the modelling of non-mechanistic biology (Saunders 1998: 55).

Confronted with the evidence of non-linear systems that are capable of self-organization, Lovelock (1988) recently proposed that what appears as self-regulation is a co-ordinated phenomenon arising from causes that are themselves co-ordinated and purposeful. An overall 'design' thus does not have to be in existence, while the system itself has to be inherently co-ordinated and purposeful, a view that ascribes autonomy and agency to non-linear organic systems, as against the dependency on external forces suggested in the mechanical description of systems.

Lifted out of biology to the world of material culture, the notion of co-ordination and purpose throws a new light on the poignancy of the knot as a metaphor for generative systems. The knot might be argued to work as a 'source', not because it is comprehended in terms of a quasi-pre-existing mathematical and spatially de-centred system of ordering, but because it is a trace of purposeful co-ordination. And it is here, in being a trace of *purposeful co-ordination*, that the loop and the knot meet, diverging 'merely' in the relative importance ascribed to either technical process or pattern in the generative reproduction of things. Following the insights of new biology, however, each manner of co-ordination, the mechanistic and the organic, would bring with it associated space-time frames that in turn would create a difference in culture and society.

Turning back to the distribution of looped and knotted artworks in the Pacific, we note with MacKenzie (1991) the neat overlapping of the two sides of binding with the spread of non-Austronesian- and Austronesian-speaking cultures. One may be reminded of Whitney Davis's (1986) argument in his 'Origins of Image Making' that images originate from mark-making, not from pre-existing concepts that are 'projected' on to materials. The story of the loop and knot may support his case and provide a new perspective on the epidemiology of cultural representations: one that draws attention to the mundane, affective, personal and yet profoundly mathematical nature of binding, which shapes ways of thinking.

Notes

1. One is reminded of Howes's (1988) poignant insight into the correspondence of a cultural emphasis on olfaction with a conceptual displacement of the dead from the realm of the living. I would add to this the observation

of the corresponding amplification of knotting as 'cognitive style' common to socio-political institutions that grow out of the finishing of the dead.

2. My understanding of knot theory is almost entirely governed by Adams's (1994) work.

3. The 'flattening' of surfaces of carvings is considered a consequence of the constraints of modern life, but is also realized to make figures much less attractive to the Western buyer.

Potent Absence and the Dynamics of Sacrificial Economy

> The transformation and contextual mutations of objects cannot be appreciated if it is presumed that gifts are invariably gifts and commodities invariably commodities (Thomas 1991:39).

Our museums are overflowing with uncounted numbers of *malanggan* figures; public institutions alone house more than ten thousand artefacts – excluding masks, which would at least double the total figure for objects collected between 1870 and today. Waldemar Stöhr (1987) estimates that for every collected artefact at least another seven *malanggan* remained uncollected, as the expeditions that collected the largest number of artefacts between 1875 and 1935 targeted only certain villages that were easily accessible by sea. Given that about 7,000 objects were collected over this sixty-year period, he considers it possible that the actual numbers of figures produced for ceremonial purposes could have amounted to between 28,000 and 35,000. As *malanggan* are still produced, this number can at least be doubled to arrive at an estimate for the numbers of *malanggan* produced during a hundred-and-twenty-year period.

Western collections, however, contain only *malanggan* figures that are carved from wood as part of the three-phase ritual process that culminates in the death and decomposition of the artefacts. Instead of being left to rot, the 'finished' remains of ritual work can be sold to collectors or visitors to the island. The money that is acquired in this way is retained for future funerary work, and is usually used for the payment of a carver. The possibility of alienating the material thing, while keeping hold of the right to reproduce its image, appears to have

167

been realized and acted upon ever since such figures attracted the attention of traders and explorers in the mid-nineteenth century.[1]

By allowing the collecting of ritual remains whenever possible to replace their decomposition, the Western collector inadvertently attained a comparable conceptual status to the sea-spirit *moroa,* in becoming, like her, the site of recollection. *Malanggan* in this way answer to the millennarian concern with the re-opening of the road to the ancestors believed to be blocked by the white man.

Malanggan is not an isolated example of object sacrifice in Oceania. Alain Babadzan (1993) reveals for Tahiti the differential material and conceptual nature of three ritually produced artefacts, of which an artefact called *to'o* appears to have played a very similar role to the wooden *malanggan* figure in being animated, killed and rendered absent; the rendering absent of these objects effected contact with the gods, while keeping them, like the dead, at a safe distance. We may also recall the *rambramb* from Malekula that, as described by Gudieri and Pellizi (1981), equally allowed deposition to be replaced by collecting.[2]

Whether ritual objects are hidden, burned, left to rot or otherwise disassembled, let alone the relation between the chosen treatment and the ritual process as whole, is hardly ever mentioned in ethnographies, which otherwise are exemplary in contextualizing the same artefacts as they are produced and appear in ritual. And yet, I want to argue, it is here in this unacknowledged process of rendering things absent that their ritual efficacy resides; this is because, when rendered invisible, *malanggan* act as an absent reflection that is simultaneously a foundation for resistance and also a vehicle of exchange between the visible and the invisible. In being made as a 'gift to the gods', *malanggan* emulate, as Krystof Pomian has argued for objects in sacrificial economies, pure exchange value (1986).[3]

On Mneme and Memoria

The inseparable part that decomposition plays in ritual work has implications for how knowledge is conceived, owned and transmitted; this is because, in being rendered absent, objects come to form images that are possessed as mental resources or assets. How images are recollected, in turn, is affected by the choice of processes of erasure, such as dismantling, burning and leaving to rot, of which each has a specific effect on the nature of the mental resource constituted. Loisy's (1920) fitting observation, that the iconic or representational nature of the thing to be destroyed visualizes the processual nature of destruction itself, and

that this is essential to the 'magical' efficacy of the ritual act, directs us
to an alternative perspective on artworks such as *malanggan*. It shows
us the way to account for the nature of the form of objects not in terms
of a content that is extraneous to form, such as the social or spiritual
context of their production and circulation, but in terms of the *logical*
relation between the iconic description of processes that may at first
glance have nothing to do with each other.

What *malanggan*, bodies, and land share is, firstly, that they are a
container; secondly, that the container and the contained – the object
and its image, the bones and the skin, the cultivated and settled land –
can, and even must, be separated; and thirdly, that the method of separation is an incremental part of the thing itself, as it resonates in its
looks, its feel, its smell or its taste. That is, they share the same iconic
translation of the process of separation, this being inversion or the act
of turning a container inside-out, as we saw in the process of carving,
in the hardening and softening of bodies during life and after death,
and in the alternate use of land as garden (skin) and settlement (womb).
Yet they also share the same processes of reversing or unleashing
containment, described as the 'stripping' of skin', that de-animate an
animate thing in ways that both distance and retain its powers. These
processes are burning and leaving to rot.

This relation between cultural form and processes of erasure has been
overlooked in earlier studies of *malanggan* that attached significance to
owning *malanggan* 'with the eye', as it appeared to confirm Western
post-Renaissance assumptions of the optical or perceptual basis of
knowledge.[4] While seeing is important for the transmission of ritual
knowledge, it is, however, not sufficient to account for 'how' it is known.
This is because a sculpted *malanggan* image merely foreshadows relationships of ownership that only come into existence with, and are
dependent upon, the disappearance of the figure.

The leaving to rot of ritually de-animated *malanggan*-skins, whose
death has dramatically 'finished' the memory of deceased persons,
creates an olfactory domain that in itself cannot be recollected, but that
engenders spontaneous remembering when re-contained in 'skins':
shared between those who made and those who 'killed' them, 'skins'
are the common substance of a remembering that is incited through
the analogical and iconic relation between a present thing and its absent
counterpart. Woven *malanggan* that are burned 'alive', on the other
hand, leave no trace and thus cannot be recalled, but are only repeated;
there remains only a bodily memory that allows anyone who ever
participated in the weaving of a *malanggan* to know it intimately and

to be able to reproduce it at any time: being for ever present, and yet forgotten; the repetitive force effected by such erasure is also eminently useful as a conceptual 'trapping' device in magical performances.

Not only is the ownership of *malanggan* images conceived as coming into force almost after the fact, that is with the death of the figure and its ultimate disappearance from view; it also facilitates a conception of social relationships as grounded in absence. Only as mental resource can 'sources' of *malanggan* have the generative and reproductive capacity ascribed to them.

Permeable and odorous 'skins' are passed on as a mobile and inherently regenerative substance between and within severed parts of a matri-clan, and recreate its unity in a point-like, momentary and non-linear frame; this frame is spatial in character and created through the analogy that is drawn between material and spiritual (mental) domains; that is between wood and the seat of the ancestral spirit *moroa* beyond the horizon, between fibre and the spirits of the slain (*pue*) that dwell invisibly, and yet tangibly, in rain clouds, and between clay and the spirits of the bush (*rulrul*) that emanate from the ground in *masalei* places.

Only the ownership of images sculpted from wood is ever contested, and is in principle capable of sheer unlimited growth; images woven from fibre or moulded from clay, on the other hand, are the undisputed secret property of matri-clans that is known only to those who know how to recall them in the process of fabrication. The two forms of ownership, one active, the other passive, are thus interdependent and co-existent.

As was suggested by Simon Harrison (1995), our problem of disentangling Melanesian economies lies in our object-centred notion of property. Not only may property be image-based, but its transmission may depend less on the 'revelation' of the image than on the way the image is possessed through the method of deposition. The possibility of severing image from object and of thereby effecting an image-centred ownership is present in Strathern's (1991, 2001) and Wagner's (1986, 1987) accounts of the Melanesian image, yet is left unacknowledged because their analysis focuses on the revelatory practice of ritual performance and thus on the presentation, rather than the decomposition, of material artefacts.[5]

Gender and Flow of Property

Malanggan figures carved from wood, in fact, are significant from a religious and economic point of view, not because of their capacity for revelation, but because they *can* be 'killed' (*luluk*). The possibility of de-animation is grounded in their conception as 'skins', which is visualized in the permeable and perishable materials that are used for the sculpting of these membrane-like figures. The death of a figure, in analogy to the human body, is incurred by the removal of skin and the freeing of life-force. Yet, we may ask, how is this 'killing' done in other than metaphorical terms? For were it just metaphorical, de-animation would surely not possess the efficacy that is clearly attributed to it.

The agent apparently capable of executing this act of flaying is shell-money (*burut*), the hardly visible, secret and forgotten ritual artefact whose role in the ritual process is at least as important as that of the figures. Despite the wide availability of monetary currency, shell-money has not relinquished its importance in the work for the dead; on the contrary, the number of strings in circulation has dramatically increased since the late 1970s, when shell-money production became a widely known and practised skill.

The source of *malanggan* on Tabar island could not be further removed from that of the shell-money known as *burut,* and it is in this physical distance of their sources that the dynamic of *malanggan* resides. The shells (*Olivia textilia*) required for the manufacture of the strings are found along the north-west coast, but in the required quantities only in the Lamusmus and Lavolai area of north-west Kara. Until recently, the skill of shell-money manufacture was exclusively in the hands of women living in this area, and manufactured strings could only be acquired through exchange or bought with money. Today anyone may purchase beer bottles filled with the raw material in the market stalls in Kavieng or in local roadside stalls and make them in their own home.

The raw material of shell-money, small shells of red colour (*Olivia textilia*), is distinguished into two categories according to size: *ruwas* (small) and *dangap* (large). *Ruwas* are used for strings of shell-money called *tingerip*, which are passed down the generations 'inside' the house and are never used in exchanges. *Tingerip* are recognizable by their consistent colouring of red discs with white discs on either end. The larger shells, called *dangap,* are used to produce the strings of shell-money called *talamai,* which consist of alternating white and red discs.

The shell-money in circulation in the North is markedly shorter and less embellished than southern strings, which occasionally find their way north through marriages; these strings are manufactured in Lihir, often re-knotted in the Mandak area, and circulate as far south as Siar.[6] The Northern *burut* measures only the length of the lower arm and has no attachments, while the Lihir *baram* measures the length of the whole arm and has attachments that increase with the increasing circulation of the string. While *baram* are considered more valuable, they are never used for the work for the dead in the north. *Baram* are exclusively used in bridewealth payments with Mandak, and are considered prerequisite for such marriages.

One may thus ask what it is about *burut* that enables them alone to be used in the work for the dead, and specifically in the final climactic 'killing' of *malanggan*. One factor is certainly the geographical positioning of shell-money and *malanggan*, which is the subject of a widely told myth; this myth also points to the second factor, to be found in the genders attributed to *malanggan* and shell-money:

Once two men were living at Tabar. One of the men was married to a woman from Simberi island, the other was married to a piece of wood that he had cut and carved. Today, this wooden piece is called Malanggan. *The wood never did anything, but slept in the house all day and all night. The real wife, on the other hand, prepared food and worked in the garden together with her husband, just as all married people do. The man married to the real wife thought, I wonder what this woman is doing all day in her house so that I have never seen her face? He decided to ask the other man about the whereabouts of his wife. The man replied, 'Oh, my wife is just here.' – 'Does she cook?', the other man demanded to know. 'No', said the husband of the piece of wood, 'she just sleeps inside the house.' Intrigued, the husband of the real woman went at night into the house of the other man to find out for himself; as he lay down next to the woman he exclaimed, 'Oah, why is she so hard?' Thus he discovered that the wife of the other man was made from wood.*

The man with the wooden wife possessed a string made out of a vine called teresi; *the man with the real wife, however, possessed shells tied on to strings. Seeing the basket of shells, the man married to the* Malanggan *became hot with desire. When once the two men were walking towards the seashore, the husband of* Malanggan *suggested that they engage in a competition as to who could dive for a longer time. He went ahead first, dived while counting, and returned to the shore. Now it was the turn of the husband of the real wife to dive. While he was under the water, the husband of the* Malanggan *grabbed the basket of shells and ran. When the other man reappeared on the surface, he discovered that his basket with the shells had been stolen. He went into the house to get a string with which people used to throw stones at times of a fight. He shot a stone towards the direction in which the man had escaped; the first stone separated Tabar into what is called today Tatau and Big Tabar, while the second stone separated Tabar from the mainland so that it became an island. The husband of the* Malanggan, *however, had already reached the north-west coast, where today there is the village Lamusmus. Since then* Malanggan *comes from Tabar, while shell-money comes from the coast of Lamusmus.*

This myth is revealing in many ways: deceit and trickery are held to be the cause of the experience of rupture and physical distance that constitutes people's perception of social relationships in New Ireland. Shell-money reveals what *malanggan* lacks; a lack that is partially reflected in the immobility of the wooden wife, partially in the bare string possessed by the *malanggan*'s husband. While the myth does not tell us what *malanggan* is lacking, it addresses the open secret that it is not *malanggan* that is desired, but shell-money, causing *malanggan* to move in search of it.

Shell-money, which was appropriated by *malanggan*'s husband, symbolizes 'female' reproductive powers in ways only implicit in the conception of *malanggan* figures as 'skins'. This is because shell-money is considered *burut* or 'pregnant', and like food prepared for those about to conceive life, it is made by women who are considered wet. And yet, shell-money is also likened to bones and thus to 'male' substance. *Burut*, moreover, incites an analogy with fertility as it smells salty (*mopak*), like the sea, which delivers *moroa*'s goodwill, and like women in their 'wet' period when they are able to conceive. The same olfactory quality comes to be embodied in *malanggan* figures as a result of the ingestion of odorous food by the carver, and is finally set free with the decomposition of the figure, but is not a primary quality of the material used for carving. It is almost as if the carving of *malanggan* seeks to emulate the manufacture of shell-money to secure the impregnation of its material with the powers that are attributed to the shells.

There are six stages to the production of shell-money, which gradually comes to life in the course of this process: (1) The shells collected in the lagoon are wrapped in leaves of the pandanus palm (*haum*). The bundles are heated over the fire (*tune*). (2) The meat is removed from the shell and the shells are left to dry. (3) The shells are broken into pieces (*wagil*). (4) Holes are drilled through the centre of the pieces by using branches of a tree called *mediget* (the tree is said to die when it has reached a certain height and is planted around the grass-free area of the *rune malei*). (5) The pieces are filed on a stone (obsidian) called *benat* buried afterwards next to a *baral*. (6) The pieces (*ruwas*) are pulled on to a string called *wuap* made out of vine. Of these stages it is the filing with obsidian that causes shell-money to come alive in the process of its production, as a *malanggan* carving does through the incising of holes with heated instruments.

Benat are either washed ashore along the west coast or have to be acquired through trade from as far away as New Britain; their most important use is as the base of a stone-oven. Frequent heating of the oven turns these stones into the white powdered substance called *but*, which is the essence of the potent white paste called *kambang* that when eaten together with areca nut has a distinct revitalizing effect, expressed in symptoms of feeling hot and active. *Benat* also encircle the uprooted tree-trunk called *baral*, and thus figuratively contain the recollective power ascribed to the spirits of the slain (*pue*). After having been treated with *benat*, shell-money is pure reproductive force, and considered too potent to be left in the open for any length of time.

Thus, unlike the necklaces or arm-rings of the Massim, *burut* is never worn on the body or displayed longer than necessary at ritual events. Almost as soon as it is put on a mat for the payment of a pig or an item of ritual paraphernalia, it is scooped up and disappears. *Burut* is guarded by elder women past the menopause for their brothers and sons, and less commonly for their husbands, in special purses (*sesewe*) that are kept hidden inside the house. This purse is made from the skin of the flying fox (*raiwung*), which is a creature that is assumed to be the embodiment of the spirits of the dead prior to their transformation into ancestors. More importantly, as was pointed out to me, the flying fox has no bones, but consists entirely of skin. Hidden inside the skin, strings of shell-money are wrapped in highly odorous leaves of plants called *hi* and *thai*, a body-like assemblage of skin and bone.

Sesewe contains both types of shell-money, yet one string of *tingerip* is separated from the rest in being pulled through a piece of tortoise shell. Over this *tingerip* a spell (*ngain*) has been performed that is thought to pull (*wangam*) back all the strings of shell-money that have left the purse. Unlike *talamai*, *tingerip* should always stay inside the house and remain hidden inside *sesewe*. Upon death, *sesewe* is secretly handed over at the time of a funeral; a father passes it on to a son who married back into his father's clan, and a mother to her eldest daughter.

There is a third type of shell-money that is contained inside this purse, never to leave it, except at death. Children of *piren* are given at birth a string of shell-money called *manun* (*ma*=active comparison, *nu(a)*=growth). *Manun* is made out of white discs with black discs on both ends. It is said to have come from Manus island in mythical times, and is not used in the exchanges of marriage or *malanggan*. The *manun* predisposes the child to become the future heir of *sesewe* upon the death of its father.

Shell-money is thus capable of killing *malanggan*-skins, because both embody female reproductive powers that, when shell-money is thrown at the base of the figure, cancel each other out. The effect of the clash of substances was likened to an account of what happens when a menstruating and 'hot' woman enters a garden during its 'hot' phase, which is marked by the appearance of the paloloworm (*mamaze*). The odour that during this time is directed to the gardens would escape, it is thought, as the clash of two things that are hot 'burns away the skin' that contains it. Yet what is left over in this clash between *malanggan* and shell-money is the 'male' substance enshrined in the 'bones' of shell-money. It is this 'left-over' that allows the process of the recollection and destruction of *malanggan* to be repeated indefinitely.

The Opening and Closing of Remembrance

The killing of *malanggan* is thus not an act that exists in isolation, nor is it the end. On the contrary, it is merely the closing stage, literally the 'return' or *sorolis*, of a preceding cycle of opening gifts, while foreshadowing new opening gifts in its wake. These opening gifts are given 'for free' or *aradem*, and are thought to create rather than respond to existing debt-relationships. Acts of *aradem* thus effect a remembrance that becomes part of the sequence of events that transforms a settlement as its work advances. Rather than a single act, *aradem* therefore denotes a continuous process of giving that is initiated with the burial of a person and returned in a momentary act of *sorolis*. *Sorolis* can occur sometimes as many as twenty years later, when the work for the dead is finished inside a local cemetery.

Since the advent of the fractal person in Melanesian anthropology, it is generally taken for granted that acts of decomposition of multiply authored persons create, for the brief space of a moment, the appearance of singly authored entities that alone are capable of reproduction (cf. Strathern 1988). While this is certainly also the case in *malanggan* (in the move from affinal, to sibling, to clan relationships in the course of the funerary cycle), the sacrifice of *malanggan* also suggests a further dimension.

Nothing could better visualize the 'dividual' person than the *malanggan*-figure, as it stands animated on the grave: it is pure 'skin' and yet resembles in its form the multiple relations of *korok* and their contribution to the animation of a person as a being with talents, names and offices. Its death and decomposition result in the 'birth' of the ancestor, reflected in the image of the clan. As singular, undifferentiated entity, the clan embraces the capacity to self-reproduce. And yet, like the skin-shedding snake identified with the clan, it is also incapable of growth and accumulation. Nothing new can come from it, as it is condemned to renew itself. This, as it is said, happens when a *malanggan* is 'killed' 'inside' a *dahun*, allowing images merely to be 'repeated' in forms that resemble the previous ones. Only when *malanggan* is 'killed' by those outside the *dahun* can effective recollection take hold and an image be projected in its 'new' and self-sufficient second or third dimension.

Thus the act of 'killing' and the process of decomposition is inseparable from the act of reproduction. It is, moreover, the material and visual nature of the thing thus decomposed that imparts its character to the entity thus created. By shifting the emphasis from person to object, and from reproduction to decomposition, *malanggan* suggests a logical development of the model of the fractal person – in that not remembrance, but forgetting ensures the future.

The Opening of *Aradem*

Between the first burial inside a new cemetery and *malanggan* many years pass, in which all thoughts are directed at inciting indebtedness. Village-based *maimai* are the spokesmen for acts of giving things as *aradem*, but it is the clan-based *maimai* that act as organizers of the massive prestation of returns at *malanggan*. Both *maimai*, who occasionally may be one and the same person, also supervise the work to be expected from anyone in the settlement and the village of the deceased person in the years following a funeral. The extent of the work, however, depends on whether anyone feels morally obliged to take on this work in more than a cursory fashion.

Detailed notebooks are kept about when, where and in what form items were either received or given as *aradem* in anticipation of their future return in *sorolis*. Acts of *aradem* are distinguished into a number of named types, of which each specifies the timing and the amount of return. These four modes of giving are called *haroien*, *hamasgibel*, *hamasak* and *wurpuran;* they address progressively encompassing and simultaneously exclusive, because clan-based, relationships built up in the course of the ritual cycle.

Haroien is the first of these acts of giving 'for free', and is performed at the funeral. The term means literally 'to cause good feeling', and addresses through the prestation *korok* relationships that were tied to the deceased person. The clan relatives of a deceased man who assisted his wife's siblings consistently during his lifetime in the work for the dead are the subject of the payment at his own funeral. *Haroien* is thought to be a return of the marriage payment retained by the bride's siblings as *aradem* during the marriage ceremony, and thus starts the gradual dismantling of *korok* relationships that defines the work to be done in the years to come.

The funeral is also the occasion of *hamasgibel*, which addresses relationships of nurture and their imminent effacement as the work for the dead progresses inside the cemetery. The presentation is made during the funeral of a person who adopted a child and is returned at the funeral of the person who had been the subject of the adoption. *Hamasgibel* can also be given for the care of the elderly or the ill. As with *haroien*, in *hamasgibel* the presentation of shell-money, currency and the head of a pig answers an existing interpersonal relationship and redefines the relationship as a debt relationship between units of siblings, rather than between individuals.

Hamasgibel literally means 'to cause parts to be one', and refers to the intermarriages encouraged between adopted offspring. Units tied through *hamasgibel* describe their relationship as one of moving together. It is not marriage that keeps them together, but the exchange of children in adoption and the exchange of *hamasgibel* at the death of a foster-parent and foster-child.

Hamasak is given during ritual events leading to marriage (*sesemangil* – 'the buying of shame') and during events leading to *malanggan* (*haram gom* and *gisong*). Those who are given *hamasak* are classified as *korok*. The return of *hamasak* is called *hamarere*. In the funerary cycle, *hamasak* is exclusive to two events, *haram gom*, the burning of the house, and *gisong*, the end of mourning, to be returned as *hamarere* at *malanggan*. In *haram gom*, *hamasak* is a presentation of raw food (taro or sweet-potato), pork and money exchanged between units of siblings of the same clan as the deceased person, of the same village, but of a different history of land-holding settlement. In *gisong*, *hamasak* is extended with a prestation of cooked food, pork and currency. It is now given separately by brothers and sisters of the deceased person to their own *korok* who have ties to the same land through *kiut*, who in turn will not consume the prestation, but pass it on to their own *korok*. Anyone who received a prestation of *hamasak* is obliged to make return on the morning of the third day of *malanggan* with prestations of raw food and live pigs given as *hamarere*, which are cooked during the last night of *malanggan* inside clan-specific cooking-houses. Each house prepares a single *rut*, a giant parcel of two metres in diameter that is wrapped in *pandanus* leafs and placed inside the cemetery next to *malanggan* after its revelation on the last day.

Hamasak is thus a process, rather than a single presentation, that aims at extending the inclusiveness of social relationships associated with the 'skin' nexus. During *malanggan, hamarere* demonstratively takes on the form of *rut,* which, as large wrapped and cooked parcels with a content exclusively consisting of taro from clan-based stock, visualize the matri-clan in an unparalleled olfactory manner that provides a telling commentary on the departure of the smell-canoe that is announced with the opening and scattering of their contents.

The more people are given *hamasak* during the events of the funerary cycle, the more spectacular will be the display of wealth associated with individual clans in the killing of *malanggan. Hamasak* thus foreshadows the spatial dimension of *malanggan* in terms of its monumentality, visible in the number of cooking-houses built around the central place, in the number of *rut,* and in the number of successive presentations of money to the *malanggan.* The exchange is distinguished from all others in that the return has to be at the same place and during the same sequence of funerary events.

Wurpuran is distinguished from *hamasak* in that both the item and the amount of the return are specified in the presentation. Its return, moreover, is not expected to be given in the same sequence of funerary events, but at the same type of event. A string of shell-money given as *purai* during a funeral, for example, has to be returned at the burial in the recipient's funerary enclosure. A pig returned as *purai* has to be of the same size and has to be accompanied with the same amount of shell-money and money as the initial presentation.

In *hamasak* the debt relationships established in the exchange correspond to an affinal or *korok* relationship based on current marriages. *Wurpuran* is given between units of siblings whose relatedness is framed much more generally in terms of remembered co-residence or remembered assistance in the work for the dead, as it sprang from such co-residence. It is thus given between settlements, rather than between individuals. Those who receive *wurpuran* thus include the widest possible extension of a *dahun* and the most spatially and temporally extended usufructory rights to land. To receive *wurpuran,* a settlement has to be known to be involved in separate, but similar types of work. *Wurpuran,* for example, is given at a funeral if the recipients are expected to have a funeral within their own cemetery some time in the future. The *wurpuran* will be returned as *susuang* at the funeral event organized in the recipient settlement. Without reference to the life-cycle marked by the event, the interval between giving and receiving seems to exempt time in favour of space. It is not how long ago *wurpuran* was given that is remembered, but which social space was marked at the occasion when it was given.

By contrast with *hamasak*, in *wurpuran* the place of giving and of return is removed in space, but ranked on the same level of the temporal sequence of events leading to marriage and *malanggan*. *Wurpuran* thus generates a spatial hierarchy in the ritual sequence, while *hamasak* generates the necessity for one event to be followed by another in the temporal hierarchy of ritual events. The differing perception of the interval between giving and returning in *hamasak* and in *wurpuran* is related to a different notion of the morality of exchange and of social sanctions following the failure to return. Should *hamasak* not be returned, the unit is excluded over time from the right to use the cultivated land by becoming unpopular marriage partners. Men have to marry out and risk not being able to stay on their own land, because of the lack of effective *korok* or debt relationships. If *wurpuran* is not returned, the sanctions are violence and the rupture of social relations between settlements. The inability to return *wurpuran* affects the ability to organize exchanges of *malanggan* with those outside the immidiate *dahun*. In *hamasak*, therefore, the obligation to return is phrased in terms of social criteria based on actual ties of *korok*. In *wurpuran*, on the other hand, the obligation to return does not involve social, but moral, criteria, and is sanctioned with expulsion and even violence.

The Closing or *Sorolis*

When the time is right to think about *malanggan* for one's own cemetery, much thought is given to reconsidering how successfully *aradem* have been placed since the first burial in its cemetery. How much is expected to be returned will decide whether one can even contemplate 'killing' *malanggan* from outside one's own *dahun* in an act called *sorolis*. The desire to do so is usually prompted by the need to expand rights to land or simply by the lack of any existing rights to *malanggan*. The decision to go outside may be taken jointly by all those resident in a settlement who have buried their dead in the same cemetery.

The planning for *sorolis* with those outside one's *dahun* is the more likely the older the initiating residents of a settlement are. Those who are younger will be intent on passing on as *meme* rights to *malanggan*-images they already own either partially or completely to their children or sister's children; *sorolis* is in this case conducted inside the *dahun*. While both forms of *sorolis* involve the 'killing' of *malanggan*, the form given to an image when it is shaped inside the enclosure will depend on for which of the two presentations it has been conceived.

Sorolis is an act of undoing or finishing that culminates in the death of *malanggan*. 'Killed' are *meut*, the mourning over the dead prior to the burial, the dancing of *buma* with the coffin to the grave, the making of the *sebedou* enclosure out of bamboo and wood (*vei a sebedou*), the 'skins' of *malanggan*, including gravestones (*smel*), the *malanggan* house (*luhu*), the songs and dances performed at any stage in the ritual process and the manner of food-distribution. As an act of finishing, *sorolis* engenders relationships that are not grounded in indebtedness, but formal sameness; those who are 'strangers' (*namsei*) are turned into those of one growth. The sharing one skin (*namam retak*) takes the form of a process that is strung out over the many stages of the ritual work.

This process is initiated with the finishing of ritual services through *sorolis* that are conducted between opposite parts of the village and between village pairs; an example is the *sorolis* of a *meut* or mourning in Panachais village on the north-west coast. Panachais is divided into an upper part, known as Belifu, and a lower part known by the name under which the village is now known in official records. Of its many resident clans, Morumbalus and Morokomaf are resident in opposite parts of the village, whose land was originally owned by Morumuna, to which both are related. At the funeral of a man of Moromuna in the cemetery of Morumbalus, Morumbalus 'killed' the *meut* carried out by Morokomaf; Morokomaf, in turn, will invite Morumbalus to carry out a *meut* in its own cemetery and seek to 'kill' it in the same manner. The passing on of ritual work between spatial domains thus effects an official neutrality and relatedness.

Gravestones, house-forms, dances and images of *malanggan*, on the other hand, are finished by villages in opposite parts of the locality (northern vs southern Kara, East vs West Kara) or between parts of New Ireland distinguished geographically (Tabar vs mainland) or linguistically (Kara vs Nalik). Their construction, death and destruction form the second phase of the ritual work that expands and consolidates the formal relation between spatial domains.

Sorolis thus precipitates the regional expansion of the matri-clan by effecting and increasing the spatial inclusiveness of endogamous units. Places that grow separate *dahun* are made alike by sharing a 'skin' of *malanggan* that was taken in a *sorolis* prestation. However, as each *sorolis* is inevitably followed by new marriages and the setting up of new *dahun* through *kiut*, the ritual conglomerates thus created are fleeting phenomena and are only too quickly superseded by the new direction of ritual work initiated in the newly created post-*malanggan* settlement.

This final act of *sorolis* is distinguished into two types. The first finishes the generative capacity attributed to a *malanggan*-source and grants those who carry out the act of 'killing' the right to generate variations of the 'skin' snatched in this way, while the second aims at the finishing of the content of a source in a bit-by-bit fashion.

The finishing of the generative capacity of a source is considered the most expensive act of *sorolis:* what is finished in *sorolis* is not just the sculpted 'skin', but the house in which it is displayed, the fence surrounding the burial place, the songs sung during its revelation, the dances and masks associated with the *malanggan*-name, and the manner of distributing food. Such a *sorolis* has to be repeated at least once for it to be completed; a *malanggan* carved for the occasion will under these circumstances be wrapped and hidden (*kowebag*) under the roof of the house, to be reused for work within the same cemetery until the *sorolis* is completed to satisfaction.

Sorolis of this kind are mostly conducted with Tabar or with clans that have known ties to one of Tabar's three islands. It is strictly possible only as a transaction that relates severed parts of a clan that may not have any existing relationships other than the memory of a common migration history that often reaches back into the distant times of warfare. The following list gives the names of Tabar clans and the known locations on the mainland to which they 'exported' sources of *malanggan* through *sorolis*:

Sipeo (Tatau/Simberi)	Lossu (Notsi), Lugagon (Nalik)
Bungpikila (Tatau)	Lamusong (Notsi), Langanir (Notsi), Hamba (Notsi), Lossu (Notsi)
Sateri (Tatau)	Lossu (Notsi), Tandis (Notsi)
Keis (Tatau/Simberi)	Kafkaf (Nalik), Lugagon (Nalik), Utu (Tigak), Lamusmus (Kara), Panamafei (Kara), Djaul island, Lihir island, Panatkin (Mandak)
Barok Zeremengis (Simberi)	Medina (Nalik), Mangai (Kara), Paruai (Kara)
Kuk (Tatau/Simberi)	Munawai (Nalik), Lugagon (Nalik), Lemakot (Kara)
Kis (Tatau)	Lugagon (Nalik)
Zizim (Tatau)	Fatmilak (Nalik)
Damok (Tatau/Simberi)	Panatkin (Mandak), Fatmilak (Nalik), Medina (Nalik), Kafkaf (Nalik),Lugagon (Nalik), Munawai (Nalik), Paruai (Kara), Mangai (Kara), Maiom (Tigak)

Whenever an image is carved into wood to be killed in *sorolis* it is called out for (*nungnung*). The owner of the image thus approached travels to the settlement in which the *malanggan* is to take place and directs the carver at every step in the shaping of the image. If the intent of his host is to kill in *sorolis* not just his sculpted image, but the generative capacity of its source, the method of recall he uses in re-calling the image will be that of 'projection'. Those who own a source in the shape of a vertical stem will recall it in the shape of a horizontal branch, and those who own it as a branch will recall it in a figurative shape likened to a leaf-bearing branch.

Thus, while the source is alienated in reproducing it for *sorolis*, the method of partitioning serves to retain effective and undiminished rights over the generative capacity of the source. The inalienability of the source allows both transacting parties to be seen as linked in a fundamental way; coming to share in a 'source' is like becoming 'one growth' and thus one clan.

While it is most prestigious to acquire source rights from outside one's *dahun* and thus to expand its range, the passing on of the contents of a source within the *dahun* is of equal importance, and likewise only accomplished through *sorolis*. There is a marked regional variation in the practice of this *sorolis* between Tabar and the mainland; this difference cannot be stressed enough, as it has a profound impact on the social relations conceptualized in terms of the ownership of *malanggan*.

On Tabar, where sources are known by their content, this content has to be finished bit by bit, or in 'bites' known as *meme*. This process of finishing starts in infancy with the simplest part of the source, and culminates in adulthood with the finishing of the most complex image in the shape of a branch or stem (Gunn 1987). Clan land and the source of *malanggan* literally stay in one place. Thus, from a Tabar perspective, nothing moves.

On the mainland, however, sources are owned in their generative capacity acquired through *sorolis* from Tabar. This generative capacity enables people to innovate variations and thus to create the content of a source over time. Yet in contrast to Tabar, the images that are thus produced out of a source for acts of *sorolis* do not stay within the *dahun* or even the village, but tend to be acquired through a network of *korok* relationships. The images linked to one source are thus dispersed across the mainland. While in Tabar one is given a string of names when inquiring into a *malanggan* source, on the mainland one is directed to the kinds of variations that were innovated, yet over which one has only limited control. This is because any one of the *korok* who have acquired an image produced out of a generative source may in turn reproduce it and pass it on at another *sorolis*.

Thus the source is passed on as *meme* on the mainland not vertically, that is from one generation to another in a sequential manner, but horizontally, that is between affinal siblings in a discontinuous and momentary fashion. One's *meme* is thus scattered, reconstituting the unity of the clan in a decidedly spatial manner.

A *malanggan* to be finished as *meme* on the mainland is re-created according to the kinds of relationships over land that become the basis for acts of remembering (*mamaluhen*) in any future work for the dead. The image is 'produced out' of the generative source as a variation if it is to be finished by a *dahun* that shares the memory of co-residence in one of the former mountain villages. Those who hold variations share specified usufructory rights to land with those who own the generative capacity of the source. Such usufructory rights, which include the right to plant gardens and the control of the allocation of plots, as well as fishing and hunting rights, have to be reasserted in every generation through repeated acts of *sorolis*.

Variations, in turn, can be passed on to others as *meme* in subsequent acts of *sorolis*. Thus, one variation of *Langmanu* has come to be shared in this way by people of different clan identity who once lived together at *Labolehai* in the Pratrehat area, but who live today in different villages along the east and west coasts. Owning different variations, rather than the same variation, is seen as marking distinctions drawn between different *dahun* while allowing them to share virtually indistinguishable land rights.

As owning a variation does not necessarily imply the capacity to generate out of the image new variations, it can only be used in a limited fashion to extend equally more limited and often local usufructory rights to land. Those who acquire a fragment of a variation through *sorolis* share rights to harvest fruit-bearing trees and the reef with those whose *malanggan* they finished.

One example is the variation of a source of a spirit canoe, with figures sitting inside, that was given as variation from Paruai to Luburue. A *malanggan* of this kind collected in Paruai around 1910, now part of the Stuttgart collection, may be the *malanggan* through which source rights were acquired from Tabar. Nobody remembers how exactly the image reached Luburue village, yet it is clear that over the last twenty years it was reproduced by the clan Morokala in Luburue in several fragments for *sorolis* with its *korok*. Today, Morokals owns merely one of the six figures that originally composed the image, which is known under the name Nowele. The other five were given away in successive *malanggan* events.

Thus, as a rule, the closer to the *dahun* in purely spatial but by implication also social terms those are to whom the call for *sorolis* is directed, the less expensive will be the anticipated act of finishing and the less complex is the image when it is recalled for carving. On the other hand, the more distant in spatial and social terms, the more self-sufficient and generative an image becomes as it is projected into its new dimensions. An example is the case of Moromah of Lamusmus 1, who used the friendship between one of their men and a man from Simberi island in Tabar that grew out of their joint period working as policemen in Rabaul around the turn of the century to elicit the carving of a Tabar *malanggan* when one of the men died in Lamusmus. While it is not verifiable, a *malanggan* that reached the Basle collection through Alfred Buhler around 1932, who collected it at Lamusmus, was locally identified as the image that is owned by Moromah in Lamusmus. The image is known as *Lalambais* of the source known as *Tsur Varim*, which is recognized by the knotting of the feather-like paloloworm and snake around the head of a bird. Lamusmus considers itself to 'own' the image, and in recalling it in new forms does not have to remember its original Tabar owners, who are, in fact, forgotten.

The analogy between the source of a *malanggan* (*wune*) and a water-well or spring illuminates the need to forget in order to remember. The analogy is even more vivid in the north, where rivers flow underground to resurface in waterholes again and again until they merge with the ocean. Like a river whose flow one cannot see, but can retrace through its point-like appearances, the interrupted flow of images of *malanggan* conditions the *mamaluhen* or remembrance through which 'gatherings' are brought into being.

Image-based sources of *malanggan* thus enable the retracing and rewriting of connections on an *ad hoc* and inherently momentary and thus fluid basis (cf. Clifford 1988: 15). This is because the closing of remembrance, enacted in the 'killing' of *malanggan*, negates all previous relations invoked by the sharing of 'skin' and replaces them with new ones. These new relations over land, labour and loyalty are now attested not by the sharing of 'skin' but by the sharing of an absent, remembered image. It is thus ultimately the sacrifice, and forgetting, of *malanggan* that enables connections to prevail where once there stood at least potentially divisive relations. In order for this as it were 'negative' remembrance to have legislative powers, however, the image needs to be recalled in new 'skins' from time to time. Over time, relations that are defined in association with image-based sources of *malanggan* thus have a tendency to expand through a process of incorporation.

At the same time, the proliferation of 'introverted' 'skins' that are recalled in a bit-by-bit fashion inside the clan, involving the repetition, rather than transformation, of the image leads to endemic conflict. In fact village courts, which meet monthly, are rife with complaints of the theft of an image. Sometimes, such accusations are brought up at a *malanggan* ceremony, when neighbouring villages may witness the display of a figure to whose image they consider themselves to have exclusive rights. Sometimes, the pressure on garden land is so great that accusations over the theft of land lead to elaborate trials about rights to images. We can see in *malanggan* in operation the effects of, as Simon Harrison has recently called it, an identity that is a 'scarce resource' (Harrison 1999). Where identity is not plentiful, but limited, tension breaks out not between, but within, groups over the material markers of this identity.

Endogamous ideology, an image-based economy of memory and a proliferation of material markers of identity thus provide an explosive nexus of social relations. And yet, *malanggan* also provides a solution to its own problem. As in fourteenth- and fifteenth-century France and England, where the rapid adoption of 'the king's two bodies' changed forms of governance into cumulative and expansive images of a self-fashioning identity, death and forgetting have opened visions of a new beginning. Expansive and image-based polities built on the sacrifice of *malanggan* and ritualized forgetting have secured the hidden abode where relations of loyalty, of labour and of land could thrive away from the eyes of colonial and missionary forces (cf. Feeley-Harnik 1991). It is the networking capacity of these polities, expanding like the knotted fishnet through a myriad of nodal points, which are always on the move to someplace else and are always looking ahead rather than behind, that supported the social relations upon which independence came to be founded.

Notes

1. Bataille (1955, 1988). See also Küchler (1988, 1997). For studies on sacrificial gift exchange see Codere (1964) and Gregory (1980). For a critique on theories of gift exchange see also Carrier (1992).

2. See also Kooijman (1984) on the ritual deposition and leaving to rot of ancestor poles among the Mimika.

3. See also my own argument on *malanggan* (Küchler 1988, 1997).

4. For a poignant discussion of the Aristotelian legacy of the relation between seeing, knowing and creating foregrounded in eighteenth- and nineteenth-century Europe see Kemp (1990: 221–59).

5. See also Foster's (1993) account of exchange in Tangan mortuary feasting as revelatory practice.

6. See B. Clay (1986: 192–5) on Mandak shell-money.

Conclusion

Death, we might say, is not without analogue in New Ireland. For *malanggan* enable one to envision a parallel world after death. It is this world that empowers and sustains the living. Perceived as a process, rather as an event, death is, moreover, not the end of the life-course, but an intrinsic part of it. In finishing 'the work for the dead', one thus does not remember a past that is gone for ever, but remembers to forget in order to re-create a new present and a new beginning.

'Made as skin', *malanggan* were shown to capture visually the workings of a body politic that seeks to replace the mortal body with an immortal soul whose legislative powers are embedded in generative and reproductive images. The notion of 'skin' emerged as the pivotal agent in the fashioning of this resource, which is capable of self-renewal as well as of accumulation. Yet 'skin' is not just a concept, but is visually and materially activated as a spatial container as well as a process of containment in ways that allow associative links to relate body, land and image. This visual amplification of a 'skin' nexus allowed matri-lineal identity to emerge alongside an ideology of endogamy that amplifies processes of growth as processes of absorption. As recollected images become 'skin' to absorb the life-force of the recent dead, they come to be seen, for a brief moment, as enduring reminders of a world 'in which one keeps to oneself', untouched by death and distinction. And yet, as is acknowledged in the 'death' of *malanggan*, it is the death of the object that alone is able to turn renewal into the potent site of re-collection.

Malanggan are a poignant example of Alfred Gell's theory of the cognitive stickiness of artworks, which allows objects to be the vehicle of a technology of enchantment (1992, 1996). This is because the synthesis, in *malanggan*, of the mental and the material, of memory and of carving, creates the basis for the quasi-'magical' efficacy of the ritual act of making and 'killing'; yet it is the iconic or representational

187

nature of the thing to be destroyed, visualizing the processual nature of destruction itself, that ensures that the process can be repeated many times over. The death of the object and the birth of an image that is self-reflexive and self-organizing provide the trajectory from which an exchange with the invisible can be subsumed under the work for the dead, allowing for the dead to be distanced and yet to remain 'attached' to the living. The form of the *malanggan*-effigy is thus not a representation that refers to something external to itself, but effects the recall of what was previously rendered absent in its own prior destruction (ancestral power being at the same time the image that is 'found' in the carving of *malanggan*). Illuminated by this power, representation in *malanggan* works like a hologram, in that the form of *malanggan* can be reflected into a second and third dimension, while still maintaining the possibility of repetition and fragmentation of a given form.

We might say that the real artwork in the North of New Ireland is the knot that is found in fishnets, in 'bound' houses and in the knotted head-dresses of *malanggan*-dancers, for it is here that the vision of alternative realities receives a tangible presence. The projecting of forms in the carving of new *malanggan* emulates the knot that can be transformed and represented in a second and third dimension while still retaining resemblance and thus connection with its basic form. Both encapsulate, materially and conceptually, a system of nodal networks on which image-based polities have come to model themselves. The proliferation of material markers of identity that was shown to be a product of an endogamous ideology, a shortage of identity, and an economy of memory, is thus turned, at least occasionally, into a source, not of tension, but of expansion.

Barbara Stafford (1999) has recently argued that analogy is inherently visual. With this statement she focuses our attention on one of the most central issues confronting our time, which is the need to re-visualize how we create attachments. We have, as she argues, unquestioningly relied on organic models of attachment, stressing notions of kinship and body, that have grown out of eighteenth-century Enlightenment thought. The model of the organism has left us with a legacy of assumptions that evoke dis-analogy, distinction and contradiction as the basis for an understanding of the nature of relation. We live surrounded by the legacy of dis-analogy and distinction when we shop and move about our daily business, faced with 'the homogeneous aloofness of cult initiates and gated communities addressing only themselves within a mosaic in which arguing groups exclusively seek to promote their separate interests' (Stafford 1999: 3).

Against the odds, however, resemblance and connection, for long banished to the pre-modern, to childhood and the feminine space of the domestic, resurfaced on the horizon of inter-media communication as key figures in a world where the material and the intellectual are not at odds. With this newly emerging notion of a relation between image and thought, the Platonic notion of the image as a 'shadow' cast on the cave wall, tricking the mind with false pretences, is becoming increasingly untenable (Mitchell 1996).

It is tempting to treat the ethnography of *malanggan* as the story of an art found in some place else, as a kind of microscopic tool from which to re-envision our own future. Yet we cannot claim that we have 'discovered' its virtues by waking up to the complexities of intellectual economy, allowing it to become a 'mirror' of our own concerns, for we are deeply implicated in what *malanggan* is or has become. *Malanggan*, as I have argued in the preceding pages, is not an ancient tradition, but an answer to oppression using the shared humanitarian concern over commemorating the dead to sustain hidden relations of labour, land and loyalty. It was, however, not just the common concern over the mortality of the body that provided the cover behind which much activity took place. At least an equally significant role was arguably played by the Modernist fascination with the animation of the present, which rendered *malanggan* figures into unique 'gifts' that facilitated an exchange between this world and an unseen, yet equally material, one. What we bought as art, New Irelanders did not 'lose', but designed as fitting agents in an exchange with the invisible through which hope for a new present and future could be envisioned. Resistance was thus built up not through confrontation, but through encompassment, by turning death, distinction and destruction into inspirational moments of a new beginning (cf. Strathern 1990).

The incredible number of figures we have in our collections might allow one to assume that *malanggan* are produced as a function of the existence of a specific 'art' institution. One could therefore think that *malanggan* could only be analysed in relation to the dynamics of an art market that is beyond the control of indigenous peoples. Unfortunately, straightforwardly true as it might at first sound, this assumption erects barriers between 'them' and 'us' that further hide the real engagement 'they' have with 'us'. It would be entirely wrong to treat *malanggan* as an instance of 'ethnographic' or 'non-Western' art whose reception and appropriation we can analyse with a sociological model, for we would thereby distort its autonomy and its agency (cf. Gell 1998: 8–9). Similarly, were we to attribute a semiotic or aesthetic analysis to *malanggan*, we would lose sight of the complex relation of resemblance between things and persons that is made visible in *malanggan*, not just in its formal but also in its performative qualities. Instead, the attribution of life and sensibility to an inanimate thing (wood and plant materials) calls for what Alfred Gell captured as an 'anthropological theory of art' that places at its centre 'problems to do with ostensibly peculiar relations between persons and "things" which somehow "appear as", or do duty as, persons' (Gell 1998: 9).

It is the visual and conceptual complexity of *malanggan* that invites us to reflect on the perhaps most central issues confronting anthropology theory in our time; these issues being exchange, memory and clearly art. Let me start with perhaps the most important of these issues, that of memory. When I first returned from fieldwork and set out to write about *malanggan*, I thought of *malanggan* as an objectified mnemonic technique that would work very much like Frances Yates's description of the workings of *memoria*. Following the classical text of *Ad Herennium*, captured by Yates's *Art of Memory*, I interpreted images as 'standing in', in a metaphorical sense, for ideas that people convey to each other in narrative form (Küchler 1987). I quickly realized, however, that one would thereby reflect on *malanggan* as if it were composed merely of the figures that we find in such abundance in our museums, when in fact these were just the hollow remains of an exchange initiated with the death of these figures (Küchler 1988). The task now was to understand much more fully the relation between representation and remembering, and to realize a very different relation between word, image and remembering, one that is not linear or referential, but point-like and re-collective. This other sense of representation was one that became increasingly important in my understanding of the data I continued to collect around the deposition of *malanggan* and the recollection of its images (Ginzburg 1991; Assmann and Harth 1993; Kantorowicz 1957).

Perhaps the most perplexing conclusion at which the study of *malanggan* is forced to arrive is that the extraordinary theatre of memory that we have enshrined in our museums is the result of a laborious and systematic work of displacement of objects by images. Unlike the increasingly object-centred notion of memory described by Pierre Nora, possessions in New Ireland are not treasured for the memories that are attached to them, but for their suitability in detaching, undoing and displacing relations between persons and things (Nora 1989). This detachment, ending in the climactic killing of *malanggan*, is not, however, creating oblivion, but a generative, image-based resource, access to which legitimized clan relations over property. It is an open secret in New Ireland that the matrilineal clan is the product of the separation of the mortal body from the immortal soul, which, as ancestrally sanctioned image, is open to intentional evocation, creating connections where divisions may once have reigned.

We find such image-based polities, that define rank and prestige, and regulate relations over land, labour and loyalty, elsewhere in the Pacific (Babadzan 1993; Guidieri and Pellizzi 1981). It might be no coincidence that they have in common an emphasis on the displacement of the dead, on ritualized forgetting through the 'un-wrapping' or 'flaying' of figurative imagery at the height of mortuary work. For it is in capturing a resemblance to corporeal processes that a material translation can be achieved between the world of the seen and the unseen so that what has been distanced through forgetting can also be 'found' in spontaneous or mnemic recollection through iconic representations that resemble the process of destruction. Thus it is that *malanggan* is not just known with the 'eye', but also with the 'nose', as its olfactory qualities entice to the recollection of what has been rendered absent.

Images that are created as resemblance achieve a translation between the material and the intellectual in ways that had profound implications for the handling of 'new' ideas such as Christianity. In New Ireland, the work of *malanggan* and Christianity were not just practised alongside each other, but Christianity found itself performed to resemble *malanggan*, in that efficacy was granted, not to words, but to images. When young New Ireland boys and girls dance up to the altar clad in *malanggan*-masks during their first communion, religious dogma is made tangible in the sights and sounds of the dancers. We may think of what *malanggan* may give to them in becoming persons, that words could not achieve. For this we need to return briefly to the two means of acquiring names and images of *malanggan*: the first, called *meme*, are names and images given to the child repeatedly as 'skins', while the second, called *sorolis*, involves going outside the group to incorporate a skin with its names and image-source attached. In both cases, images are learned deeply and significantly, since they are taking into themselves what is already in themselves as potential. One is reminded of Janet Coleman's (1992) exposition on Plato's theory of memory, in which she argues that, for Plato, nothing new of importance was ever learnt during life (cf. Bloch 1998–70). Learning is merely recalling what one already knew, but had forgotten, and is guided by what in Islamic theory is called 'mnemonic domination', using rote remembering as the technique of learning (Eickelman 1978: 489). Returning to the *malanggan*, we can see that it works very much like a text that is learnt by rote, memorized to the extent that merely smelling the pages and touching the spine of the book effects instant recall, making reading unnecessary. The point is not so much to see this concept of memory and of person in opposition to the Aristotelian model, which accentuates the accumulation of new memories throughout life, but to realize the importance assigned to the material and synaesthetic qualities that facilitate learning (Connerton 1992; Vinograd 1991). Clearly, models of semantic memory that have informed theories of learning have made the move of *malanggan* into the classrooms exceedingly difficult and have allowed the Churches to exploit a fertile ground (Bartlett 1932; Wertsch 1985; Luria 1976; Olsen 1977).

It should thus come as no surprise to find that the proliferation of different religious organizations on the island is increasing all the time. Thus, although villages were once divided up between the Methodist and the Catholic Churches, people have largely taken matters into their own hands. They search for and adopt what appears best suited to achieve the work of translation of new things and knowledge into an internalized potential, once exclusively carried out by *malanggan*. Some villages, or within certain villages, some settlements, thus may appear to have given up the work of *malanggan* in favour of whatever appears to 'work' equally well in relation to the realm of the 'unseen'. As some of these new ways involve the negation of exchange, this allows one in addition to fulfil the ideal of remaining by oneself. Yet, as this is not always very satisfactory for long, disenfranchising villagers from developing politically and economically important relations with those outside the village, very few villages have given up *malanggan* for any extended period of time.

Malanggan also engages questions of exchange, in that it forces us to reconsider the relation between persons and property forms. For in *malanggan* exchange value is grounded not in the object of exchange itself, but in an image that is the product of object sacrifice. The image's ability to move back and forth between the realm of the visible and the invisible through recollection reminds one of Annette Weiner's (1992) work on inalienable possessions, which accounts for the possibility of 'keeping while giving' with the presence of identity markers that somehow form an incremental part of objects of exchange. Annette Weiner thought of Pacific cloth, which, malleable and soft, portable and collectible, is also visually and conceptually analogous both to the body and to regenerative processes of life. Indeed, the perception of *malanggan* as knot suggests an interesting connection between cloth that is used for binding ties between two kinship groups, or different generations, and the 'bound' *malanggan*-image. Yet unlike cloth, *malanggan* allows for connections to be created beyond the immediate realm of kinship, because its connections only take root after its destruction. While Weiner's theory on the force behind the notion of reciprocity hinged on the assumption that proprietary rights are attached to the material carrier of heritage, *malanggan* illustrates the fact that the inverse may be the case, where the object in question represents the processes of its own destruction. Here, proprietary rights are attached to knowledge technologies that form an inseparable part of a political economy of memory. Its 'knowhow' is constantly transferred; in fact, it is dependent upon this process of transference (Strathern 2001).

The battle that ensues under these conditions, where ideas, not their expression, are copyrighted, was discussed recently by Simon Harrison (1999). He argued that the proliferation of identity markers is a symptom of identity's being a 'scarce resource', thus generating conflict within, and not between, social groups. This certainly is a valid description of the problems people encounter in New Ireland when faced with a myriad of recollections, each not much different from the other, and yet so intensely contested. And yet this perspective ignores something that is evident in *malanggan*, and this is the possibility of incorporating 'new' markers by 'forgetting' where they came from, while simultaneously using them to forge new connections. From a perspective that realizes the possibility of separating material expression and idea, a political economy of memory and a technology of enchantment could be said to provide the fuel for expansive social systems.

Perhaps the most important insight gained from studying *malanggan* is the realization that surfaces can be vehicles of thought in ways that we ascribe to living kinds only. The animate 'skins' of *malanggan* remind one of Nietzsche's exclamation 'Oh, those Greeks. They knew how to live. What is required for that is to stop courageously at the surface, the fold, the skin, to adore appearances, to believe in forms, tones, words, the whole Olympus of appearance. Those Greeks were superficial – out of profundity' (Nietzsche 1968[1886]). In New Ireland, as in pre-modern thought, nothing is inanimate, but able to affect thinking and being as it is fashioned as resemblance.

Bibliography

Adams, C. (1994), *The Knot Book: An Elementary Introduction to the Mathematical Theory of Knots*. New York: W. H. Freeman and Company.

Assmann, A., and D. Harth (eds) (1993), *Mnemosyne: Formen und Funktionen der kulturellen Erinnerung*. Frankfurt am Main: Fischer Taschenbuch Verlag.

Babadzan, A. (1993), *Les dépouilles des dieux: Essai sur le religion tahitienne à l'époque de la découverte*. Paris: Editions de la Maison des sciences de l'homme.

Barrow, J. (1992), *Pie in the Sky: Counting, Thinking and Being*. Oxford: Oxford University Press.

Bartlett, F. C. (1932), *Remembering: A Study in Experimental and Social Psychology*. Cambridge: Cambridge University Press.

Bataille, G. (1955), 'Hegel, la mort et le sacrifice.' *Deucalion* 5: 21–43.

—— (1988), *The Accursed Share: An Essay on General Economy*, trans. Robert Hurley. New York: Zone Books.

Battaglia, D. (1990), *On the Bones of the Serpent*. Chicago: University of Chicago Press.

Beaumont, C. H. (1972), 'New Ireland Languages: A Review.' *Papers in Linguistics of Melanesia, Pacific Linguistic Series A* 35: 1–41. Canberra: Australian National University.

—— (1976), 'Austronesian Languages: New Ireland.' *Papers in Linguistics of Melanesia, Pacific Linguistic Series A 41*: 387–97. Canberra: Australian National University.

Bickerman, E. (1929), 'Die römische Kaiserapotheose.' *Archiv für Religionswissenschaft* 27: 1–34.

Billings, D. (n.d.), 'Styles of Culture.' Unpublished Ph.D. thesis, University of Wichita.

Billings, D., and N. Peterson (1967), 'Malangan and Memai in New Ireland.' *Oceania* 38: 24–32.

Biskop, P. (1975), *Memoirs of Dampier*. Canberra: Australian National University, Pacific History Series.

Bloch, M. (1991), 'Language, Anthropology and Cognitive Science.' *Man (n.s.)* 26, no. 2: 183–98.

—— (1998), 'Internal and External Memory: Different Ways of Being in History,' in his *How We Think They Think: Anthropological Approaches to Cognition, Memory and Literacy*, pp. 67–85. Boulder, CO: Westview.

Bloch, M., and J. Parry (1982), 'Death and the Regeneration of Life,' in *Death and the Regeneration of Life*, ed. Maurice Bloch and Jonathan Parry, pp. 1–45. Cambridge: Cambridge University Press.

Blum, H. (1900), *Neu-Guinea und das Bismarckarchipelago: eine wissenschaftliche Studie*. Berlin: Schoenfeld and Co.

Bodrogi, T. (1967), 'Malangans in North-New Ireland: L. Biro's Unpublished Notes.' *Acta Ethnographica Academiae Hungaricae* 16: 66–77.

—— (1971), 'The Religious Significance of the Malangan Rites in North-New Ireland.' *Murelt Hagyomany* 13–14: 127–40.

Boluminski, F. (1904), 'Bericht des kaiserlichen Stationschefs Boluminski über den Bezirk Neu Mecklenburg.' *Deutsches Kolonialblatt* 15: 127, 134, 166–8.

Bolyanatz, A. H. (1994), 'Matriliny and Mortuary Feasting among the Susurunga of New Ireland, PNG.' Ph.D. diss., University of California, Berkeley.

Boyer, P. (1994), *Cognitive Perspectives on Religious Symbolism*. Cambridge: Cambridge University Press.

Braunholtz, H. J. (1927), 'An Ancestral Figure from New Ireland.' *Man* 27: 217–19.

Bredekamp, H. I.(1991), 'Du lebst und thust mir nichts,' in *Anmerkungen zur Aktualität Aby Warburgs. Aby Warburg: Akten des internationalen Symposions Hamburg*, ed. Horst Bredekamp, Michael Diers, and Charlotte Schoell-Glass, pp. 1–7. Weinheim: Acta Humaniora.

Brignoni, S. (1995), *Kunst der Südsee* (Exhibition catalogue, 1 February–8 March 1959). Lucerne: Kunstmuseum Luzerne.

Brown, G. (1877), 'Notes on the Duke of York Group, New Britain and New Ireland.' *Royal Geographical Society* 47: 137–50.

—— (1881), 'A Journey Along the Coast of New Ireland and Neighbouring Islands.' *Royal Geographical Society, Proceedings* 3: 213–320.

Brückner, W. (1966), *Bildnis und Brauch: Studien zur Bildfunktion der Effigies*. Berlin: Erich Schmidt Verlag.

Bühler, A. (1933), 'Totenfeste in Neuirland.' *Verhandlungen der schweizerischen Naturforscher Gesellschaft* 114: 243–70.

—— (1948), *Neuirland und Nachbarinseln*. Basle: G. Krebs.

Burkert, W. (1983), *Homo Necans: The Anthropology of Ancient Greek Sacrificial Ritual and Myth*, trans. Peter Bing. Berkeley, CA: University of California Press.

Carrier, J. G. (1992), 'The Gift in Theory and Practice in Melanesia: A Note on the Centrality of Gift Exchange.' *Ethnology* 31, no. 2: 185–93.

Carruthers, M. (1990), *The Book of Memory: The Study of Memory in Medieval Culture*. Cambridge and New York: Cambridge University Press.

Casey, E. S. (1987), *Remembering: A Phenomenological Study*. Bloomington, IN: Indiana University Press.

Chinnery, E. W. P. (1932), 'Studies of the Native Population of the East Coast of New Ireland.' *Anthropological Report of the Territory of New Guinea, 6*. Canberra: Government Printer.

Classen, C. (1993), *Worlds of Sense: Exploring the Senses in History and Across Cultures*. London and New York: Routledge.

Classen, C., D. Howes and A. Synnott (1994), *Aroma: The Cultural History of Smell*. London and New York: Routledge.

Clay, B. J. (1977), *Pinikindu: Material Nurture, Paternal Substance*. Chicago: University of Chicago Press.

—— (1986), *Mandak Realities: Person and Power in Central New Ireland*. New Brunswick, NJ: Rutgers University Press.

—— (1992), 'Other Times, Other Places: Agency and the Big Man in Central New Ireland.' *Man* (n.s.) 27, no. 4: 719–35.

Clay, R. B. (1974), 'Archaeological Reconnaisance in Central New Ireland.' *Archaeological and Physical Anthropology in Oceania* 9: 1–17.

Clifford, J. (1988), *The Predicament of Culture*. Cambridge, MA: Harvard University Press.

Codere, H. (1964), *Fighting With Property: A Study of Kwakiutl Potlatching and Warfare,1792–1930*, American Ethnological Society Monographs, 18. New York: [American Ethnological Society].

Coleman, J. (1992), *Ancient and Medieval Memories: Studies in the Reconstruction of the Past*. Cambridge: Cambridge University Press.

Connerton, P. (1992), *How Societies Remember*. Cambridge and New York: Cambridge University Press.

Corbin, A. (1986), *The Foul and the Fragrant: Odor and the French Social Imagination*. Cambridge, MA: Harvard University Press.

Davies, J. (1994), 'Introduction: Ancestors – Living and Dead,' in *Ritual and Remembrance: Responses to Death in Human Societies*, ed. Jon Davies, pp. 11–22. Sheffield: Sheffield Academic Press.

Davis, W. (1986), 'The Origins of Image Making.' *Current Anthropology* 27, no. 3: 193–214.

De Certeau, M. (1984), *The Practice of Everyday Life*, trans. Steven Rendall. Berkeley, CA: University of California Press.

De Coppet, D. (1980), 'The Life Giving Death,' in *Morality and Immortality*, ed. S. C. Humphreys and H. King, pp. 175–205. London: Academic Press.

Derlon, B. (1990), 'L'objet Malanggan dans les anciens rites funéraires de Nouvelle Irlande.' *Res* 19–20: 45–96.

Deutsches Kolonialblatt (1885), *Nachrichten über Kaiser Wilhelmland und dem Bismarck Archipelago*. Berlin.

Eickelman, D. F. (1978), 'The Art of Memory: Islamic Education and Social Reproduction.' *Comparative Studies in Society and History* 20: 485–516.

Elsner, J. and R. Cardinal (eds) (1994), *The Cultures of Collecting*. Cambridge, MA: Harvard University Press.

Feeley-Harnick, G. (1991), *A Green Estate: Restoring Independence in Madagascar*. Washington, DC: Smithsonsian Institution Press.

Forty, A. and S. Küchler (1999), *The Art of Forgetting*. Oxford: Berg.

Foster, R. J. (1990), 'Nurture and Force-Feeding: Mortuary Feasting and the Construction of Collective Individuals in a New Ireland Society.' *American Ethnologist* 17, no. 3: 431–48.

—— (1993), 'Dangerous Circulation and Revelatory Display: Exchange Practices in a New Ireland Society,' in *Exchanging Products, Producing Exchange*, ed. Jane Fajans, pp. 15–31 (Oceania Monograph 43). Sydney: University of Sydney.

Foy, W. (1910), 'Tanzobjekte vom Bismarck Archipel, Nissan und Buka.' *Publikationen – Museum Dresden* 13: 1–40.

Francis, G., with B. Collins (1995), 'On Knot-spanning Surfaces: An Illustrated Essay on Topological Art,' in *The Visual Mind: Art and Mathematics*, ed. M. Emmer. Cambridge, MA: The MIT Press.

Frazer, J. (1922), *Beliefs in Immortality and Worship of the Dead*, 3 vols. London: Macmillan.

Freedberg, D. (1989), *The Power of Images: Studies in the History and Theory of Response*. Chicago: University of Chicago Press.

Friederici, G. (1910), *Wissenschaftliche ergebnisse einer amtlichen Forschungsreise nach dem Bismarck-Archipel im Jahre 1908*, Erganzungsheft der Mitteilungen aus den Deutchen Schutzgebeiten, 3,5,7.

Funkenstein, A. (1989), 'Collective Memory and Historical Consciousness.' *History and Memory: Studies in the Representation of the Past* 1, no. 1: 5–26.

Gell, A. (1975), *Metamorphosis of the Cassowaries: Umeda Society, Language and Ritual*. London: Athlone Press.

—— (1977), 'Magic, Perfume, Dream,' in *Symbols and Sentiments*, ed. I. Lewis, pp. 25–39. London: Academic Press.

—— (1992), 'The Technology of Enchantment and the Enchantment of Technology,' in *Art, Anthropology and Aesthetics*, ed. J. Coote and A. Shelton, pp. 40–67. Oxford: Oxford University Press.

—— (1993), *Wrapping in Images: Tattooing in Polynesia.* Oxford: Clarendon Press.

—— (1996), 'Vogel's Nest: Traps as Artworks and Artworks as Traps.' *Journal of Material Culture*, Vol. 1 No. 1: 15–38.

—— (1998), *Art and Agency: A New Anthropological Theory.* Oxford: Oxford University Press.

Giesey, R. E. (1960), *The Royal Funerary Ceremony in Renaissance France.* Geneva: Mouton.

Gifford, D. C. (1974), 'Iconology of the Uli Figure in Central New Ireland.' Ph.D. diss., University of California, Berkeley.

Ginzburg, C. (1983), 'Clues: Morelli, Freud, and Sherlock Holmes,' in *The Sign of Three: Dupin, Holmes, Peirce,* ed. Umberto Eco and Thomas Sebeok, pp. 256–310. Bloomington, IN: Indiana University Press.

—— (1991), 'Repräsentation: das Wort, die Vorstellung, der Gegenstand.' *Freibeuter* 22: 3–23.

Girard, F. (1954), 'L'importance sociale et religieuse des ceremonies executées pour les Malangganes sculptes de Nouvelle Irelande.' *L'Anthropologie* 58: 241–67.

Girard, R. (1977), *Violence and the Sacred,* trans. Patrick Gregory. Baltimore, MD: Johns Hopkins University Press.

Graebner, F. (1905), 'Einige Superformen des Bismarck Archipel.' *Globus* 88: 333–36.

Gregory, C. A. (1980), 'Gifts to Men and Gifts to God: Gift Exchange and Capital Accumulation in Contemporary Papua.' *Man* 15: 626–52.

Groves, W. C. (1933a), 'Divazukmit – A New Ireland Ceremony.' *Oceania* 3: 297–312.

—— (1933b), 'Report on Fieldwork in New Ireland.' *Oceania* 3: 325–61.

—— (1936), 'Secret Beliefs and Practices in New Ireland.' *Oceania* 7: 220–46.

—— (1937), 'Settlement of Disputes in Tabar.' *Oceania* 7: 501–20.

Guidieri, R., and F. Pellizi (1981), 'Nineteen Tableaux on the Cult of the Dead in Malekula, Eastern Melanesia.' *Res* 2: 1–97.

Gunn, M. (1987), 'The Transfer of Malangan Ownership on Tabar,' in *Assemblage of Spirits: Idea and Image in New Ireland,* ed. Louise Lincoln, pp. 74–83. New York: George Braziller in association with The Minneapolis Institute of Arts.

—— (1998), *Ritual Arts of Oceania New Ireland in the Collection of the Barbier-Mueller Museum.* Milan: Skira Editore.

Hahl, A. (1907), 'Das mittlere Neu-Mecklenburg'. *Globus* 91: 310–16.

—— (1942), *Deutsch Neuguinea.* Berlin: Verlag Dietrich Reimer.

Halbwachs, M. (1925), *Les Cadres Sociaux de la mémoire.* Paris: Alcan.

—— (1950), *La M¾moire collective*. Paris: Presses Universitaires de France.

Hallam, E. *et al.* (2000), *Death, Memory and Material Culture*. Oxford: Berg.

Harrison, S. (1992), 'Intellectual Property and Ritual Culture'. *Man* (n.s.) 21 (2): 435–56.

—— (1993), 'The Commerce of Cultures in Melanesia.' *Man (n.s.)* 28, no. 1: 139–58.

—— (1993), *The Masks of War*. Cambridge: Cambridge University Press.

—— (1995), 'Anthropological Perspectives on the Management of Knowledge'. *Anthropology Today* 11, no. 5: 10–14.

—— (1999), 'Identity as a Scarce Resource.' *Social Anthropology* 7 (3): 239–51.

Hauser-Schaublin, B. (1996), 'The Thrill of the Line, the String, and the Frond, or why the Abelam are a non-cloth culture'. *Oceania* Vol. 67(20): 81–106.

Heckscher, W. S. (1974), 'Petites Perceptions: An Account of Sortes Warburgianae'. *The Journal of Medieval and Renaissance Studies* 4, no. 1: 101–34.

Heintze, D. (1969), *Ikonographische Studien zur Malanggan-Kunst Neuirlands*. Frankfurt: Himmelsthuer.

—— (1987), 'On Trying to Understand Some Malangans,' in *ed. Assemblage of Spirits: Idea and Image in New Ireland*, ed. Louise Lincoln, pp. 42–55.New York: George Braziller in association with The Minneapolis Institute of Arts.

Helfrich, K. (1973), *Malanggan: Bildwerke von Neuirland*, Abteilung Südsee, 10. Berlin: Museum für Völkerkunde Berlin.

Hertz, R. (1907), 'Contribution à une étude sur la representation collective de la mort.' *Année Sociologique* 10: 48–137.

Hocart, A. (1927), *Kingship*. Oxford: Clarendon Press.

—— (1970), *Kings and Councillors: An Essay in the Comparative Anatomy of Human Society*. Chicago: University of Chicago Press.

Hoskins, J. (1993), *The Play of Time. Kodi Perspectives on Calendars, History and Exchange*. Berkeley, CA: California University Press.

Howes, D. (1982), 'The Bounds of Sense: An Inquiry into the Sensory Orders of Western and Melanesian Society.' Ph.D. diss., Université de Montréal.

—— (1987), 'Olfaction and Transition: An Essay on the Ritual Uses of Smell.' *The Canadian Review of Sociology and Anthropology* 24, no. 3: 398–416.

—— (1988), 'On the Odor of the Soul: Spatial Representation and Olfactory Classification in Eastern Indonesia and Western Melanesia.' *Bijdragen Tot de Taal-, Land- en Volkenkunde* 144: 84–113.

—— (ed.) (1991), *The Varieties of Sensory Experience: A Sourcebook in the Anthropology of the Senses*. Toronto: University of Toronto Press.

Hubert, H., and M. Mauss (1964[1906]), *Sacrifice: Its Nature and Function*. Chicago: University of Chicago Press.

Humphreys, S. C., and H. King (1980), *Mortality and Immortality: The Anthropology and Archaeology of Death*. London: Academic Press.

Huntington, R., and P. Metcalf (1979), *Celebrations of Death: The Anthropology of Mortuary Ritual*. Cambridge: Cambridge University Press.

Hutchisson, D. (1983), 'A Bibliography of Anthropological and Related Writings on the Province of New Ireland, Papua New Guinea.' *Research in Melanesia* 7, nos. 1–2: 35–87.

Kantorowicz, E. H. (1957), *The King's Two Bodies: A Study in Mediaeval Political Theology*. Princeton, NJ: Princeton University Press.

Kaplan, M. (1990), 'Meaning, Agency and Colonial History: Navosavakadua and the Tuka Movement in Fiji.' *American Ethnologist*, 17(1): 3–22.

—— and J. D. Kelly (1994), 'Rethinking Resistance: Dialogics of "Disaffection" in Colonial Fiji.' *American Ethnologist* 21 (1): 123–51.

Keesing, R. M. (1982), *Kwaio Religion: The Living and the Dead in a Solomon Island Society*. New York: Columbia University Press.

Kemp, M. (1990), *The Science of Art: Optical Themes in Western Art from Brunelleschi to Seurat*. New Haven, CT and London: Yale University Press.

Kemp, W. (1991), 'Visual Narratives, Memory, and the Medieval *Esprit du System*,' in *Images of Memory: On Remembering and Representation*, ed. Susanne Küchler and Walter Melion, pp. 87–108. Washington, DC: Smithsonian Institution Press.

Kooijman, S. (1984), *Art, Art Objects and Ritual in the Mimika Culture*, Mededelingen van het Rijksmuseum voor Volkenkunde, Leiden, 24. Leiden: E. J. Brill.

Krämer, A. (1907), 'Die Deutsche Marine Expedition, 1907–1909.' *Marine Rundschau* 18: 1067–9.

—— (1925), *Die Malanggane von Tombara*. Munich: Georg Mueller.

—— (1927), 'Tombaresisches, altes und neues.' *Anthropos* 22: 4–21.

Krämer-Bannow, E. (1916), *Bei den kunstsinnigen Kannibalen der Südsee*. Berlin: Himmelsthuer..

Krieger, M. (1899), *Neuguinea*. Berlin: Max Schall.

Küchler, S. (1983), 'Malangan of Nombowai.' *Oral History, Journal of the Institute of P. N. G. Studies* 11: 65–98.

—— (1987), 'Malangan: Art and Memory in a Melanesian Society.' *Man (n.s.)* 22, no. 2: 238–55.

—— (1988), 'Malangan: Objects, Sacrifice and the Production of Memory.' *American Ethnologist* 15, no. 4: 625–37.

—— (1992), 'Making Skins: Malanggan and the Idiom of Kinship in Northern New Ireland,' in *Anthropology, Art and Aesthetics*, ed. J. Coote and A. Shelton, pp. 94–112. Oxford: Clarendon Press.

—— (1994), 'Landscape as Memory: The Mapping of Process and its Representation in a Melanesian Society,' in *Landscape: Politics and Perspectives*, ed. B. Bender, pp. 85–106. Providence, RI: Berg.

—— (1997), 'Sacrificial Economy and Its Objects: Rethinking Colonial Collecting.' *Journal of Material Culture*, Vol. 2 (1): 39–60.

—— (1999), 'Binding in the Pacific: The Case of Malanggan.' *Oceania* Vol 69 (3): 145–57.

Küchler, Susanne, and Walter Melion (eds) (1991), *Images of Memory: On Remembering and Representation*. Washington, DC: Smithsonian Institution Press.

Leach, E. R. (1967), 'The Language of Kachin Kinship: Reflections on a Tikopia model,' in. *Social organization*, ed. M. Friedman, pp. 125–52. London: Cass.

Levinson, S. (1992), 'Primer for the Field-Investigation of Spatial Description and Conception'. *Pragmatics* 2 (1): 5–47.

Lévi-Strauss, C. (1964), *Totemism,* trans. R. Needham. London: Merlin Press.

—— (1969), *The Elementary Structures of Kinship*, trans. James Harle Bell, John Richard von Sturmer, and Rodney Needham. Boston: Beacon Press.

Lewis, P. (1969), *The Social Context of Art in Northern New Ireland*, Fieldiana: Anthropology, 58. Chicago: Field Museum of Natural History.

—— (1973), 'Changing Memorial Ceremonial in Northern New Ireland.' *Journal of the Polynesian Society* 82: 141–53.

—— (1979), 'Art in Changing New Ireland,' in *Exploring the Visual Art of Oceania*, ed. S. Mead, pp. 378–92. Honolulu: University of Hawaii Press.

Lincoln, L. ed. (1987), *Assemblage of Spirits: Idea and Image in New Ireland*, New York: George Braziller in association with The Minneapolis Institute of Arts.

Lindstrom, L. (1990), *Knowledge and Power in a South Pacific Society*. Washington, DC: Smithsonian Institution Press.

Loisy, A. F. (1920), *Essai historique sur les sacrifices*. Paris: E. Nourry.

Lomas, Peter W. (n.d.), 'Economic and Political Organisation in a Northern New Ireland Village.' Ph.D. dissertation, University of Vancouver.

Lovelock J. E. (1988), *The Ages of Gaia*. Oxford: Oxford University Press.

Lowenthal, D. (1993), 'Memory and Oblivion.' *Museum Management and Curatorship* 12: 171–82.

Luria, A. (1976), *Cognitive Development: Its Structural and Social Foundations*. Cambridge, MA: Harvard University Press.

MacDonald, Ronald R. (1987), *The Burial-Places of Memory: Epic Underworlds in Virgil, Dante, and Milton*. Amherst, MA: University of Massachusetts Press.

MacKenzie, M. (1991), *Androgynous Objects: Stringbags and Gender in the Pacific*. Berlin: Harwood Press.

Malinowski, B. (1922), *Argonauts of the Western Pacific*. New York: Dutton.

Marcus, G. and F. Myers (1995), 'The Traffic in Art and Culture: An Introduction,' in eds. *The Traffic in Culture: Refiguring Art and Anthropology*, ed. G. Marcus and F. Myers, pp. 1–55. Berkeley, CA: University of California Press.

Mauss, Marcel (1954 [1924]), *The Gift*. London: Cohen & West.

—— (1968–69), *Oeuvres*, 3 vols. Paris: Editions de Minuit.

McKinnon, S. (1991), *From a Shattered Sun: Hierarchy, Gender, and Alliance in the Tanimbar Islands*.

Madison, WI: University of Wisconsin Press.

Messner, G. F. (1983), 'The Friction Block Lounuat of New Ireland: Its Use and Socio-Cultural Embodiment.' *Bigmaus* 4: 49–56.

Meyer, A. B., and R. Parkinson (1895), *Schnitzereien und Masken aus dem Bismarck Archipel und Neu Guinea*, Dresden: Königliches Ethnographisches Museum zu Dresden, 10.

Mitchell, W. J. T. (1996), 'What do Pictures Really Want?' 77(October): 45–72.

Morphy, H. (1991), *Ancestral Connections: Art and an Aboriginal System of Knowledge*. Chicago: Chicago University Press.

Moses, J. A. (1969), 'The German Empire in Melanesia, 1884–1914.' *History in Melanesia*, Canberra: Australian National University Press.

Mosko, Mark S. (1983), 'Conception, De-conception and Social Structure in Bush Mekeo Culture,' in *Mankind* Special issue, *Concepts of Conception: Procreative Ideologies in Papue New Guinea*, ed. D. Jorgensen, pp. 78–104.

Munn, N. (1986), *The Fame of Gawa: A Symbolic Study of Value Transformation in a Massim (Papua New Guinea) Society*. Cambridge: Cambridge University Press.

Myers, F. (1995), 'Representing Culture: The Production of Discourses for Aboriginal Acrylic Art', in *Traffic in Culture*, ed. F. Myers and G. Marcus, pp. 55–95. Berkeley, CA: University of California Press.

Needham, R. (1965), 'Percussion and Transition.' *Proceedings of the Royal Anthropological Society*, Vol. 6(2): 30–65.

Neuhaus, P. K. (1962), 'Beiträge zur Ethnographie der Pala in mittel Neuirland.' *Kölner Ethnologische Mitteilungen 2*, Cologne: Kölner Universitäts Verlag.

Neuhaus, R. (1911), *Deutsch Neu-Ginea*. Weimar: Alexander Dunder Verlag.

Nietzsche, F. W. (1968[1886]), 'Zur Genealogie der Moral: Eine Streit-schrift.' *Studienausgabe in 4 Bänden*, ed. H. H. Holz. Frankfurt am Main: Fischer-Bücherei.

Nora, P. (1989), 'Between Memory and History: Les Lieux de Mémoire.' *Representations* 26: 25–68.

Olsen, D. R. (1977), 'From Utterance to Text: The Bias of Language , in Speech and Writing.' *Harvard Educational Review*, 47: 257–81.

Orgel, S. (1975), *The Illusion of Power: Political Theatre in the English Renaissance*. Berkeley, CA: University of California Press.

Parkinson, R. H. P. (1907), *Dreissig jahre in der Südsee: land und leute, sitten und gebräuche im Bismarckarchipel und auf den deutschen Salomoinseln*. Stuttgart: Strecker & Schroeder.

Patrol Reports (1946–1980), Port Moresby: National Archives.

Peekel, P. G. (1908), 'Die Verwandtschaftsnamen des mittleren Neu Mecklenburg.' *Anthropos* 3: 456–81.

—— (1910), 'Religion und Zauberei auf dem mittleren Neu Mecklen-burg.' *Anthropos* 21, 22: 806–24, 16–44.

—— (1928), 'Lang Manu,' in *Festschrift, Publikation d'hommage offerte au P. Schmidt*, ed. W. Kopplers, pp. 542–55. Vienna:

—— (1931), 'Religiöse Tänze auf Neuirland.' *Anthropos* 26: 513–32.

—— (1932), 'Uli und Ulifeier oder vom Mondkultus aus Neu Mecklen-burg.' *Archiv für Ethnologie* 23: 41–75.

Pellizzi, F. (1995), 'Editorial, Remains.' *Res* 27: 5–10.

Pomian, K. (1986), *Der Ursprung des Museums, Vom Sammeln*. Berlin: Verlag Klaus Wagenbach.

Powdermaker, H. (1931) 'Mortuary Rites in New Ireland.' *Oceania* 2: 26–43.

—— (1931) 'Report on Fieldwork in New Ireland.' *Oceania* 1: 357.

—— (1931), 'Vital Statistics in New Ireland.' *Human Biology* 3: 351–75.

—— (1932), 'Feasts in New Ireland: The Social Function of Eating.' *American Anthropologist* 34: 236–47.

—— (1933), *Life in Lesu: The Study of a Melanesian Society in New Ireland*, with a foreword by Clark Wissler. London: William & Norgate.

Radstone, S. (2000), 'Working with Memory: An Introduction' in *Memory and Methodology*, ed. S. Radstone, pp. 1–24. Oxford: Berg.

Ranni, D. (1889), 'New Ireland.' *Royal Geographical Society of Australia, Proceedings of the Old Branch* 3: 72–92.

—— (1912), *My Adventures Among the South-Seas Cannibals*. London: Seely, Service and Co. Ltd.

Romilly, H. H. (1886), *The Western Pacific and New Guinea: Notes on the Natives, Christian and Cannibal, with some Account of the Old Labour Trade*. London: John Murray.

Rosenfield, I. (1992), *The Strange, Familiar, and Forgotten: An Anatomy of Consciousness*. New York: Knopf.

Rowlands, M. (1993), 'The Role of Memory in the Transmission of Culture.' *World Archaeology* 25, no. 2: 141–51.

Rowley, C. D. (1958), *The Australians in German New Guinea*. Melbourne: Melbourne University Press.

Ryan, P. (n.d.) 'New Ireland.' *Encyclopedia of Papua New Guinea*: 481. Port Moresby: Government of Papua New Guinea.

Saunders, P. (1998), 'Nonlinearity: What it is and Why it Matters'. *Architectural Design* No. 129:52–7

Schneider, D. (1961), 'Introduction: The Distinctive Features of Matrilineal Descent Groups,' in *Matrilineal Kinship*, ed. D. M. Schneider and K. Gough. Berkeley, CA: University of California Press.

Schnepel, B. (1995), *Twinned Beings: Kings and Effigies in Southern Sudan, East India and Renaissance France*. Göteborg, Sweden: Institute for Advanced Studies in Social Anthropology (IASSA).

Scragg, R. (1954), 'Depopulation in New Ireland: A Study of Demography and Fertility.' Thesis presented to the University of Adelaide.

Smith, W. R. (1892), 'Sacrifice'. *Encyclopaedia Britannica*, 9th edition, pp. 132–8. Chicago: Encyclopaedia Britannica.

Sperber, D. (1975), *Rethinking Symbolism*. Cambridge: Cambridge University Press.

—— (1985). 'Anthropology and Psychology: Towards an Epidemiology of Representation.' *Man* (n.s.) 20 (1985): 73–89.

Stafford, B. M. (1996), *Good Looking: Essays on the Virtue of Imagery*. Cambridge, MA: MIT Press.

—— (1999), *Visual Analogy: Consciousness as the Art of Forgetting*. Cambridge, MA: MIT Press.

Stephan, E. I., and F. Graebner (1907), *Neu-Mecklenburg (Bismarck-Archipel). Die Kueste von Umuddu bis Kap St. Georg*. Berlin: D. Reimer.

Stöhr, W. (1987), *Kunst und Kultur aus der Südsee: Sammlung Clausmeyer Melanesien*, Ethnologica (Cologne, Germany); n.F., 6. Cologne: Rautenstrauch-Jöst-Museum für Völkerkunde.

Strathern, M. (1988), *The Gender of the Gift: Problems With Women and Problems With Society in Melanesia*, Studies in Melanesian Anthropology, 6. Berkeley, CA: University of California Press.

—— (1990), 'Artefacts of History: Events and the Interpretation of Images,' in *Culture and History in the Pacific*, ed. Jukka Siikala, pp. 25–44 (Suomen Antropologisen Seuran toimituksia, 27). Helsinki: Finnish Anthropological Society.

—— (1991), *Partial Connections*, ASAO Special Publications, 3. Savage, MD: Rowman & Littlefield.

—— (2001), 'The Patent and the Malanggan,' in *Beyond Aesthetics: Art and the Technologies of Enchantment*, ed. C. Pinney and N. Thomas, pp. 259–87. Oxford: Berg.

Strauch, H. (1877), 'Algemeine Bemerkungen ethnologischen Inhaltes über Neu Guinea, die Admiralitäts, Neu Hannover, Neu Irland und Bougainville.' *Zeitschrift für Ethnologie* Vol. 9, 9–63, 81–105.

Summers, D. (1989), 'Form: Nineteenth-Century Metaphysics and the Problem of Art Historical Description.' *Critical Inquiry* Vol. 15: 372–407.

Taylor, A. C. (1993), 'Remembering to Forget: Identity, Mourning and Memory among the Jivaro.' *Man* (n.s.) 28: 653–78.

Thilenius, G. (1903), 'Ethnographische Ergebnisse aus Melanesien: die westlichen Inseln des Bismarck Archipel.' *Acta Nova*, Halle.

Thomas, N. (1991), *Entangled Objects: Exchange, Material Culture, and Colonialism in the Pacific*. Cambridge, MA: Harvard University Press.

Thompson, M. (1979), *Rubbish Theory: The Creation and Destruction of Value*, Foreword by E. C. Zeeman. Oxford and New York: Oxford University Press.

Trompf, G. W. (ed.) (1990), *Cargo Cults and Millenarian Movements: Transoceanic Comparisons of New Religious Movements*, Religion and Society (Mouton Publishers), 29. Berlin and New York: Mouton de Gruyter.

Tylor, E. B. (1889), *Primitive Culture*, Vol. 2. New York: Halt.

Valeri, V. (1985), *Kingship and Sacrifice: Ritual and Society in Ancient Hawaii*. Chicago: University of Chicago Press.

—— (1994), 'Wild Victims: Hunting as Sacrifice and Sacrifice as Hunting in Huaulu.' *History of Religions* 34, no. 2: 101–31.

Vinograd, R. E. (1991), 'Private Art and Public Knowledge in Later Chinese Painting,' in *Images of Memory: On Remembering and Representation*, ed. S. Küchler and W. Melion, pp. 176–202. Washington, DC and London: Smithsonian Institution Press.

Wagner, R. (1980), 'Cultural Artefacts at Omara and Kistobu Caves, New Ireland.' *Oral History* 13: 57–8.

—— (1986), *Asiwinarong: Ethos, Image, and Social Power Among the Usen Barok of New Ireland*. Princeton, NJ: Princeton University Press.

—— (1987), 'Figure–Ground Reversal among the Barok,' in *Assemblage of Spirits*, ed. L. Lincoln, pp. 56–63. Minneapolis, MN: Minneapolis Museum of Art.

—— (1991), 'New Ireland is Shaped Like a Rifle and We are at the Trigger: The Power of Digestion in Cultural Reproduction,' in *Clio in Oceania*, ed. A. Biersack, pp. 329–47. Washington, DC: Smithsonian Institution Press.

—— (2001), *An Anthropology of the Subject: Holographic Worldview in New Guinea and its Meaning and Significance for the World of Anthropology*. Berkeley, CA: California University Press.

Walden, E. (1911), 'Die ethnographischen und sprachlichen Verhältnisse im nördlichen Teil Neu Mecklenburgs und auf den umliegenden Inseln.' *Korrespondenz Blatt der Deutschen Gesellschaft für Anthropologie, Ethnologie, und Urgeschichte* 42: 28–31.

Walden, E. and H. Neverman (1940), 'Totenfeiern und Malangane von Neu Mecklenburg. Feldaufzeichnungen zusammengestellt von Neverman, H.' *Zeitschrift für Ethnologie* 72: 11–38.

Wassman, J. (1994), 'The Yupno as Post-Newtonian Scientists: The Question of What Is "Natural" in Spatial Description'. *Man* (n.s.), 29 (3): 645–67.

Weiner, A. B. (1976), *Women of Value, Men of Renown: New Perspectives in Trobriand Exchange*. Austin, TX: University of Texas Press.

—— (1985), 'Inalienable Wealth.' *American Ethnologist* 12, no. 2: 210–27.

—— (1992), *Inalienable Possessions: The Paradox of Keeping-While-Giving*. Berkeley, CA: University of California Press.

Wertsch, J. V. (1985), *Vigotsky and the Social Formation of Mind*. Cambridge, MA: Harvard University Press.

White, P., and J. Downie. (1978), 'Balof Shelter, New Ireland: Report on a Small Excavation.' *Records of the Australian Museum* 31: 762–802.

White, P., J. Downie and W. Ambrose (1978), 'Mid-recent Human Occupation and Resource Exploitation in the Bismarck Archipelago.' *Science* 199: 877–79.

White, P., and J. Specht (1973), 'Prehistoric Pottery from Ambitle Island, Bismarck Archipelago.' *Asian Perspective* 14: 88–93.

Whitehouse, H. (1992), 'Memorable Religions: Transmission, Codification and Change in Divergent Melanesian Contexts.' *Man* (n.s.) 27, no. 4: 777–97.

Wilkinson, G. N. (1978), 'Carving a Social Message: The Malanggans of Tabar,' in *Art in Society: Studies in Style, Culture and Aesthetics*, ed.

Michael Greenhalg and Vincent Megaw, pp. 227–41. London: Duckworth.

Yates, F. A. (1966), *The Art of Memory*. London: Routledge & Kegan Paul.

Yayii, P. Lamasisi (1983), 'Some Aspects of Traditional Dance Within the Malanggan Culture of North New Ireland.' *Bikmaus* 4, no. 3: 33–48.

Young, J. E. (1993), 'The Countermonument: Memory against Itself in Germany,' in his *The Texture of Memory: Holocaust Memorials and Meaning*, pp. 27–49. New Haven, CT: Yale University Press.

Index

DATE DUE

NOV 2 5 2010			

Demco, Inc. 38-293